Dehumanization in the Global Migration Crisis

Dehumanization in the Global Migration Crisis

Adrienne de Ruiter

OXFORD
UNIVERSITY PRESS

Great Clarendon Street, Oxford, OX2 6DP,
United Kingdom

Oxford University Press is a department of the University of Oxford.
It furthers the University's objective of excellence in research, scholarship,
and education by publishing worldwide. Oxford is a registered trade mark of
Oxford University Press in the UK and in certain other countries

© Adrienne de Ruiter 2024

The moral rights of the author have been asserted

All rights reserved. No part of this publication may be reproduced, stored in
a retrieval system, or transmitted, in any form or by any means, without the
prior permission in writing of Oxford University Press, or as expressly permitted
by law, by licence or under terms agreed with the appropriate reprographics
rights organization. Enquiries concerning reproduction outside the scope of the
above should be sent to the Rights Department, Oxford University Press, at the
address above

You must not circulate this work in any other form
and you must impose this same condition on any acquirer

Published in the United States of America by Oxford University Press
198 Madison Avenue, New York, NY 10016, United States of America

British Library Cataloguing in Publication Data

Data available

Library of Congress Control Number: 2023945984

ISBN 9780198893400

DOI: 10.1093/oso/9780198893400.001.0001

Printed and bound in the UK by
Clays Ltd, Elcograf S.p.A.

Links to third party websites are provided by Oxford in good faith and
for information only. Oxford disclaims any responsibility for the materials
contained in any third party website referenced in this work.

For the drowned and the saved

Acknowledgements

Looking at the name on the cover, it might seem like this book is the work of just one person. This is of course far from true. The insights developed in these pages have been shaped by encounters and conversations with many people, as well as ideas that were inspired by thoughts written down by others who contemplated these issues before me. It will not be possible for me to thank all those who have influenced me throughout the process of writing this book, but I hope to at least acknowledge those who have left the greatest imprint on me.

This work would not have been the same without the stories of the refugees and asylum seekers I spoke with about their experiences with practices of exclusion. The persons who shared with me their stories impressed me with their spirit and humanity. I hope that the way in which I describe and theorize their accounts does justice to the experiences they have lived through. I also would like to express my gratitude to the organizations that helped me set up the interviews and with which I spoke to get a more general sense of the challenges that refugees and asylum seekers face. Special thanks are due to Rami Emad as my translator and guide in Beirut.

The research for this book not only benefited from the fieldwork I did in Germany, Lebanon, and Italy, but also from the various academic environments I was lucky enough to reside in for shorter or longer periods. My interest for dehumanization was sparked during an undergraduate course on Conflict Studies at Utrecht University. Reading Herbert Kelman's work on dehumanization in state-sanctioned massacres, I wondered how people could stop recognizing the humanity of others and mistreat them in unimaginable ways. This question never left me. I take it as an evident sign of the great quality of the teaching carried out by the Conflict Studies staff that their courses raise issues that keep haunting former students.

A few years later, I had the chance to research dehumanization in greater detail as part of my postgraduate studies at the *École Normale Supérieure* in Paris. I am thankful for Jean-Claude Monod for giving me the opportunity to analyse this complex topic for my thesis and for the helpful feedback provided by him and Frédéric Worms on my initial philosophical musings on the subject.

viii Acknowledgements

At the European University Institute, I was so fortunate to be a part of a group of doctoral students supervised by Jennifer Welsh. Her keen eye for interesting ideas and sound reasoning aided me in sharpening my analysis of dehumanization, while her encouragement to study this theme in the context of the ongoing migration crisis helped me bring in the stories of people who experienced dehumanization and related forms of social and moral exclusion first-hand. The enthusiastic responses and constructive feedback from the members of the committee, Bert van den Brink, Andrea Sangiovanni, and Nick Vaughan-Williams, gave me the confidence to pursue the project of turning my dissertation into a book.

My academic path took me to the Goethe University in Frankfurt, the University of Newcastle, and the University of Humanistic Studies in Utrecht where different parts of this research were discussed and took shape. I am grateful for all those who shared their ideas and advice with me along the way. Bert van den Brink has been a constant pillar from the very beginning of my academic trajectory. Since my bachelor studies in Philosophy at Utrecht University, Bert has been an important mentor for me, presenting valuable support and encouragement without which I would not be where I am today.

I would also like to thank the delegates of Oxford University Press, the anonymous reviewers, and the editorial and production teams for their support and assistance. Dominic Byatt has been particularly supportive as commissioning editor. As a first-time author, I greatly benefited from his advice and encouragement throughout the process of writing this book.

As always, I owe the greatest thanks to my family and friends. As I travelled to various places in Europe and a little beyond, I met many inspiring and lovely people. I feel grateful for all the friends I made along the way and particularly for those bonds that remain strong even with distance. My parents have a unique role in my life. I am thankful for their encouragement to always be curious and learn about the unfamiliar and for giving me the confidence to go out into the world and explore. I am grateful for my sister for being an example in life, combining a demanding job with a loving family and writing a book on the side, and for my parents-in-law who have always welcomed me with open arms. Lastly, I want to thank Matteo for having been there for me throughout all the steps of this book. We both know writing a book is not easy, but having you on my side definitely helps.

Contents

Background stories	xiii
Introduction	**1**
'Humanity washed ashore'	1
Dehumanization in the migration crisis	3
Analysing dehumanization	5
A first look at dehumanization	8
The global migration crisis	10
Outline of the book	13
1. Dehumanization in the Migration Crisis	**23**
Introduction	23
Frames of dehumanization	24
Threat and deviance	25
De-individualization and disengagement	31
Denials of dignity	34
Three forms of moral exclusion	37
Conclusion	39
2. Animalization	**45**
Introduction	45
Animalization in the global migration crisis	46
Portraying people like animals	49
Vermin, lovebirds, and chickens	50
War propaganda and moral disengagement	52
Treating people like animals	54
As if	56
Hunting refugees	58
Making people resemble animals	61
Viewing people as animals	62
The evolutionary scale	63
Human animals	64
The moral dimension	66
Animalizing migrants	66
Conclusion	70

x Contents

3. Objectification   77

Introduction   77
Objectification in the global migration crisis   78
Portraying people like objects   80
    Indigestible food, poison, and waste   81
    From floods to flows   82
    The 'refugee' category   84
Treating people like things   86
    Bargaining chips and pawns   87
    Warehousing refugees   88
    Failing to care   89
    Torture and abuse in prison camps   90
Viewing people like objects   93
    The curious case of Dr P.   93
    Its and Thous   94
    Reification   95
Objectifying migrants   96
Conclusion   98

4. Brutalization   105

Introduction   105
Brutalization in the global migration crisis   106
Breaking humans   109
    Alienation in Auschwitz   110
    Kafka, zombies, and ghosts   113
    Inhumane detention conditions   117
    Brutal audiences   120
Brutalizing migrants   121
Conclusion   123

5. Dehumanization   129

Introduction   129
Denying the moral relevance of human subjectivity   130
Dehumanization as a denial of moral status   133
    Recognizing people as minimally human   133
    From indifference to hate   136
    Recognizing human subjectivity without recognizing its moral value   137
    Entering the mind of the perpetrator   138
Dehumanizing migrants   142
    Definite dehumanization   142
    Recognizing dehumanization   147
Conclusion   151

Conclusion 155

Countering dehumanization	155
Persuasion against dehumanization	156
Standing with the victims	160
Ending dehumanization through coercive means	163
The wrongs that remain	165

References	171
Index	185

Background stories

The analysis of dehumanization in this book is informed and illustrated by the accounts of the experiences of the refugees and asylum seekers with whom I spoke. I share brief descriptions of the persons whom I mention in the book here. The names mentioned are not their real names.

Abdul

Abdul is a young Syrian who lives in Beirut. He comes from a Bedouin family and grew up in the countryside near Aleppo. He never attended school since he had to help his father on the land. Abdul came to Lebanon in 2014 and had difficulties finding a job but now works in a cafeteria. Before, he was living in the streets. Abdul says that some Lebanese people treat Syrians well, but others humiliate them. He wants to find a place where he can feel at home. He remembers how different it was in his hometown: 'In my village, we felt one. Here everybody is alone. We are not friends. No one cares about another'.

Amadou

Amadou comes from Guinea-Buissau and was living in Italy at the time of our meeting. He recounts the difficulties he encountered on his way to Europe, particularly in Libya. He was imprisoned in Tripoli and Sebha, where he was subjected to extortion and abuse. Amadou believes that racism lies at the root of all inhumane treatment. He wishes that people would realize that people are all the same: 'We should not treat each other unequally. That creates all the problems between people'.

Amira

Amira is a young Syrian student who fled with her family from Damascus to Germany after the army took possession of their house. She notes that people sometimes seem to be afraid of refugees. She explains that refugees are fleeing war and come to live in freedom. She believes it is not shameful to be a refugee

xiv   Background stories

since they cannot help the fact they had to flee. In Europe, she finds that she is treated with humanity: 'Everyone respects me, no matter if I am big or small. I can express my opinion'.

Ammar

Ammar is a teacher who fled from Aleppo to evade military service. He finds it hard to rebuild his life in Germany. He stresses that he wants to feel normal but struggles with loneliness and the lack of meaningful social contact. Ammar notes that in Germany, people handle him with respect. He is no longer afraid of the police or that people will exploit him. Still, he notes that although people do not harm him, it is still difficult to feel at ease. He encountered discrimination and feels out of place in his new country. For Ammar, respect is the basis of humanity: 'If you give respect to the other, you cannot be bad to the other'.

Hanan

Hanan is a young Syrian woman who came from Aleppo to Germany. Her family left before, while Hanan and her sister were staying with their aunt and uncle to try to finish high school. When the situation became too dangerous, Hanan and her sister crossed to Turkey. They travelled on to join their family who had requested asylum in Germany. Hanan is upset about how refugees are depicted in the media. She feels that media portrayals show refugees as weak and lowly, and do not represent them as normal human beings. Humanity stands in her eyes for helping others: 'When someone does not know me and he helps me, he empathizes with me and helps me, that is for me humanity'.

Hassan

Hassan is a Syrian man who fled with his family to Lebanon. He illegally sells fruit in the streets of Beirut and is distraught about the situation he finds himself in. He is not allowed to work and struggles to provide for his wife and children. He considers the possibility of travelling back to Syria but is worried about the fees that he would need to pay for forfeiting the payment for a residence permit, if checked at the border. Hassan thinks humanity entails that you welcome people fleeing from war without subjecting them to complex rules and high fees.

Joseph

Joseph fled from Senegal to Europe out of fear of persecution on religious grounds. He was staying in Italy at the time of our encounter. He believes dignity and freedom are important for people's humanity. Humanity, for Joseph, stands for helping others: 'Humanity means to help a person in need. To accommodate the person, to give him food, to take of him when he is ill, to help him find work'.

Musa

Musa is a Gambian electrician who came to Libya for work and who fled to Italy due to the civil war. He recounts that his life in Libya was very hard. People robbed him in the street. He decided it would be better to go to Europe. He stayed in Sabrata for three weeks, where he was beaten and given little food. Sometimes gangs would come in the warehouses to steal the belongings of the people who were waiting for the boats. Humanity, for Musa, stands for virtue: 'Humanity means to be someone good. A human being should be a special kind of being with empathy and feeling. A human being should not be like a river, freely making yourself do things without accountability'. The virtue of humanity, in his eyes, is connected to solidarity: 'Humanity is also about helping each other, not leaving one another. Not making each other suffer. Not seeing that I have more power and I use it against you'.

Salim

Salim is a young Iraqi who left Mosul shortly before the takeover by the so-called Islamic State. He was living in Italy at the time of our meeting. Salim thinks that people sometimes are afraid of him because he comes from Iraq. Yet, he points out that Iraqi refugees are fleeing from violence and war: 'What happens now in my country has happened before in your country'. A big problem in his eyes is the lack of concern for the fate of refugees. In his view, difficulties in communication play an important role in this failure to connect: 'If I don't speak good language they don't respect me. I know language is key to everything'.

Suha

Suha is a Syrian woman who came to Germany with her children to join her husband, who had requested asylum there. She feels it is difficult to be a refugee. She notes that it is hard to leave behind one's home, possessions, and memories. It is difficult to accept that all these things belong to one's past: 'We should embrace the fact that we have two homelands, two memories, but eventually we live one life'. It also feels shameful for her to be a refugee. It presents the impression of being weak, whereas refugees are capable and strong. She notes that refugees are not taken serious and that politicians should speak *with* refugees and not just *about* them: 'If we are part of your crisis, we should be part of the solution'.

Tariq

Tariq is an asylum seeker from Pakistan who left his country out of fear of persecution for his atheist worldview. He spoke with me in Italy, explaining that he feels bad to be called a refugee. He wishes he would not be a refugee and that he could have stayed in his country. He recounts how some countries that he travelled through treated refugees inhumanely. He was incarcerated in Bulgaria, where the only way out was to file for asylum. For Tariq, inhumanity is related to discrimination and racism: 'Inhumanity is thinking someone is below you. Perhaps because of colour: that person is brown, or black, so he should not be in my country'. Inhumanity is expressed through a failure to help others in need: 'If the person has a problem, you are on purpose not helping them. You can, but you won't. That is inhumanity'.

Introduction

> Humanity is in crisis—and there is no exit from that crisis other than solidarity of humans.
>
> **Zygmunt Bauman, *Strangers at Our Door***

'Humanity washed ashore'

On 2 September 2015, twelve people died when two boats carrying refugees sank in the Aegean Sea. Among the dead was three-year-old Alan Kurdi, whose body was found on the coast not far from Bodrum. A picture portraying the boy, who drowned together with his five-year old brother, Ghalib, and their mother, Rehan, while trying to reach the Greek island of Kos after the family had fled from war-torn Syria, was soon shared all over the internet and published by hundreds of newspapers. The little boy's body, lying face down in the sand of a Turkish beach, came to stand for the plight of refugees everywhere, facing severe risks to their life and safety in their attempts to reach secure grounds, even after having managed to flee from countries afflicted by violent conflict, or rife with persecution and severe human rights violations. In an outburst of indignation, the picture of Alan went viral on Twitter, as it was disseminated under the hashtag 'Humanity washed ashore'.

The photograph and the discussion it sparked about policies regarding the accommodation of asylum seekers spoke of a failure to alleviate the suffering of people in difficult circumstances and to protect their fundamental human rights. For a brief moment, the predicament of persons whose life and well-being were not secured by their country of origin, or in the places to which they had fled and who decided to undertake yet another dangerous journey to find a safe haven elsewhere, became the central point of focus in the popular media. News about the event replaced reports on concerns about the security of the local population or the allegedly detrimental effects that a great influx of asylum seekers might have on the economy and social cohesion of destination countries.[1] In his individuality, Alan appealed to empathy without diffusing this sense of identification through the abstraction of large

Dehumanization in the Global Migration Crisis. Adrienne de Ruiter, Oxford University Press. © Adrienne de Ruiter (2024).
DOI: 10.1093/oso/9780198893400.003.0001

2 Dehumanization in the Global Migration Crisis

numbers. In his innocence, he appealed to compassion without raising difficult questions about the responsibility that migrants and asylum seekers themselves may hold for their misfortune.

This moment of widely shared grief was exceptional in that people from diverging political, social, and cultural backgrounds responded in seemingly similar ways to the powerful visual imagery of the dead child. Alan became the symbol of a loss of humanity. On the one hand, the evocative notion of 'humanity washed ashore' reiterated the fact that the little boy was himself part of humankind, who drowned in the sea. On the other, it provocatively suggested that human solidarity had come to nothing as the international community had failed to instil trust in his parents that an alternative was available, other than carrying their children on an unstable rubber boat to cross the sea. Notably, his family had requested asylum in Canada, but their application had been declined as it was incomplete.[2]

Due to this general lack of international solidarity in the face of the hardships faced by asylum seekers, this crisis has sometimes been called a 'crisis of humanity'.[3] One reason to speak of a 'crisis of humanity' is the scope of the refugee question, which affects people in all parts of the world. One only needs to glance at the list of countries that hosted the largest number of refugees at the height of the so-called European refugee crisis in 2015, led by Turkey, Pakistan, Lebanon, Iran, and Ethiopia, to realize the global dimensions of the issue.[4] A second reason why the dysfunctional political response to the unprecedented levels of mass displacement over the past years can be considered a 'crisis of humanity' is that humanity as a moral ideal seemingly faltered, given that even countries that have vowed to safeguard human rights and protect the dignity and equality of all look away, as people continue to die in their attempts to find safety and meet increasingly stringent asylum requirements. In a similar way, the sociologist and philosopher Zygmunt Bauman characterizes the migration crisis as a crisis of humanity.[5] 'Humanity is in crisis', he notes, as the general public response to the plight of strangers in need seeking to reach Europe, and other 'developed' parts of the world, is marked by hostility, alienation, and indifference.[6] Both of these aspects—that is, the global dimension and the apparent decline of humanity as a moral guideline for political action—are important for understanding this crisis as a product of policies that seek to discourage potential asylum seekers from making onward journeys to safe havens, which seem to imply that asylum can only be won through risking one's life. Such policies suggest that the lives of the people involved are insufficiently valued as worthy of protection.[7]

The tragic death of Alan and so many like him thus reflect not only an incapacity to overcome domestic and international political cleavages and to uphold the moral and legal obligations that states have towards asylum seekers under the human rights framework, but may also entail a prior failure to engage with the pleas that refugees make on us as fellow human beings. In fact, one reason why the picture of Alan may have been considered so shocking by many is that it forcefully reaffirmed the fundamental similarity we share with people who for a long time have been portrayed predominantly as a risk to our way of life or as little more than pitiable creatures who in their despair do not constitute our moral counterparts. In the case of Alan, on the other hand, it was only too easy to imagine that he could have been one's son, brother, nephew, or grandchild.[8] Such identification generated an emotional engagement with his death, which does not usually befall migrants and asylum seekers.

This book is concerned with this dynamic of moral exclusion through which refugees, asylum seekers, and other (forced) migrants oftentimes find themselves deprived of concern and consideration. Various modes of exclusion are involved here, including discrimination, marginalization, and stigmatization, which play an important role in physical and structural forms of violence involved in policies of border control, the general reluctance of states to accept large numbers of strangers in need, and the challenges involved in political efforts to establish international schemes of solidarity to provide more effective assistance to people who are forcibly displaced. While these exclusionary practices are important and will be given due attention, the main focus of this book is on dehumanization. Through a close analysis of dehumanization in the global migration crisis, this book examines the role that denials of humanity play in processes of moral disengagement that condone the deaths of hundreds of thousands of people who are forcibly displaced worldwide as a tragic side effect of political regimes that seek to curb irregular migration.

Dehumanization in the migration crisis

In reporting on the hardships that refugees and migrants face, journalists, scholars, commentators, and forcibly displaced persons themselves have frequently described their treatment using the term of dehumanization. The widespread use of the concept can be seen reflected, for example, in the fact that the rhetoric used by politicians to portray the arrival of migrants in terms reminiscent of plagues, the destitute living conditions in certain refugee camps, and the hostile policies devised by some countries to keep newcomers out have all been called dehumanizing.[9] In a similar vein, acts of labelling people 'migrants', 'frauds', 'criminals', or 'queue-jumpers' have been characterized in this way,[10] as have policies that seek to facilitate the

4 Dehumanization in the Global Migration Crisis

provision of aid to asylum seekers, including the use of wristbands to signal their right to food and the distribution of pre-paid grocery cards.[11]

Certain asylum seekers have also decried the harsh treatment they have received at the hands of countries they believed would offer them protection. One of them is Hadish, a young Eritrean, who lost his wife in a shipwreck off the coast of Lampedusa in October 2013. He tried to make his way to Switzerland, only to be returned to Italy, where he was homeless and eating garbage. In detention in Germany, after a failed attempt to get to Sweden, he wonders why refugees and migrants are treated like this, asking '[a]ren't we human beings?'[12] Another allusion to dehumanization can be found in the testimony of Ibrahim, a detainee in one of the immigration detention centres off the shores of Australia, who speaks about having been treated worse than an animal. He claims that he needs '[t]o be respected as a human. To be treated as a human. So you can feel your humanity and dignity. ... they treated us as an animal, ... the manager of the camp has a dog, and I think the dog, he was luckier than me. Seriously.'[13]

These examples illustrate how the concept of dehumanization features both explicitly and implicitly in commentaries on the current refugee situation and testimonies by refugees and asylum seekers.[14] This book examines whether, in fact, we should speak of dehumanization in all these cases. The appeal to dehumanization in situations where displaced persons are subjected to harmful treatment is understandable, as this notion holds great moral force. To say that people are not treated as human beings is a powerful indictment, given that the moral category of humanity delimits the ways in which we believe others may be treated.[15] While appeals to this notion help draw attention to the plight of the mistreated, my concern is that using this concept in underdetermined, vague, or overly inclusive ways obscures its distinct meaning. If we use this term in an imprecise manner, it becomes more difficult to see what is unique to dehumanization as a form of moral exclusion, which in turn is likely to undermine the effectiveness of our efforts to counteract it.

This book explores what it means to deny people's humanity in a dehumanizing way and seeks to develop a clearer understanding of what dehumanization entails and establish when refugees, asylum seekers, and migrants are dehumanized. It is important to look more closely at dehumanization in the global migration crisis, I believe, because the denials of humanity to which forcibly displaced persons are at times exposed form a formidable obstacle to our assessment of what they are due. When we do not consider the costs involved in the current international border regime as genuinely human costs, we are unlikely to see and appreciate the dire need for change.

Even if it turns out that we do not necessarily actively dehumanize refugees, asylum seekers, and unwanted migrants ourselves—an outcome I believe is quite likely—it is relevant to consider how structures, institutions, and policies may contribute to the dehumanization of the displaced and what may be done to put an end to this. Understanding what dehumanization is and why it is uniquely wrong is crucial to finding ways to mitigate, resist, and counteract this detrimental mode of exclusion.

My good news is that—on my view—dehumanization is less common than is generally assumed. My bad news is that dehumanization is far worse than we often tend to think. Because this notion is frequently used as an umbrella term to reject a wide variety of practices that undermine the social, legal, or moral standing of forced migrants, dehumanization comes across as a routine practice. This obscures the fact that dehumanization is a uniquely radical form of exclusion. Dehumanization, on my understanding, involves expelling people from the moral category of humanity, rather than assigning them a low or marginal position within this category. Dehumanization therefore allows for people to be treated in ways that otherwise would not be deemed acceptable forms of conduct towards fellow human beings. People who are humiliated, marginalized, stigmatized, or subjected to inhumane treatment, but not dehumanized, continue to be recognized as normatively human, which constitutes an important form of moral inclusion that sets limits to the ways in which perpetrators believe they may treat them.[16] It is therefore vital to distinguish dehumanization from such related practices, I argue, to recognize the particularity of this form of exclusion and the extreme forms of mistreatment which it allows for.

Analysing dehumanization

The main aim of this book is to clarify what dehumanization entails by considering its role in the global migration crisis. In developing my account, I examine how people can fail to recognize the human status of persons through the way they perceive, represent, or treat them. It is important to emphasize that dehumanization can be conceptualized in different ways and that I do not pretend to develop a uniquely 'right' way of thinking about dehumanization. Since people hold divergent views of what it means to be human and to be considered human, dehumanization can mean different things to different persons. This does not entail, however, that all these understandings are equally compelling. Some of these understandings, for example, will depend on controversial notions of what it means to be human, which

6 Dehumanization in the Global Migration Crisis

exclude certain individuals from the human category, while others may not be able to clearly explain why animals cannot be dehumanized. A convincing account of dehumanization, I argue, should be able to spell out what a failure to recognize people's humanity entails without drawing on vague, idealist, or otherwise controversial claims about what it means to be human.

The more specific aim of this book is to develop an account of dehumanization that not only helps us understand what this failure to recognize humanity involves but also contributes to a better understanding of its unique moral wrong and what should be done against it. In order to develop this account, the book will set out what the bare minimum of consideration is that people owe to one another and identify how this consideration manifests itself in the way we perceive, represent, and treat those persons we regard as human.

To develop this account I engage in normative theorizing. 'Theorizing' consists in formulating a conceptual framework for understanding a particular subject matter. 'Normative' refers to what is (considered) good and bad or right and wrong. 'Normative theorizing' therefore involves the practice of developing an account of the evaluative characteristics of a subject matter in ethical terms. The aim of this book is thus to set out what dehumanization entails with particular attention to its moral dimensions. The outcomes of this process can be evaluated on the basis of the consistency of the developed arguments, the relation between the premises and observations of facts or general knowledge about the world, and the extent to which the conclusions reached appear reasonable and acceptable to us. What is produced by this method is a theory that provides an account of the analysed subject matter that can be considered more or less persuasive. This corresponds to the claim, made above, that this book does not pretend to offer a uniquely 'right' way of thinking about dehumanization. Rather, it aims to provide an account that is compelling to a large and diverse audience by avoiding, as much as possible, controversial claims about what it means to be human.

The conviction that normative theorizing should focus on providing arguments to convince people of reasonable conclusions, rather than endeavour to uncover moral truths, follows from my meta-ethical standpoint. While, on the one hand, I hold that there exist no moral facts in the Platonist sense of the term, on the other hand, I maintain that moral norms and principles are not completely relativist either. Moral norms and principles, in my view, are sustained by universal characteristics of human existence and generally seek to promote peaceful coexistence (at least between members of one's social group) and lessen suffering (of those who are considered worthy of moral consideration). Moral norms and principles thus neither mirror moral truths that are accessible through pure reason, nor consist of subjective opinions.

Rather, normativity arises in an intersubjective way as moral norms and principles are established, negotiated, and rejected through interpersonal processes of claim-making.

To develop my normative account of dehumanization, I base my arguments not just on general knowledge, experience, and observation but also on academic literature. Theoretical and empirical studies on dehumanization are considered to draw from the insights of other authors on its nature and dynamics.[17] As this book seeks to develop an account of dehumanization in the global migration crisis, it is also important to consider the work of scholars who identify dehumanization in various aspects of this crisis.[18]

To map out how dehumanization and related forms of social and moral exclusion of refugees, asylum seekers, and other migrants are portrayed in media and taken up by non-governmental organizations, Chapter 1 presents a critical discourse analysis of the ways in which the terminology of dehumanization is employed in scholarship and in reporting by journalists and human rights organizations on the global migration crisis. The account of dehumanization that this book presents draws furthermore from stories of refugees and asylum seekers who have experienced dehumanization and related exclusionary practices, as either victims or witnesses. These stories serve to empirically ground, illustrate, and refine this account.[19]

The analysis in this book is informed by interviews I held with refugees and asylum seekers in Germany, Lebanon, and Italy in 2017, which present first-hand accounts of dehumanization and related forms of social and moral exclusion, such as marginalization, stigmatization, and inhumane treatment.[20] The aim of these interviews was to learn about the experiences of forcibly displaced persons with dehumanization and related practices of rejection and exclusion. These conversations focused on what it means for them to be a refugee, how their life has changed since they became a refugee, what challenges they face as a refugee, and other questions related to the impact being a refugee has had on them.[21]

Throughout this work, testimonies from refugees and asylum seekers, drawn from the interviews and taken from views cited in newspaper articles, scholarly works, and NGO reports, are presented to bring in the voices of forced migrants. I deem it important to include their viewpoints, first, to recognize and value the insights of persons who have undergone dehumanization or related forms of social and moral exclusion. Second, it is relevant to note that their ways of describing the challenges they face at times differ from the analyses put forward by scholars, journalists, and other commentators. These personal stories are presented in this book to gain deeper insight into the various forms of exclusion that refugees, asylum seekers, and other

8 Dehumanization in the Global Migration Crisis

forced migrants experience, reveal the ways in which they make sense of these practices, and illustrate the account of dehumanization that this work develops. Short background stories of the persons with whom I spoke and whom I mention in the chapters can be found at the beginning of the book.

A first look at dehumanization

This book seeks to understand better what dehumanization entails. In scholarly literature, diverse accounts have been developed that offer valuable insights into this phenomenon.[22] While most, if not all, scholars agree that dehumanization involves a process, practice, or act through which something human is denied, undermined, or otherwise negatively affected, less agreement exists on what this means precisely. Some scholars claim, for example, that dehumanization is an ordinary phenomenon because people tend to regard only few persons as 'people like us', while all others are seen as less human.[23] Others argue, by contrast, that dehumanization constitutes a pathological form of engagement with people, which is brought about through propaganda or ideologies that distort the ordinary emotional and moral mechanisms through which we recognize other persons as fellow human beings.[24] Disagreement exists not only about how 'normal' dehumanization is but also about what it involves precisely. Some authors claim that dehumanization entails a denial that people have a rich mental life typical of human beings,[25] while others believe it concerns harming people's fundamental human interests.[26] There are scholars who maintain that dehumanization involves attributing to people a subhuman essence,[27] and those who contend that the language of dehumanization should be taken less literally and be seen as a discursive tool to encourage moral disengagement.[28]

This book seeks to contribute to this debate by developing an account of dehumanization that emphasizes the denial of the moral relevance of people's human subjectivity as central to understanding this phenomenon.[29] On my view, dehumanization is an extraordinary and pathological form of (dis)engagement with human beings through which their experiences are no longer considered to matter, or at least not as moral reasons that weigh in on decisions concerning how to treat them. More specifically, following my account, dehumanization constitutes a distinct type of moral exclusion that is characterized by disregard for the moral status of human beings, which expresses itself in blindness for the significance of the human subjectivity of victims as a moral factor that warrants consideration. While this may sound abstract, it means that when persons are dehumanized, their experiences, particularly in terms of suffering, no longer matter in the eyes of the dehumanizer(s), or at least not as moral factors that count against their mistreatment.

This account will be developed throughout the book. It is important, however, to briefly introduce a set of underlying assumptions that orient my analysis in order to clarify the premises on which my perspective rests. First, I consider it essential to maintain a restrictive understanding of dehumanization that is limited to practices that cast people as *less than* human, and not *less* human. A crucial difference exists between regarding people as inferior human beings or as not human at all, as I will set out in greater detail in Chapter 1. An account of dehumanization that ignores this conceptual difference cannot adequately capture the distinct nature and wrong of this practice or offer precise guidance on what should be done to counter it.

Second, the perspective I develop regards dehumanization as a denial of a particular *moral* sense of humanity. Humanity holds different meanings and can refer, for example, to people's biological status, the quality of possessing particular traits that are considered characteristic of human beings, or to one's belonging to the moral order of humankind.[30] This last, normative, understanding is key to dehumanization. This may not be immediately intuitive. Dehumanizing rhetoric that likens people to animals might seem to deny their human status in a biological sense, for example. Yet, to understand dehumanization we need to look beyond the terminology that is used to deny the humanity of victims. This becomes clear when we take an example in which stark differences exist between humans and the animals to which victims are likened. When perpetrators of genocide call them lice, for instance, they evidently do not seek to challenge their biological status in the sense that they declare that their victims belong to the species *phthiraptera* rather than *homo sapiens*. Instead, they express the idea that these persons are like lice in terms of their moral standing, that is, filthy, parasitic creatures. By calling them lice, perpetrators say something about how they believe these persons may (or should) be treated, given the lowly moral standing that they hold (if any) and the nuisance they form for others. This point will be explored in greater detail in Chapter 2.

Third, I assume that dehumanization can be expressed in three forms: by failing to *perceive* of people as human beings, by *representing* them in ways that fail to recognize their humanity, or by *treating* them as if they were not human or in ways that take away or obscure their humanity. Perception, I understand here as the viewpoints that people hold. Dehumanized perception refers, then, to viewpoints that fail to recognize people as human and conceive of them as less than human. Representation involves the way

10 Dehumanization in the Global Migration Crisis

in which things or beings are portrayed. Dehumanized, or dehumanizing, representation thus entails that people are portrayed in ways that do not acknowledge their humanity and cast them as less than human. Treatment means acting with and on others. Dehumanizing treatment therefore involves treating people in ways that fail to recognize their humanity or that severely undermine their humanity.

Based on these premises, I start out from an understanding of dehumanization as involving acts of viewing, portraying, or treating people as less than human. People are viewed as less than human when they fail to be attributed the moral status of human beings, and the moral status that they are ascribed instead, if any, is lower than that of human beings.[31] People are portrayed as less than human when they are likened to animals, objects, or entities that hold a moral status lower than that of human beings, such as, for example, cockroaches, garbage, or zombies, in ways that imply that they hold the moral status of that animal, object, or entity. People are treated as less than human when they are treated in ways that signal that they are attributed a lower moral status than that of human beings.

This view will be developed, expanded, and amended throughout the book. Personal stories of refugees, asylum seekers, and unwanted migrants and prevailing accounts of their treatment in the global migration crisis offer rich material to reconsider not only conceptually, but also in terms of lived experience, what dehumanization entails. This brief overview of guiding assumptions sheds light on the ideas, beliefs, and concerns that form the point of departure for this analysis. With these fundamental ideas in place, we are almost ready to begin our analysis of what dehumanization is.

The global migration crisis

Before turning to an outline of the book, it will be helpful to reflect briefly on how we should call the 'crisis' that is the focus of this study. Various labels could be used to describe the chain of ongoing emergency situations related to the rise in the number of refugees and other (forcibly) displaced persons in the world, challenges involved in the management of migration, and increasing strains on the effective control of international borders.

'Refugee crisis' is the name most often used to denote the political pressures and human suffering that follow from this rise in mobility, at least within the European context over the past years.[32] This name is based on the fact that the sharp rise in the number of refugees, asylum seekers, and undocumented migrants travelling to Europe over the past decade was caused in large part by the violent aftermath of the revolutions of the Arab Spring that occurred in the early 2010s and the political instability, sectarian violence, and systematic human rights violations that jeopardize the life and well-being of civilians in Afghanistan and Iraq after the armed interventions of the early 2000s. At the peak of the European crisis, in 2015, refugees from Syria, Afghanistan, and Iraq constituted over 75 per cent of arrivals in Europe.[33] Since refugees made up the large majority of those who came to Europe, the term 'refugee crisis' appears particularly suitable to describe the crisis. This naming has been criticized, however, for its Eurocentric focus and its depiction of the loss of life and large-scale suffering as a consequence of unforeseeable catastrophe rather than as the outcome of (a lack of effective) policies for dealing with the international movements of people in need.[34]

While these criticisms are well taken, the main issue with the term 'refugee crisis' for the purposes of this book is that it unduly limits our focus to an emergency situation that appears to lie in the past. Using this denomination may provide a false sense of closure. This is mistaken in my view since the European crisis has not reached a resolution, but only an impasse, brought about by political agreements with Europe's neighbours that impede undocumented migrants from crossing to Europe. Crucial to limiting the arrivals of asylum seekers and other migrants to Europe was the EU–Turkey deal that came into force on 20 March 2016.[35] This agreement stipulated that Turkey would take in rejected asylum seekers from Greece and police its coastline in exchange for 6 billion euro for humanitarian assistance to the Turkish refugee camps, consideration of a proposal that would allow Turkish citizens to travel within the EU without a visa, and the EU admitting one refugee from the Turkish camps for every rejected asylum seeker that would be sent from Greece to Turkey. Similar agreements have been reached with countries in North Africa. Notably, the Italy–Libya Memorandum of Understanding, signed on 2 February 2017, sets out regulations regarding financial and technical support from Italy for Libya to halt irregular migration to Europe.[36] These agreements have not addressed the root causes of the crisis but merely moved the crisis out of sight from the European public.

This false sense of closure furthermore ignores the fact that in many parts of the world issues are ongoing and in some cases have significantly worsened over the past years. In the United States, for example, the situation for many refugees, asylum seekers, and irregular migrants became more dire with the introduction of a 'zero tolerance' approach, adopted by President Donald Trump in June 2018. While his successor President Joe Biden has sought to release strict immigration policies at the US–Mexico border, tensions continue.[37] Examples are plenty, including the Rohingya crisis in South

12   Dehumanization in the Global Migration Crisis

East Asia and the rise in refugees after the takeover of power of the Taliban in Afghanistan over the summer of 2021. The war in Ukraine furthermore produced large numbers of refugees within Europe in early 2022. The term 'migration crisis' is therefore used in this book as it lacks the strong association with a series of past events restricted to a particular geographical area.

Some authors have suggested that it would be better to speak of a 'border crisis', in recognition of the fact that widespread suffering is caused by restrictions to free movement.[38] While this shift in focus helps elucidate the key role that policies and institutions play in bringing about the crisis, it is the sharp rise in people on the move that brings to the fore more clearly the violence and injustice involved in international border control. Another suggestion has been to call the emergency situation that has emerged a 'humanitarian crisis' in recognition of the fact that this labelling firmly places the responsibility to mitigate the harm caused by this crisis in the hands of state authorities.[39] Although I am sympathetic to the motivation behind this proposal, it seems that we would still need to refer to 'refugees' or 'migration' to elucidate what kind of humanitarian crisis we are talking about given the variety of humanitarian crises the world faces. The labels 'refugee crisis' and 'migration crisis' are in this sense more helpful to indicate the type of crisis we are dealing with. Furthermore, there is no logical or conceptual impediment that entails that a 'refugee crisis' or 'migration crisis' cannot constitute a humanitarian crisis as well.

The term 'migration crisis' has been criticized for suggesting that the choices of individuals have led to the crisis situation. The term 'migration' lacks the sense of urgency and inevitability that 'refugee' possesses. After all, a refugee is per definition a person who has to flee because his or her life, liberty, or security is threatened. While migrants may have been forced to leave their home country, they could also have decided to leave to see if better opportunities may be found in other countries, although it should be remembered that decisions to uproot one's life are never taken lightly.[40] This ties into the fact that throughout the crisis, the emphasis on the concept of 'refugee' has led to a devaluation of the meaning of 'migrant'.[41] In spite of these reservations, I use 'migration crisis' because it highlights the central role of international mobility in the crisis without linking closely to a specific geographically and temporally delineated emergency situation. This term also indicates that the crisis affects people who have left their country of origin for various reasons without denying the fact that many of them were forced to flee due to war, prosecution, and fundamental rights violations.

Lastly, it may be said that the use of the term 'crisis' itself is problematic because what we are dealing with here concerns a form of prolonged injustice resulting from structural and systematic flaws in the international border regime. I believe there is something to say for avoiding the term 'crisis' to emphasize the fact that the harms and wrongs done to people who are forced to leave their homes are not exceptional, but structural. While this reality should not be ignored, the term 'crisis' evokes a sense of urgency that is helpful in turning attention to the plight of refugees, asylum seekers, and other people who suffer the consequences of this regime. The origin of this term, furthermore, refers to a decisive moment when change must come, for better or worse.[42] A 'crisis' therefore confronts us with a critical choice, whether or not the underlying problem is structural or accidental. I therefore opt for the term 'global migration crisis' to signal the urgent need to respond to a long chain of ongoing emergency situations around the world through which the human rights of the displaced are not adequately respected.

Outline of the book

The main aim of this book is to develop an original philosophical account of dehumanization that is grounded in the lived experiences of refugees, asylum seekers, and other migrants and prevailing accounts of their treatment. To advance this account, it is important to lay the theoretical groundwork for the analysis and set out the problem that the book addresses in greater detail. Chapter 1 therefore critically examines the various ways in which the terminology of dehumanization is used in reporting on the global migration crisis and introduces a number of key conceptual distinctions that help bring dehumanization into sharper focus. This chapter shows how a wide range of exclusionary practices is considered dehumanizing and zooms in on the central themes of threat and deviance; de-individualization and disengagement; and denials of dignity, which feature prominently in the debate on the dehumanization of refugees, asylum seekers, and other (forced) migrants. The central argument in this chapter is that sharper distinctions should be made between dehumanization and related forms of social and moral exclusion, such as marginalization, stigmatization, and criminalization, in other to clarify its distinct nature. This chapter, lastly, introduces animalization, objectification, and brutalization as helpful, alternative lenses to study dehumanization in the global migration crisis. This lays the theoretical groundwork for the subsequent chapters, which look at the animalization, objectification, and brutalization of the forcibly displaced and examine when, if ever, these turn into dehumanization.

Chapter 2 examines the so-called 'animalization' of refugees, asylum seekers, and migrants. This chapter starts with an overview of the various ways in which refugees, asylum seekers, and unwanted migrants are portrayed, treated, and viewed like animals and then examines how each of these relates to dehumanization. A close look at animalization shows that the act of likening people to animals is not always morally problematic, let alone dehumanizing. Central to dehumanizing forms of animalization is the idea that the distinctively human quality of the feelings, thoughts, and life of the person(s) involved is discredited by attributing to it a lower, animalistic, status. Through dehumanizing forms of animalization, people are usually seen, portrayed, or treated as mere vermin or other lowly animals, who are devoid of a human inner life, or as dangerous predators, whose experiences need not concern us because of their viciousness or depravity. The main argument of this chapter is that the moral sense of humanity is central to understanding when animalization turns into dehumanization as this occurs when victims are viewed, portrayed, or treated as less than human in a normative sense.

Chapter 3 focuses on the objectification of refugees, asylum seekers, and unwanted migrants. While objectification is often presented—together with animalization—as a paradigm case of dehumanization, it is far less commonly used as a conceptual lens to make sense of the experiences of the internationally displaced by journalists, scholars, commentators, and refugees, asylum seekers, and other migrants themselves. This chapter considers forms of objectification that portray migrants like waste, natural disasters, or diseases, treat them as mere things, or view them as objects without intrinsic moral value. Objectification turns into a form of dehumanization, so I argue, when treating, portraying, or viewing people as objects entails a failure to ascribe them human subjectivity.

Chapter 4 looks into the brutalization of refugees, asylum seekers, and unwanted migrants. Brutalization entails that people become less humane or lose touch with their own sense of humanity through severe forms of mistreatment or deprivation. In the global migration crisis, brutalization may take the form, for example, of abuses that take place in immigration detention centres, as recounted by (former) detainees. This chapter examines the dynamics of brutalization and how it impacts on human subjectivity. This analysis affirms the strength and resilience of human subjectivity, which tends to resist denials of its existence even under the direst of circumstances. It presents a warning to not too easily follow the logic of perpetrators of dehumanization who hold that victims can truly be made less than human through brutalizing treatment. In most cases of brutalization, victims are not turned into something less than human but impeded from enjoying or expressing their full range of human qualities. Only when the human spirit is utterly broken is it possible to claim that brutalization dehumanizes people in the sense that they come to fail to recognize their own humanity. Nonetheless, brutalization can serve as a form of dehumanizing representation since brutalizing treatment can portray people as less than human. Brutalization thus amounts to dehumanization when it serves as a performative act of representation that portrays the victim as less than human.

Chapter 5 presents the account of dehumanization this book develops, building on the insights set out in the previous chapters. This chapter draws from key works in philosophy and social psychology to reconceptualize the notion of moral exclusion that is central to understanding dehumanization. Dehumanization, on my view, consists in a particular form of moral exclusion that is characterized by neglect of or contempt for the moral status of human beings, which expresses itself in blindness for the significance of the human subjectivity of victims as a moral factor that should be taken into consideration in decisions on how to treat them. This means that when persons are dehumanized, their experiences no longer matter in the eyes of the dehumanizer(s), or at least not as moral factors that count against their mistreatment. Those who are dehumanized are thereby not simply attributed a lower moral standing than persons whom we include in our inner moral circle(s), but excluded from the moral category of humanity altogether. Dehumanization, therefore, constitutes a uniquely radical form of exclusion. The last part of the chapter illustrates how this perspective can help clarify when refugees, asylum seekers, and other migrants are dehumanized.

The final chapter considers what should be done to bring an end to dehumanization. The ultimate aim of any normative theory of dehumanization should be to understand it better in the hopes that it may one day be dispelled altogether. The last chapter therefore considers what could and should be done to resist dehumanization through measures to counteract, challenge, or mitigate its exclusionary logic. More specifically, the chapter identifies three constitutive elements of our response to dehumanization—persuasion, support, and coercion—and illustrates how each of these could be implemented. Strategies of persuasion, I argue, should be the cornerstone of our approach since dehumanization is a social process that is upheld by ideology and propaganda. Support to the victims of dehumanization is also required to affirm the moral significance of their human subjectivity and rebuild trust in the moral human community. Beyond persuasion and support, coercive means, directed against perpetrators, may be needed to resist dehumanization in

16 Dehumanization in the Global Migration Crisis

light of its detrimental impact on the lives of victims. The chapter therefore considers what forms of coercion, aimed at restricting the space for action and expression available to perpetrators, are conceivable and permissible to counteract dehumanization.

Notes

1. For an analysis of the changes in news coverage in Europe in this period, see: Lilie Chouliaraki and Rafal Zaborowski, 'Voice and Community in the 2015 Refugee Crisis: A Content Analysis of News Coverage in Eight European Countries', *The International Communication Gazette* 79 (2017): 613–35, https://doi.org/10.1177/1748048517727173. For an overview of the changes in media reporting and political policies one year after the event, see: Patrick Kingsley, 'The Death of Alan Kurdi: One Year On, Compassion towards Refugees Fades', *The Guardian*, 2 September 2016, https://www.theguardian.com/world/2016/sep/01/alan-kurdi-death-one-year-on-compassion-towards-refugees-fades. For a critical analysis of the role of images in eliciting solidarity, see: Zakaria Sajir and Miriyam Aouragh, 'Solidarity, Social Media, and the "Refugee Crisis": Engagement Beyond Affect', *International Journal of Communication* 13 (2019): 550–77, https://ijoc.org/index.php/ijoc/article/view/9999.

2. Jennifer Welsh, *The Return of History: Conflict, Migration, and Geopolitics in the Twenty-first Century* (Toronto: House of Anansi Press, 2016), p. 110.

3. Zygmunt Bauman, *Strangers at Our Door* (Cambridge: Polity Press, 2016), p. 19. In a similar way, the President of the European Commission Jean-Claude Juncker stated in an address to the European Parliament that dealing with this crisis is a 'matter of humanity and human dignity'. See: BBC, 'Migrant Crisis: EU's Juncker Announces Refugee Quota Plan', 9 September 2015, http://www.bbc.com/news/world-europe-34193568.

4. For a global perspective on the crisis, see: Reece Jones, *Violent Borders: Refugees and the Right to Move* (London and New York: Verso, 2016).

5. Bauman, *Strangers at Our Door*, 19.

6. Bauman argues that these responses of hostility, alienation, and indifference are fuelled by opportunistic politics. He criticizes short-sighted strategies of political gain at the expense of refugees and other migrants that seek to capitalize on the desires of the downtrodden in society to see others still worse off than themselves and the fears of those in less precarious positions facing people who symbolize the decline of order. In opposition to divisive rhetoric, Bauman calls for communication to promote mutual understanding and mitigate estrangement and disregard. See: Bauman, *Strangers at Our Door*, 1–25.

7. This claim is supported by Tugba Basaran's insightful study of the way in which legal proceedings against people who have engaged in rescue at sea in the Strait of Sicily produces 'a distinction between worthy lives that fall within the duty to rescue and charitable lives becoming a question of benevolence' (205). See: Tugba Basaran, 'The Saved and the Drowned: Governing Indifference in the Name of Security', *Security Dialogue* 46 (2015): 205–20, https://doi.org/10.1177/09670106145575. The work of the political scientist Nick Vaughan-Williams on so-called 'push-back actions' and cases where irregular migrants are abandoned at sea also endorses this point. According to Vaughan-Williams,

Introduction **17**

such cases reflect a political decision 'on the status of the lives of some "irregular" migrants as being unworthy of protection'. See: Nick Vaughan-Williams, *Europe's Border Crisis: Biopolitical Security and Beyond* (Oxford: Oxford University Press, 2015), p. 67.

8. This sense of identification was also captured in the hashtag *#CouldBeMyChild*, which was used to spread the picture. See: Nadine El-Enany, 'Aylan Kurdi: The Human Refugee', *Law Critique* 27 (2016): 13, https://doi.org/10.1007/s10978-015-9175-7.

9. See, for example: Jessica Elgot and Matthew Taylor, 'Calais Crisis: Cameron Condemned for "Dehumanising" Description of Migrants', *The Guardian*, 30 July 2015, https://www.theguardian.com/uk-news/2015/jul/30/david-cameron-migrant-swarm-language-condemned, Emina Ćerimović, 'Asylum Seekers' Hell in a Greek "Hotspot"', *Human Rights Watch*, 30 November 2017, https://www.hrw.org/news/2017/11/30/asylum-seekers-hell-greek-hotspot, and Lauren Wroe, 'Social Workers Have a Duty to Speak Up about the Humanitarian Crisis in Calais', *The Guardian*, 4 August 2015, https://www.theguardian.com/social-care-network/2015/aug/04/social-workers-humanitarian-crisis-calais. The question as to whether these different examples amount to dehumanization will be discussed in more detail in later chapters.

10. See: Barry Malone, 'Why Al Jazeera Will Not Say Mediterranean "Migrants"', *Al Jazeera English*, 20 August 2015, http://www.aljazeera.com/blogs/editors-blog/2015/08/al-jazeera-mediterranean-migrants-150820082226309.html, Victoria Esses, Scott Veenvliet, Gordon Hodson, and Ljiljana Mihic, 'Justice, Morality, and the Dehumanization of Refugees', *Social Justice Research* 21 (2008): 4–25, https://doi.org/10.1007/s11211-007-0058-4, and Victoria Esses, Stelian Medianu, and Andrea Lawson, 'Uncertainty, Threat, and the Role of Media in Promoting the Dehumanization of Immigrants and Refugees', *Journal of Social Issues* 69 (2013): 518–36, https://doi.org/10.1111/josi.12027.

11. See: BBC, 'Food Wristbands Scrapped for Cardiff Asylum Seekers', 25 January 2016, http://www.bbc.com/news/uk-wales-35397109, Scottish Refugee Policy Forum, 'A Fairer Scotland for Asylum Seekers and Refugees in Times of Austerity?' February 2012, p. 6, https://scottishrefugeecouncil.org.uk/wp-content/uploads/2019/10/A-fairer-Scotland-for-asylum-seekers-and-refugees-in-a-time-of-austerity-Scottish-Refugee-Policy-Forum-report-PDF.pdf.

12. Juliana von Mittelstaedt and Maximilian Popp, 'One Year after the Lampedusa Tragedy' (translated by Christopher Sultan), *Spiegel Online*, 9 October 2014, http://www.spiegel.de/international/europe/lampedusa-survivors-one-year-after-the-refugee-tragedy-a-994887.html.

13. Lucy Fiske, 'Human Rights and Refugee Protest against Immigration Detention: Refugees' Struggles for Recognition as Human', *Refuge* 32 (2016): 22, https://doi.org/10.25071/1920-7336.40380.

14. In this book, the terms 'refugee' and 'asylum seeker' are used for the most part interchangeably, although an asylum seeker officially becomes a refugee only after he or she has been granted this status by the authorities of the country of reception. It should be noted as well that there might be asylum seekers who are not refugees in the common-sense meaning of the term: that is, people who have fled their country of origin because of danger to their life or safety or the risk of persecution. In these cases, their claim for asylum will probably be rejected, but for as long as legal decisions are pending, they fall within the category of asylum seekers. For the purposes of this work, both terms are used to refer to people who have reached or are travelling towards a country that

18   Dehumanization in the Global Migration Crisis

is not their country of origin and claim to have fled from persecution, armed conflict, or severe human rights violations, irrespective of whether the legal status of 'refugee' has been granted to them or not. In cases where people have not filed for asylum, the term 'refugee' is used. In cases where people have filed for asylum but the grounds for these claims are less clear, the term 'asylum seeker' is used. The term 'migrant' is used only to refer to reports and scholarly works that do not focus specifically on refugees and asylum seekers but on people who move to and settle in countries for various reasons.

15. The political theorist Norman Geras highlights, for example, that to be considered a fellow human being guarantees people inclusion in a moral order that governs interpersonal relations: 'The widespread tendency to dehumanize potential victims tells ... that the notion "(fellow) human being"—as opposed to infidel dog and devil, to demonic force or poison, to parasite, to vermin—is, for human beings, an extremely powerful mode of moral inclusion'. See: Norman Geras, *Solidarity in the Conversation of Humankind: The Ungroundable Liberalism of Richard Rorty* (London: Verso, 1995), p. 97.

16. Ibid.

17. Central works that have informed the analysis in this book include, but are not limited to: Paul Bain, Jeroen Vaes, and Jacques-Philippe Leyens (eds.), *Humanness and Dehumanization* (New York and London: Routledge, 2014), Nick Haslam, 'Dehumanization: An Integrative Approach', *Personality and Social Psychology Review* 10 (2006): 252–64, https://doi.org/10.1207/s15327957pspr1003_4, Axel Honneth, *Reification: A New Look at an Old Idea* (Berkeley Tanner Lectures) (Oxford: Oxford University Press, 2012), Herbert Kelman, 'Violence Without Moral Restraint: Reflections on the Dehumanization of Victims and Victimizers', *Journal of Social Issues* 29 (1973): 25–61, https://doi.org/10.1111/j.1540-4560.1973.tb00102.x, Maria Kronfelder (ed.), *The Routledge Handbook of Dehumanization* (London and New York: Routledge, 2021), Johannes Lang, 'Questioning Dehumanization: Intersubjective Dimensions of Violence in the Nazi Concentration and Death Camps', *Holocaust and Genocide Studies* 24 (2010): 225–46, https://doi.org/10.1093/hgs/dcq026, Jacques-Philippe Leyens, Stéphanie Demoulin, Jeroes Vaes, Ruth Gaunt, and Maria Paola Paladino, 'Infra-Humanization: The Wall of Group Differences', *Social Issues and Policy Review* 1 (2007): 139–72, https://doi.org/10.1111/j.1751-2409.2007.00006.x, Kate Manne, *Down Girl: The Logic of Misogyny* (Oxford: Oxford University Press, 2019), Avishai Margalit, *The Decent Society*, translated by Naomi Goldblum (Cambridge, Massachusetts and London: Harvard University Press, 1996), Anne Phillips, *The Politics of the Human* (Cambridge: Cambridge University Press, 2015), Richard Rorty, 'Human Rights, Rationality, and Sentimentality', in *Truth and Progress: Philosophical Papers. Volume 3* (Cambridge: Cambridge University Press, 1998), pp. 167–85, David Livingstone Smith, *Less than Human: Why We Demean, Enslave and Exterminate Others* (New York: St. Martin's, 2012), and Karen Stollznow, 'Dehumanization in Language and Thought', *Journal of Language and Politics* 7 (2008): 177–200, https://doi.org/10.1075/jlp.7.2.01sto.

18. For scholarly work on the dehumanization of refugees, asylum seekers, and migrants, see: Daniela DeBono, '"Less than Human": The Detention of Irregular Migrants in Malta', *Race & Class* 55 (2013): 60–81, https://doi.org/10.1177/0306396813497880, Esses, Veenvliet, Hodson, and Mihic, 'Justice, Morality, and the Dehumanization of Refugees', Esses, Medianu, and Lawson, 'Uncertainty, Threat, and the Role of Media', Victoria Esses, Stelian Medianu, and Alina Sutter, 'The Dehumanization and Rehumanization

of Refugees', in *The Routledge Handbook of Dehumanization*, edited by Maria Kronfelder (London and New York: Routledge, 2021) pp. 275–91, Fiske, 'Human Rights and Refugee Protest', Lisa Hartley and Caroline Fleay, '"We Are like Animals": Negotiating Dehumanising Experiences of Asylum-Seeker Policies in the Australian Community', *Refugee Survey Quarterly* 36 (2017): 45–63, https://doi.org/10.1093/rsq/hdx010, Sverre Varvin, 'Our Relations to Refugees: Between Compassion and Dehumanization', *Academic Journal of Psychoanalysis* 77 (2017), 359–77, https://doi.org/10.1057/s11231-017-9119-0, and Nick Vaughan-Williams, '"We Are Not Animals!" Humanitarian Border Security and Zoopolitical Spaces in EUrope', *Political Geography* 45 (2015): 1–10, https://doi.org/10.1016/j.polgeo.2014.09.009.

19. This approach is fairly similar to the one employed by the political theorist Michael Walzer, who draws on historical illustrations to develop and clarify his normative arguments on the ethics of war in *Just and Unjust Wars*. An important difference lies, however, in the fact that this book does not make use of historical examples but draws from personal stories, which were recounted to me during interviews that I conducted with refugees and asylum seekers. See: Michael Walzer, *Just and Unjust Wars: A Moral Argument with Historical Illustrations* (New York: Basic Books, 2006).

20. The interviews took place in Frankfurt am Main from 12 until 20 June 2017, in Beirut from 12 until 28 July 2017, and in Milan on 26 and 27 September 2017. Most of the interview participants came from Syria, but I also spoke with people from Iraq, Pakistan, Senegal, Guinea-Bissau, Nigeria, and Gambia. The interviewees included refugees and asylum seekers who were living in Lebanon at the time of the interview or reached Europe through the Balkan or Libyan route. The interviews in Germany and Italy were conducted in English, German, French, or Italian. The interviews in Lebanon were conducted in Arabic with the help of a Syrian translator. Citations found throughout this book correspond to what the participants said in the interviews (or to the translation given by the translator). In the case of interviews conducted in German, French, or Italian, the statements of the participants have been translated by the author.

21. Given that the purpose of the interviews was to understand better how refugees and asylum seekers experience dehumanization and other forms of exclusionary treatment, the most suitable approach for the interviews was deemed to be interpretative phenomenological analysis. This approach focuses on the way in which people make sense of important events in their lives. The interview guide was drawn up with the basic principles of interpretative phenomenological analysis in mind, which set out that questions should encourage participants to speak at length. The interview guide therefore included predominantly open questions that allowed participants to recount detailed stories and indicate which topics they felt comfortable speaking about. Follow-up questions were asked to encourage participants to speak about issues that were particularly relevant for the research.

While interpretative phenomenological analysis generally does not object to stating the precise phenomenon under study, it was decided that the term 'dehumanization' would not be mentioned during the interview to avoid upsetting, unsettling, or confusing the participants. Instead, the participants were asked at the end of the interview if they had experience with being treated 'inhumanely'. To avoid imposing a particular understanding of this term on the interviewees, they were first asked what they took 'humanity' and

20 Dehumanization in the Global Migration Crisis

'inhumanity' to mean. Some participants said they had no experience with inhumane treatment, while others recounted stories of the inhumane treatment of others. Several participants also said they had no idea of what 'humanity' or 'inhumanity' meant, but could give concrete examples of having been treated inhumanely.
See: Jonathan Smith, Paul Flowers, and Michael Larkin, *Interpretative Phenomenological Analysis: Theory, Method and Research* (London: Sage, 2009).

22. Recent publications on dehumanization include, for example: Bain, Vaes, and Leyens (eds.), *Humanness and Dehumanization*, Nicholas Epley, *Mindwise: Why We Misunderstand What Others Think, Believe, Feel, and Want* (New York: Vintage Books, 2015), Megan Glick, *Infrahumanisms: Science, Culture, and the Making of Modern Non/personhood* (Durham and London: Duke University Press, 2018), Haslam, 'Dehumanization', Honneth, *Reification*, Kronfelder (ed.), *The Routledge Handbook of Dehumanization*, Nour Kteily, Emile Bruneau, Adam Waytz, and Sarah Cotterill, 'The Ascent of Man: Theoretical and Empirical Evidence for Blatant Dehumanization', *Journal of Personality and Social Psychology* 109 (2015): 901–31, https://doi.org/10. 1037/pspp0000048, Lang, 'Questioning Dehumanization', Johannes Lang, 'The Limited Importance of Dehumanization in Collective Violence', *Current Opinion in Psychology* 35 (2020): 17–20, https://doi.org/10.1016/j.copsyc.2020.02.002, Leyens et al., 'Infra-Humanization', Manne, *Down Girl*, Mari Mikkola, *The Wrong of Injustice: Dehumanization and Its Role in Feminist Philosophy* (Oxford: Oxford University Press, 2016), Harriet Over, 'Seven Challenges for the Dehumanization Hypothesis', *Perspectives on Psychological Science* 16 (2021): 3–13, https://doi.org/10.1177/1745691620902, Phillips, *The Politics of the Human*, Tage Rai, Piercarlo Valdesolo, and Jesse Graham, 'Dehumanization Increases Instrumental Violence, But Not Moral Violence', *Proceedings of the National Academy of Sciences* 114 (2017): 8511–16, https://doi.org/10.1073/pnas.1705238114, John Rector, *The Objectification Spectrum: Understanding and Transcending Our Diminishment and Dehumanization of Others* (Oxford: Oxford University Press, 2014), Smith, *Less than Human*, David Livingstone Smith, *On Inhumanity: Dehumanization and How to Resist It* (Oxford: Oxford University Press, 2020), David Livingstone Smith, *Making Monsters: The Uncanny Power of Dehumanization* (Cambridge: Harvard University Press, 2021), Johannes Steizinger, 'The Significance of Dehumanization: Nazi Ideology and Its Psychological Consequences', *Politics, Religion & Ideology* 19 (2018): 139–57, https://doi.org/10.1080/21567689.2018.1425144, Stollznow, 'Dehumanization in Language and Thought', Cristian Tileagă, 'Ideologies of Moral Exclusion: A Critical Discursive Reframing of Depersonalization, Delegitimization and Dehumanization', *British Psychological Society* 46 (2007): 717–37, https://doi.org/10.1348/014466607X186894, Lynne Tirrell, 'Genocidal Language Games', in *Speech and Harm: Controversies over Free Speech*, edited by Ishani Maitra and Mary Kate McGowan (Oxford: Oxford University Press, 2002), pp. 174–221, and Philip Zimbardo, *The Lucifer Effect: How Good People Turn Evil* (London: Rider, 2008).

23. Rorty, 'Human Rights, Rationality, and Sentimentality'.
24. Honneth, *Reification*.
25. Epley, *Mindwise*.
26. Mikkola, *The Wrong of Injustice*.
27. Smith, *Less than Human*.
28. Stollznow, 'Dehumanization in Language and Thought'.

29. I also present this account in two articles in which I explain what matters most about human beings in terms of moral recognition and present my view of dehumanization as a solution to the so-called 'paradox of dehumanization'. See: Adrienne de Ruiter, 'Failing to See What Matters Most: Towards a Better Understanding of Dehumanisation', *Contemporary Political Theory* (2022), https://doi.org/10.1057/s41296-022-00569-2 and Adrienne de Ruiter, 'To Be or Not to Be Human: Resolving the Paradox of Dehumanisation', *European Journal of Political Theory* 22 (2023): 73–95, https://doi.org/10.1177/1474885120984605.

30. These meanings correspond to the various senses that 'humanity' holds following dictionary definitions. Merriam-Webster indicates that 'humanity' can refer to: (1) the collective of human beings, or humankind; (2) the quality or condition of being human, or human nature; (3) the quality of being humane, or benevolence. Merriam-Webster also adds a fourth sense of 'humanities' as a branch of learning. Since this applies to a field of study, rather than people, this meaning is not directly relevant for the study of this book. See: 'Humanity', *Merriam-Webster Online*, https://www.merriam-webster.com/dictionary/humanity.

31. The addition that the moral status that the dehumanized are attributed is lower than that of human beings is important because dehumanization can consist in regarding people as either subhuman or supra-human. The philosopher Avishai Margalit insightfully makes this point through his discussion of the historical case of the Egyptian pharaohs who were seen as deities. In exceptional cases where people are considered divine, they are attributed a status not below that of human beings, but higher and more exalted. This book focuses on forms of dehumanization that ascribe people a less than human status, given that this kind is more relevant for the analysis of forms of moral exclusion in the migration crisis. See: Margalit, *The Decent Society*, 90.

32. Chouliaraki and Zaborowski, 'Voice and Community in the 2015 Refugee Crisis': 632, note 1.

33. William Spindler, '2015: The Year of Europe's Refugee Crisis', *UNHCR*, 8 December 2015, https://www.unhcr.org/news/stories/2015/12/56ec1ebde/2015-year-europes-refugee-crisis.html.

34. Chouliaraki and Zaborowski, 'Voice and Community in the 2015 Refugee Crisis': 632, note 1.

35. European Parliament, *Resolution of 14 April 2016 on the 2015 Report on Turkey*, 2015/2898(RSP), https://www.europarl.europa.eu/doceo/document/TA-8-2016-0133_EN.html?redirect.

36. Ministry of Foreign Affairs of the Italian Republic, *Memorandum d'Intesa Sulla Cooperazione nel Campo dello Sviluppo, del Contrasto all'Immigrazione Illegale, al Traffico di Esseri Umani, al Contrabbando e sul Rafforzamento della Sicurezza delle Frontiere tra lo Stato della Libia e la Repubblica Italiana*, 2 February 2017, itra.esteri.it/vwPdf/wfrmRenderPdf.aspx?ID=50975.

37. Ashley Parker, Nick Miroff, Sean Sullivan, and Tyler Pager, '"No End in Sight": Inside the Biden's Administration's Failure to Contain the Border Surge', *The Washington Post*, 22 March 2021, www.washingtonpost.com%2fpolitics%2fbiden-border-surge%2f2021%2f03%2f20%2f21824e94-8818-11eb-8a8b-5cf82c3dffe4_story.html.

38. Patrick Kingsley, *The New Odyssey: The Story of Europe's Refugee Crisis* (London: Guardian Faber Publishing, 2016), pp. 289–90.

22 Dehumanization in the Global Migration Crisis

39. Izzy Tomico Ellis, 'Don't Call It the "Refugee Crisis", It's a Humanitarian Issue—Failing to Recognise That Creates Even More Suffering', *The Independent*, 13 November 2019, https://www.independent.co.uk/voices/refugee-migrant-crisis-humanitarian-greece-syria-turkey-eu-a9201006.html.
40. Chandran Kukathas, 'Are Refugees Special?' in *Migration in Political Theory: The Ethics of Movement and Membership*, edited by Sarah Fine and Lea Ypi (Oxford: Oxford University Press, 2016), pp. 249–68.
41. Malone, 'Why Al Jazeera'.
42. 'Crisis', *Online Etymology Dictionary*, https://www.etymonline.com/word/crisis.

1
Dehumanization in the Migration Crisis

> Some countries are not treating refugees as human beings but as animals or something like that, like intruders.
> **Tariq, asylum seeker from Pakistan**

Introduction

Tariq is a young Pakistani who left his country out of fear for persecution for his atheist worldview. We speak with each other at a charity in Milan that offers a place for the night for asylum seekers. Tariq recounts how some countries that he travelled through treated refugees inhumanely, like intruders. In stating that countries do not treat refugees as human beings he explicitly links this treatment to dehumanization.

In reporting on the global migration crisis, the term dehumanization is also frequently used to denounce practices that are detrimental to the well-being of refugees, asylum seekers, and unwanted migrants.[1] Among the array of depictions that have been called dehumanizing are representations that link immigrants to the spread of (contagious) diseases, portray them as queue-jumpers, or depict them as potential terrorists.[2] Portrayals that fail to individualize refugees have been said to be dehumanizing,[3] as have policies that seek to facilitate the provision of aid to asylum seekers through the use of wristbands.[4]

This chapter critically examines the various ways in which the terminology of dehumanization is used in reporting on the global migration crisis. The central argument is that sharper distinctions should be made between dehumanization and related forms of social and moral exclusion, such as marginalization, stigmatization, and criminalization, in other to clarify the distinctive nature and wrong of dehumanization. It is important to distinguish between these concepts, I argue, since dehumanization takes a unique position in the spectrum of exclusionary practices, as it excludes people from the moral community we share as human beings rather than simply weakens

Dehumanization in the Global Migration Crisis. Adrienne de Ruiter, Oxford University Press. © Adrienne de Ruiter (2024).
DOI: 10.1093/oso/9780198893400.003.0002

24   Dehumanization in the Global Migration Crisis

their position within it. Our understanding of dehumanization should therefore be restricted to acts of perceiving, portraying, or treating people as *less than* human, thereby excluding forms of rejection and exclusion that relate to them as *lesser* human beings. Delimiting our understanding in this way is necessary to do justice to the fact that dehumanization constitutes a distinctively radical form of exclusion.

The chapter starts with an overview of how the terminology of dehumanization has been used by scholars, journalists, and other commentators on the global migration crisis, as well as by refugees, asylum seekers, and other migrants themselves. This analysis focuses on three themes to which dehumanization is often linked, which relate to threat and deviance; de-individualization and disengagement; and denials of dignity. This discussion illustrates how dehumanization tends to be used in an overly broad sense to describe portrayals and treatments that deny the *full* humanity of refugees, asylum seekers, and migrants. By drawing from the conceptual distinction between dehumanization and infra-humanization, I argue for the need to limit our understanding of dehumanization to ways of viewing, portraying, or treating people as *less than* human. The final part of the chapter introduces the notions of animalization, objectification, and brutalization and explains why these provide helpful lenses to direct our analysis of dehumanization in the global migration crisis in the following chapters.

Frames of dehumanization

In recent years, much has been written on the position of refugees and asylum seekers in the contemporary world.[5] While some authors expose injustices that mark current political regimes of dealing with people who are fleeing from war, persecution, or severe human rights violations,[6] others highlight how the stigmatization of asylum seekers and migrants in popular media encourages moral disengagement, which makes populations of receiving countries less inclined to support accommodating policies towards people requesting asylum.[7] In this field, the term 'dehumanization' is commonly used to denounce practices that are detrimental to the well-being of refugees, asylum seekers, and unwanted migrants.[8]

The notion of dehumanization is used in diverse ways to describe the predicament of the displaced. Appeals to dehumanization in this field roughly cluster around three broad themes, which relate to threat and deviance; de-individualization and disengagement; and denials of dignity. Threat and deviance involve representations and forms of treatment that cast refugees, asylum seekers, and other migrants as a risk to security or social cohesion. (Forced) migrants are presented as a danger, for instance, when they are depicted as criminals or as carriers of disease. These portrayals seem related to dehumanization because the depictions of displaced people as a threat draws attention away from their needs and standing as fellow human beings and cast them in a pejorative light.

De-individualization and disengagement entail that refugees, asylum seekers, and migrants are presented in ways that distract from their personal characteristics and weaken affective and moral responses to their plight. De-individualization occurs, for example, when refugees are depicted in media photographs in large groups. The appeals of forced migrants as people in need lose force through this kind of portrayal. De-individualization and disengagement can therefore be linked to dehumanization as these processes impair recognition of the individual humanity of displaced persons and undermine feelings of concern and care.[9]

Denials of dignity are involved in portrayals or treatments that express disregard for the standing that displaced persons hold as human beings. This may take the form of representations that portray refugees, asylum seekers, and other migrants as undeserving of respect or treatments that impede them from meeting their basic needs. While all three themes contain certain links to dehumanization, it will be helpful to consider each individually to examine this relation more closely and determine when it makes sense to speak of dehumanization, and when it does not.

Threat and deviance

Refugees, asylum seekers, and unwanted migrants are often linked to danger. In European media coverage of the 2015 crisis, immigrants were, for instance, likened to tidal waves or invading hordes and suspected of being potential terrorists.[10] Alarmist reporting on the arrival of newcomers is of long standing, however. Scholars have noted, for example, how immigrants and refugees have been depicted in Western media as 'enemies at the gate' for decades.[11]

The perceived danger of displaced persons does not necessarily involve an existential threat to the population. As the social psychologists Victoria Esses, Stelian Medianu, and Andrea Lawson note, threat can relate not only to straightforward risks to public health and the physical safety of the population (as exemplified in the threats of contagious diseases or terrorism), but also to fears about economic loss or undesirable social transformations, as taking in people who do not play by the rules may undermine social cohesion.

26 Dehumanization in the Global Migration Crisis

These authors note how 'such depictions grab the publics' attention, alerting them to potential physical, economic, and cultural threats'.[12] In this cultural and social sense, threat is related to deviance.

The view that refugees are sometimes perceived as threatening is also expressed by forcibly displaced persons themselves. Tariq echoes this idea when he speaks about the period that he was held in an immigration detention centre in Bulgaria. This treatment made him feel like a criminal, even though he did not do anything illegal: 'They put me behind bars. You could not call it a camp. I am a human. I am not going to kill people'.

Amira, a young woman who fled with her family from Damascus to Germany after the army took possession of their house notes that interactions with people in everyday life are also sometimes marked by suspicion. This fear of refugees as a destructive force is uncalled for, she claims, as she explains that 'we do not come here to break something. We are coming because of the war. We come to live in freedom'.

Other refugees also speak about the fear that certain people seem to have for asylum seekers as they associate them with the destructive and dangerous environment from which they flee. Salim, who left Mosul shortly before the takeover by the so-called Islamic State and who lived in Italy at the time of our meeting, observes, for instance, that some people respond in negative ways to Iraqi refugees: 'They think you are bad because you come from Iraq. You have war. You have black hair'. Salim notes how certain Europeans seem to fear the coming of people from Iraq because they identify them with militants and terrorists, although many of the refugees who have come from Iraq are actually among the principal victims of IS. Salim points to the absurdity that people in Europe seem to be afraid of him, whereas he is the one who is alone in an unknown country: 'Who must be frightened, you or me? Me. I can't do anything against you. I don't know anything here. You know everything here!'

The notions of threat and deviance play a central role in the study of Esses, Medianu, and Lawson about dehumanization of migrants in media reporting. These authors maintain that people can be dehumanized in various ways, which involve 'the denial of full humanness to others, and their exclusion from the human species'.[13] One indication of dehumanization is when people are only attributed primary emotions (such as pleasure or fear), but not secondary emotions (such as hope or remorse). Another is when their values are considered base, which entails that their moral thinking has failed to transcend basic animal sensibilities and lacks, for example, more complex pro-social values related to equality and forgiveness. When people are considered barbarians, this is another marker of dehumanization, following their account.

Drawing from this notion of dehumanization as a denial of full human-ness that can be seen reflected in denials of secondary emotions, higher-order social values, or civilization, Esses and her colleagues argue that representations of immigrants in media that link them to the spread of (contagious) diseases, portray them as queue-jumpers, or represent them as potential terrorists are dehumanizing.[14] While this analysis importantly draws attention to the ways in which migrants may be stigmatized, marginalized, and criminalized through the media and resonates with some of the experiences of refugees, recounted above, my concern is that the classification of these representations as dehumanizing fails to clearly distinguish dehumanization from these related concepts.

Let us consider first the portrayal of migrants as spreading (contagious) diseases. Traditionally there has been a strong link between diseases and dehumanization. For example, Nazi propaganda represented Jewish people as a cancer. A chilling example of this may be found in a statement by the camp doctor from Auschwitz and Bergen-Belsen, Fritz Klein, who used the dehumanizing image of Jews as an infectious disease to reconsider his medical responsibilities: 'My Hippocratic oath tells me to cut a gangrenous appendix out of the human body. The Jews are the gangrenous appendix of mankind. That's why I cut them out.'[15]

It is important to note, however, that likening people to a disease and portraying them as carriers of an illness is not the same thing. Although representing people as a disease—as in the case of Klein—is clearly dehumanizing, because it denies them even minimal human status (as the Jews were considered not part of mankind, but 'the gangrenous appendix to mankind'), the same is not necessarily true for portraying them as carriers of a disease. This representation marginalizes people by conveying the idea that contact with asylum seekers and migrants would threaten the health of the local population. Through marginalization, the position that persons hold in relation to others is lowered as they are relegated to the outer circles of a society, moral community, or social group, banned to a sphere where their interests and concerns matter significantly less than those of others. Claiming migrants have (contagious) diseases thus marginalizes them through the suggestion that people better stay away from them and by allegedly justifying measures of isolation and quarantine.

This portrayal can also be considered stigmatizing, as stigmatization entails marking people as bad or tainted by a characteristic of which to be ashamed. The sociologist Erving Goffman thus describes stigma as 'an attribute that is deeply discrediting' through which people are set apart from a majority that is considered 'normal'.[16] The accusation that migrants are the spreaders of (contagious) diseases is stigmatizing because it represents them as unhealthy, unclean, and dangerous. This portrayal can furthermore invoke disgust, which makes dehumanization more likely.[17] To be the carrier of a disease does not automatically jeopardize people's human status, however, since we generally do not fail to regard the sick in our midst as fellow human beings. A tension therefore exists in the account of dehumanization of Esses, Medianu, and Lawson as it includes both 'the denial of full humanness to others' and 'their exclusion from the human species'.[18] People may well be denied full humanness and thereby seen as inferior, I hold, without necessarily being excluded from the human category altogether.

These authors argue that portraying immigrants and refugees as queue-jumpers is dehumanizing as well. Given their understanding of dehumanization as a denial of full humanness that may be expressed as a denial of higher-order social values, this argument makes sense. After all, the portrayal of refugees 'as bogus queue-jumpers who are attempting to gain entry to western countries through illicit means',[19] as Medianu and her colleagues summarize this depiction, presents them as selfish and lacking respect for fairness and social rules. My concern is that something is lost in this broad understanding of dehumanization as encompassing any portrayal or treatment that casts others as inferior human beings. It is important to distinguish here between portrayals through which people are cast as *less than* human and portrayals that depict them as *less* human.

This distinction is introduced by the social psychologist Jacques-Phillipe Leyens and his colleagues, who claim that a qualitative difference exists between conceiving of others as less human or considering them less than human:

> [P]eople are inclined to perceive members of outgroups as somewhat less human, or more animal-like, than themselves; such a view corresponds to the word infra-humanization (although we could also have used 'subhumanization'). By contrast, dehumanization of an outgroup implies that its members are no longer humans at all.[20]

Leyens and his colleagues suggest that the difference between viewing people as less human or regarding them as less than human is not just gradual. Instead, this distinction signals a qualitative difference. If we consider people lesser human beings, we do still consider them human, whereas if we regard them as less than human, we exclude them from the category of humanity.

Some scholars have argued that this distinction is hard to maintain in practice, as it is often difficult to tell whether someone is viewed as less than human or a lesser human being, and that it is therefore more helpful to think of dehumanization as a scale, which includes more relative and absolute denials of humanity.[21] While it indeed can be hard to distinguish sharply between dehumanization and infra-humanization in practice, I believe that the conceptual distinction should be maintained because viewing, portraying, or treating people as less than human significantly differs from viewing, portraying, or treating them as less human.

Dehumanization does not simply lower the position victims hold among fellow human beings, but excludes them from this moral category altogether. This distinction matters theoretically, normatively, and practically. Someone who is dehumanized is no longer considered normatively human and thereby loses the moral protection that this label provides. To be considered a fellow human being guarantees people inclusion in a moral order that governs interpersonal relations. The political theorist Norman Geras highlights this point as he insightfully notes how '[t]he widespread tendency to dehumanize potential victims tells ... that the notion "(fellow) human being"—as opposed to infidel dog and devil, to demonic force or poison, to parasite, to vermin—is, for human beings, an extremely powerful mode of moral inclusion'.[22]

It is important, furthermore, to distinguish between situations where persons are treated or portrayed in degrading ways because they are regarded as inferior human beings and situations where this treatment or depiction follows from a perception of the victims as less than human. This difference matters, not only for understanding the precise wrong that is done, beyond the degradation inherent in this treatment or portrayal, but also for deciding how to dissuade perpetrators from continuing engaging in these actions. Emphasizing human equality and human rights may be helpful, for example, in cases where victims are viewed as inferior human beings, but not in cases where they are regarded as less than human, given that the victims are excluded from the moral category of humanity.[23] To maintain this conceptual distinction, dehumanization should therefore be defined as a practice or process, which involves relating to people as *less than* human, and not just *less* human.

A weakness of Esses, Medianu, and Lawsons's argument, in my view, is that it fails to uphold this distinction. When refugees and migrants are represented as people who 'cheat' to get ahead, they are portrayed as inferior human beings but not necessarily as less than human.[24] After all, queue-jumping is a uniquely human activity. The accusation of queue-jumping indeed blemishes the reputation of refugees, but this label fits better with stigmatization than dehumanization, since it marks asylum seekers and refugees as tainted by a negative quality, but does not in itself exclude them from the human category. The portrayal of asylum seekers as frauds and cheats is thus not dehumanizing in itself, I claim—as their depiction as a disease, plague, or pestilence, for example, would be.

The act of representing migrants and refugees as potential terrorists fails to be dehumanizing for the same reason. It is important to distinguish here between the question whether (potential) terrorists are (sometimes) dehumanized and whether portraying people as (potential) terrorists is dehumanizing in and of itself. In my view, it is reasonable to claim that terrorists and terrorist suspects are sometimes dehumanized. For example, the portrayal of terrorists as 'unlawful combatants', which was used after 9/11 as a strategy to justify the exclusion of detainees in Guantanamo Bay from the protection of human rights and international law, can be viewed as a form of dehumanization.[25] By labelling prisoners as 'unlawful combatants', terrorists and terrorist suspects have been denied the moral status of human beings who as such are entitled to fundamental human rights.

Although terrorists and terrorist suspects thus indeed face a risk of dehumanization, which is sometimes realized in practice, this does not entail that the portrayal of people as (potential) terrorists is de facto dehumanizing as well. Depicting people as (potential) terrorists does not necessarily constitute a form of dehumanization, in my view, because this depiction does not automatically cast them as less than human. If this would be the case, there could be no calls, for example, to negotiate with (potential) terrorists.[26] While I believe that representing migrants and refugees as potential terrorists would be dehumanizing in cultural settings where potential terrorists are granted a less than human status, it cannot be assumed that such representations are universally dehumanizing. A contextual analysis that considers the status attributed to (potential) terrorists would be required to establish whether this is the case or not in a particular situation.[27]

In brief, dehumanization, on my view, should be restricted to perceiving, portraying, or treating people as *less than* human. There is something special about dehumanization as a form of moral exclusion because it expels people from the moral order of humanity rather than attributing them a lower position within it. While it may indeed often be difficult to distinguish between situations in which people are perceived, portrayed, or treated as less human and situations in which people are cast as less than human, ignoring this distinction entails disregarding the qualitative difference that exists between these types of exclusionary practices.

De-individualization and disengagement

A second theme in reporting on the dehumanization of refugees, asylum seekers, and unwanted migrants revolves around de-individualization and disengagement. Scholars have noted that media representations often portray refugees in medium or large groups rather than individually or in small groups.[28] International development scholar Annabelle Wilmott, who studied pictures of Syrian refugees that were published in September 2015 by three online British newspapers, found, for example, that photographs often depicted refugees in large groups from afar, which contributes to a sense of emotional distance and avoids identification with people in need.[29] Similar conclusions were drawn by communication scholars Xu Zhang and Lea Hellmueller in their study of photographs of refugees published on the website of *Der Spiegel*, in contrast to CNN International. Zhang and Hellmueller found that *Der Spiegel* frequently used pictures that framed the 2015 European refugee crisis in xenophobic ways and as a threat to law and order by depicting refugees as an anonymous mass.[30] CNN International, instead, emphasized the humanitarian dimensions of suffering and loss and humanized refugees by portraying them with family members and recognizable facial expressions.

Disengagement is mentioned in the personal stories of refugees as well. Salim, for instance, expresses the feeling that some migration officials do not care about the people they are dealing with: 'If you died in this room, they don't worry. If you have a problem, they don't care'. Abdul, a young Syrian who works in a cafeteria in Beirut, contrasts his life in Lebanon with the life he led in his home town and appeals to a sense of belonging and concern that is lacking in his current situation as a refugee: 'In my village, we felt one. Here everybody is alone. We are not friends. No one cares about another'. Abdul's testimony points to the idea that disengagement cannot only arise through de-individualization but also through a lack of social contact through which people come to feel that they stand alone.

The themes of de-individualization and disengagement are also central to an article on the visual dehumanization of refugees in Australian media by the political scientists Roland Bleiker, David Campbell, Emma Hutchison, and Xzarina Nicholson.[31] These authors contend that the lack of images depicting individual asylum seekers leads to their dehumanization. They explain how Australian media coverage demonstrates dehumanizing visual patterns that 'have framed the refugee "problem" such that it is seen not as a humanitarian disaster that requires a compassionate public response, but rather as a potential threat that sets in place mechanisms of security and border control'.[32]

This article importantly identifies the ways in which media reports on refugees influence how the broader audience morally and emotionally engages with their plight, but it fails to distinguish clearly between dehumanization and de-individualization. Although it is true that individualizing images and narratives may lead to the humanization of the displaced, in the sense that they become more easily recognizable as persons whose claims deserve consideration, I argue that the reverse, that is to say, a failure to depict people as individuals, is not necessarily dehumanizing.

Bleiker and his colleagues do not explain what makes the visual patterns used in Australian media reports on refugees specifically dehumanizing. Given that the examples they provide only fail to individualize those portrayed, and do not, for instance, depict them as diseases or parasites, it seems that the images used indeed create emotional distance, as the authors observe, but do not directly deny the status that refugees hold as human beings.[33] Although these reports do not engage with the individuality of asylum seekers, they do not necessarily exclude them from a shared moral community either.

Regarding this point, we may consider the influential work of the anthropologist Liisa Malkki on typical representations of refugees.[34] She points out that visual portrayals of mass displacement often take the shape of 'a spectacle of "raw", "bare" humanity', which 'in no way helps one to realize that each of the persons in the photograph has a name, opinions, relatives, and histories, or that each has reasons for being where he is now'.[35]

Malkki draws here from the concept of 'bare life', which has been introduced by the philosopher Giorgio Agamben to describe a state in which people are excluded from consideration as subjects under law, politics, and religion.[36] The idea behind this concept is that human life can be rendered 'bare' by the reduction of an ordinary human life with political, social, and religious meaning (*bios*) to a (virtually) naked biological existence (*zoë*), which is excluded from any sociopolitical and legal order.[37] Despite the reduction to that 'raw', 'bare' humanity, Malkki points to the complexity of deciding whether such framing should be considered dehumanizing in her reflections on the different ways in which the notion of humanity features in this practice:

> The visual conventions for representing refugees and the language of raw human needs both have the effect of constructing refugees as a bare humanity—even as a merely biological or demographic presence. This mode of humanitarianism acts

> to trivialize and silence history and politics—a silencing that can legitimately be described as dehumanizing in most contexts. And yet the mechanisms involved here are more complex than that. For one might argue that what these representational practices do is not strictly to dehumanize, but to humanize in a particular mode. A mere, bare, naked, or minimal humanity is set up. This is a vision of humanity that repels elements that fail to fit into the logic of its framework.[38]

Malkki's reflections highlight the complexities involved in determining whether reductive representations of people's humanity should be considered dehumanizing. If refugees are humanized in a mode that allows them only to be seen through the lens of 'a mere, bare, naked, or minimal humanity', the question is whether this includes them in the moral order of human beings. Are people attributed moral human status when they are seen through this lens of mere, bare, naked humanity? The tension here is one between a biological and a normative sense of humanity.

On my reading, Malkki's reasoning points to the idea that de-individualization can indeed amount to dehumanization, but also indicates that this process needs to be carried through to an extreme degree to achieve the sense of mere, naked, bare humanity described. It is important to note that de-individualization is not a sufficient condition to turn pictures of refugees into depictions of 'bare' humanity. Consider, for example, that media reporting on music festivals or, for example, after terrorist attacks, such as those in Paris or Cannes, at times publishes similar-looking images of masses of people. People do not object to such images on the ground that they dehumanize the people portrayed or represent them as 'bare life'. The failure to portray refugees in individualizing ways may therefore reinforce already existing perceptions of refugees as belonging to a category of 'bare life', especially if such portrayals focus on the aspects of human beings that we share with animals, but the aspect of de-individualization itself does not lie at the core of this reduced view of people's humanity and can therefore also not be seen to be de facto dehumanizing, even if it may contribute to it.

This conclusion is supported by the findings of a study on the effect of visual framing on the dehumanization of refugees. Cognitive neuroscientist Ruben Azevedo and his colleagues found that this effect appears to be connotative, rather than denotative, which means that de-individualizing visual framings of refugees may lead to dehumanization due to cultural and historical meanings that are already attributed to a certain image. These authors claim that it is not the case that 'seeing any anonymous group literally hinders the identification of human subjects. Cognitive processes of categorial

34 Dehumanization in the Global Migration Crisis

perception and stereotyping are subject to historical and social contexts and the saliency of the refugee crisis in western media over the recent years may explain the selective effect we observed.'[39]

De-individualization is thus not necessarily dehumanizing but may become so when it is applied to groups that are already seen as less fully human and closer to a 'mere, bare, naked, or minimal humanity', as described by Malkki. What this discussion shows is that humanity holds different meanings and that dehumanization does not require for all of these meanings to be denied. Recognition of a (minimal) biological sense of humanity may thus coincide with dehumanization, as the latter revolves around casting the victim as less than human in a moral sense.[40]

Denials of dignity

A third theme that is central to the debate on dehumanization in the ongoing migration crisis concerns denials of dignity. Broadly speaking, there are two ways of conceiving of denials of dignity in this context. First, denials of dignity are involved in depictions that portray refugees, asylum seekers, and unwanted migrants as undeserving of respect and consideration. Second, denials of dignity are concerned in treatments, policies, or structural conditions that impede people from meeting even their basic needs.

An example of the first type of denial of dignity can be found in the claim by Bill Frelick, the director of the Refugee Programme of Human Rights Watch, that the practice of labelling migrants as illegal is dehumanizing.[41] Although Frelick does not specify what he takes dehumanization to mean, he seems to draw from an understanding of dehumanization as a violation of human dignity, according to which the depiction of a human being as illegal should be understood as an affront to the moral status that migrants hold as people. He explains, for example, that calling people 'illegal immigrants' presupposes that 'a particular event in someone's life, such as irregularly crossing an international border or overstaying a visa, irrevocably taints that person's character as illegitimate or criminal'.[42]

An example of the second type is reflected in the appeal by Salil Shetty, Secretary General of Amnesty International, that 'people who have fled war are now enduring dehumanizing living conditions and dying of entirely treatable diseases. They escaped bombs to die of infections, diarrhoea, or pneumonia'.[43] Dehumanization is linked here to living conditions that do not correspond to minimally decent standards. Although Shetty does not explicitly mention dignity, what allegedly makes such living conditions dehumanizing is the fact that they do not correspond to even a minimal threshold that allows people to live their life as a *human* life.

These two understandings of dignity—as linking to a certain moral status that requires both respect and resources to live a minimally decent life—may coincide. This is reflected in the statement by Filippo Grandi, the United Nations High Commissioner for Refugees, that dehumanization constitutes a political strategy which leads to denials of dignity and disregard for basic human needs:

> Humanity is losing ground. The language of politics has become ruthless, giving licence to xenophobia. Refugees and migrants have become the catalysts of a 'dehumanization trend', whose sole purpose is immediate political gain. People uprooted by war are branded as a threat. The consequences are chilling: refugees turned back at borders, imprisoned indefinitely or left to perish at sea. Entire groups have been pushed to the margins of society, their dignity denied and their basic human needs for sustenance and security disregarded.[44]

Dignity is also mentioned by forcibly displaced persons themselves. Ibrahim, as noted in the Introduction, ties dehumanization to a denial of dignity in claiming that he needs '[t]o be respected as a human. To be treated as a human. So you can feel your humanity and dignity'.[45] Dignity is sometimes seen as a requirement for being fully human. This idea is expressed by Joseph, who fled from Senegal to Europe out of fear for persecution on religious grounds, and claims that 'it is one's dignity and freedom that determine the individual. When a person loses one of the two, he becomes like an animal'.

Linking dehumanization to denials of dignity seems promising, at least at first sight, because the concept of human dignity speaks to the idea of an intrinsic and inalienable worth that people possess by virtue of being human, which proscribes particular ways in which human beings may be treated and requires for a minimal standard of life to be provided. Yet, a closer look at the aforementioned examples shows that the notion of dignity is complex as its precise meaning is difficult to pinpoint.

Frelick, as noted above, claims that calling migrant 'illegal' is dehumanizing and seems to implicitly appeal in his argument to a notion of dignity. While he does not specify what he takes dehumanization to mean, his arguments indicate that the portrayal of a human being as illegal should be understood as an affront to the moral status that migrants hold as people. Although it can be rightly questioned whether the label of illegality should be applied to human beings at all, this term does not straightforwardly deny

36 Dehumanization in the Global Migration Crisis

people's humanity in a meaningful sense. After all, this affront does not directly affect a person's *human* status, but rather the standing that people hold within a particular legal framework. While it places undocumented migrants and asylum seekers in a low position in a hierarchy of human subjects, which may make them more vulnerable to dehumanization, labelling someone as 'illegal' does not in itself entail treating, viewing, or representing them as *less than* human. I therefore believe that the practice of characterizing people as 'illegal' migrants should be understood as stigmatizing and criminalizing, but not necessarily dehumanizing.

Barry Malone, editor of *Al Jazeera English*, takes Frelick's argument one step further and contends that the term 'migrant' is dehumanizing. Malone argues that 'migrant' has become an umbrella term that can be used as 'reductive terminology' that renders the lives of refugees virtually valueless:

> The umbrella term migrant is no longer fit for purpose when it comes to describing the horror unfolding in the Mediterranean. It has evolved from its dictionary definitions into a tool that dehumanises and distances, a blunt pejorative. It is not hundreds of people who drown when a boat goes down in the Mediterranean, nor even hundreds of refugees. It is hundreds of migrants. It is not a person—like you, filled with thoughts and history and hopes—who is on the tracks delaying a train. It is a migrant. A nuisance. It already feels like we are putting a value on the word. Migrant deaths are not worth as much to the media as the deaths of others—which means that their lives are not. Drowning disasters drop further and further down news bulletins. We rarely talk about the dead as individuals anymore. They are numbers.[46]

Malone importantly reflects on the way in which the meaning of terms can change, allowing for a notion that is not intrinsically dehumanizing to become so over time. In my view, he overstates his case, however, given that migrants are not necessarily excluded from a shared moral compact of human beings. People who are migrants may indeed be dehumanized when their lives are not considered valuable and when they are seen as mere statistics, but in that case they are dehumanized, not because they are viewed as migrants, but because they are no longer considered to matter. It is important to note, furthermore, that not all migrants are necessarily seen in this way, and that it therefore cannot be claimed that the term 'migrant' itself is dehumanizing. Malone seems to think that something happens with the status of persons when a label is attributed to them that does not adequately reflect their moral standing as human beings. This argument draws implicitly from a concept of human dignity, which proscribes the portrayal of people in ways that are devoid of even minimal concern for their plight. This discrediting meaning cannot be attributed to the term 'migrant' in general, however, because people can be called migrants without this necessarily entailing that they are excluded from the moral category of humanity.

In the case of Shetty's statement, dehumanization is seen as a characteristic of living conditions that threaten the health and well-being of refugees, where this risk could be taken away with relatively little effort. The fact that people are dying of 'entirely treatable diseases' indicates that the lives of these people are not sufficiently valued.[47] Dignity may be seen to perform a dual function here: since the minimal dignity of refugees is not acknowledged, politicians consider it permissible to let them subsist in dehumanizing living conditions that in turn undermine and violate their dignity in a practical lived sense. This also speaks to Grandi's claim that denials of dignity and disregard for basic rights can constitute detrimental consequences of dehumanizing policies and perceptions.

This discussion shows that a wide range of alleged denials of dignity are linked to dehumanization by commentators on the global migration crisis. While some of these ties are intuitively appealing, such as Shetty's claim that living conditions under which refugees die from easily treatable diseases are dehumanizing, others are less so, such as Malone's position that the term 'migrant' is dehumanizing in and of itself. This supports the claim that the notion of dehumanization is used in too broad and inclusive a way by commentators on the global migration crisis and that a more nuanced account of what dehumanization entails in this context could contribute to drawing more precise distinctions between portrayals, treatment, and perceptions that are dehumanizing and those that are not.

Three forms of moral exclusion

This discussion of scholarly writing, human rights commentary, and journalistic (opinion) pieces that have been published over the past years on the dehumanization of refugees and migrants shows that dehumanization is often conflated with related processes. De-individualization, stigmatization, marginalization, criminalization, and infra-humanization unsettle the social and moral position that refugees, asylum seekers, and migrants hold in the current world order and the interpersonal relations they maintain with others. Still, these practices only turn into dehumanization when morally degrading portrayals deny the moral status that victims hold as human beings.

38 Dehumanization in the Global Migration Crisis

The imprecise use of the term is problematic because it may well render claims that refugees, asylum seekers, and unwanted migrants are dehumanized less convincing. There is a risk involved in the tendency of advocates for the rights of the displaced to resort to a broad notion of dehumanization to bring home the point that certain treatments and portrayals of refugees and migrants are inadmissible. In using this term in underdetermined, vague, or overly inclusive ways, the distinct nature and wrong of dehumanization become more difficult to discern. In turn, it becomes easier, and more reasonable, for parties that are more reluctant to aid refugees, asylum seekers, and other migrants to dismiss criticisms of their stance and practices if critiques are not based on compelling arguments.

To develop our understanding of dehumanization in the global migration crisis, an alternative approach is needed that can help us distinguish between various forms of moral exclusion and allows us to leave the umbrella term behind. A suitable starting point for this analysis, I believe, can be found in three prevalent frames in the scholarly literature, which link dehumanization to animalization, objectification, and brutalization.[48] Animalization entails identifying people with non-human animals, usually ones that are held in low esteem, such as rats or cockroaches. Objectification involves viewing, portraying, or treating people as objects, lacking in fundamental human traits or qualities, such as a will of one's own or (deep-felt) emotions. Brutalization speaks to a process through which people allegedly become less human(e), in the sense that they become insensitive to the suffering of fellow (human) beings.

These three prisms can be recognized in reporting on the global migration crisis. In his testimony, mentioned in the Introduction, Ibrahim objected, for example, to the treatment he and his fellow detainees were given in an immigration detention centre, stating that 'they treated us as an animal'.[49] Other examples of animalization may be found in the work of the anthropologist Ruben Andersson, who describes interactions between undocumented migrants and (vigilante) border guards as relations between 'hunter and prey',[50] or the writings of Bridget Anderson on depictions of refugees and migrants as a pestilence.[51] Objectification can be recognized in rhetorical depictions of refugees and migrants as natural disasters,[52] or waste products,[53] or in the instrumentalist treatment of asylum seekers as 'bargaining chips' for political negotiations.[54] Brutalization is a theme in the testimonies of people who have been detained in immigration detention centres and who recount their sense of a loss of humanity through prolonged periods of inhumane treatment.[55] Salim also alluded to brutalization in recounting how he sometimes feels like a zombie, being unable to make contact with others.[56]

The next three chapters will zoom in on the animalization, objectification, and brutalization of refugees, asylum seekers, and other migrants to analyse when these turn into dehumanization. By considering the moral exclusion of the (forcibly) displaced through these prisms, the following chapters will provide critical insights to further develop our account of dehumanization and clarify the way(s) in which refugees, asylum seekers, and migrants are perceived, portrayed, or treated as less than human in the global migration crisis.

Conclusion

This chapter took us from a critical appraisal of the way in which the term 'dehumanization' has been used in reporting on the global migration crisis to a foreshadowing of the analysis of animalization, objectification, and brutalization that lies ahead. This chapter set the stage for the analysis of dehumanization that runs through this book by identifying the problem of the overly broad use of this notion in reporting on the global migration crisis.

The study of academic literature, human rights commentary, and journalistic (opinion) pieces on the dehumanization of refugees, asylum seekers, and migrants showed that the notion of dehumanization is frequently used as an umbrella term to refer to a wide variety of practices and processes of social and moral exclusion. De-individualization, stigmatization, marginalization, criminalization, and infra-humanization unsettle the social and moral position that refugees hold. Still, these practices only turn into dehumanization when morally degrading portrayals fundamentally deny the moral status that victims hold as human beings. This is the case when people are excluded from the moral order that we share as human beings. Dehumanization thus takes a unique position within the family of moral exclusionary practices and processes in that it entails an exclusion from the moral category of humanity as such.

To narrow down, a more careful analysis is needed to examine what dehumanization involves more precisely. The following chapters will therefore take a closer look at animalization, objectification, and brutalization to deepen our understanding of dehumanization.

Notes

1. See, for example: BBC, 'Food Wristbands Scrapped', Ćerimović, 'Asylum Seekers' Hell', DeBono, '"Less than Human"', Elgot and Taylor, 'Calais Crisis', Esses, Medianu, and Lawson, 'Uncertainty, Threat, and the Role of Media', Esses, Veenvliet, Hodson,

40   Dehumanization in the Global Migration Crisis

and Mihic, 'Justice, Morality, and the Dehumanization of Refugees', Fiske, 'Human Rights and Refugee Protest', Hartley and Fleay, '"We Are like Animals"', Bill Frelick, 'Dispatches: Why We Should Outlaw "Illegal"', *Human Rights Watch*, 24 June 2014, https://www.hrw.org/news/2014/06/24/dispatches-why-we-should-outlaw-illegal, Malone, 'Why Al Jazeera', von Mittelstaedt and Popp, 'One Year after the Lampedusa Tragedy', Hugh Muir, 'Indefinite Detention Is Dehumanizing For Refugees: This Practice Must End', *The Guardian*, 19 July 2017, https://www.theguardian.com/commentisfree/2017/jul/19/indefinite-detention-refugees-journeys-refugee-tales, Varvin, 'Our Relations to Refugees', Vaughan-Williams, '"We Are Not Animals!"', Wroe, 'Social Workers', and Barçın Yinanç, 'Treating Migrants Like Natural Disasters "Dehumanizing"', *Hürriyet*, 7 September 2015, http://www.hurriyetdailynews.com/treating-migrants-like-natural-disasters-dehumanizing.aspx?PageID=238&NID=88054&NewsCatID=359.

2. Esses, Medianu, and Lawson, 'Uncertainty, Threat, and the Role of Media'.

3. Roland Bleiker, David Campbell, Emma Hutchison, and Xzarina Nicholson, 'The Visual Dehumanisation of Refugees', *Australian Journal of Political Science* 48 (2013): 398–416, https://doi.org/10.1080/10361146.2013.840769.

4. See: BBC, 'Food Wristbands Scrapped'.

5. See, for example: Michel Agier, *On the Margins of the World: The Refugee Experience Today*, translated by David Fernbach (Cambridge: Polity, 2008), Michel Agier, *Managing the Undesirables: Refugee Camps and Humanitarian Government*, translated by David Fernbach (Cambridge: Polity, 2010), Alexander Betts and Paul Collier, *Refuge: Transforming a Broken Refugee System* (London: Allen Lane, 2017), Alexander Betts and Gil Loescher, *Refugees in International Relations* (Oxford: Oxford University Press, 2010), and Peter Gatrell, *The Making of the Modern Refugee* (Oxford: Oxford University Press, 2015).

6. Médecins Sans Frontières, *Obstacle Course to Europe: A Policy-Made Humanitarian Crisis at EU Borders*, January 2016, https://www.doctorswithoutborders.org/sites/usa/files/2016_01_msf_obstacle_course_to_europe_-_final_-_low_res.pdf and Jones, *Violent Borders*.

7. Greg Philo, Emma Briant, and Pauline Donald, *Bad News for Refugees* (London: Pluto Press, 2013) and Bleiker et al., 'The Visual Dehumanisation of Refugees'.

8. See, for example: Ćerimović, 'Asylum Seekers' Hell', Elgot and Taylor, 'Calais Crisis', Yinanç, 'Treating Migrants', and Wroe, 'Social Workers'.

9. It is important to note here that refugees and asylum seekers are entitled to a fair response, not just a humanitarian one. Countries who take up asylum seekers should not be seen so much as good Samaritans who take up asylum seekers as poor people in need. It is a duty of states to offer asylum to people fleeing persecution and war. The willingness to perform this duty is affected, however, by processes of disengagement, and it is therefore important to consider the affective dynamics that underpin political responses to claims for asylum.

10. For studies of the securitization of asylum and migration in the 2015 European refugee crisis see, for example: Mike Berry, Inaki Garcia-Blanco, and Kerry Moore, *Press Coverage of the Refugee and Migrant Crisis in the EU: A Content Analysis of Five European Countries. Report Prepared for the United Nations High Commission for Refugees*, 2015, https://www.unhcr.org/protection/operations/56bb369c9/press-coverage-refugee-

migrant-crisis-eu-content-analysis-five-european.html, Chouliaraki and Zaborowski, 'Voice and Community', Simon Goodman, Ala Sirriyeh, and Simon McMahon, 'The Evolving (Re)Categorisations of Refugees throughout the "Refugee/Migrant Crisis"', *Journal of Community and Applied Social Psychology* 27 (2017): 105–14, https://doi.org/10.1002/casp.2302, Seth M. Holmes and Heide Casteñada, 'Representing the "European Refugee Crisis" in Germany and Beyond: Deservingness and Difference, Life and Death', *American Ethnologist* 43 (2016): 12–24, https://doi.org/10.1111/amet.12259, Billy Holzberg, Kristina Kolbe, and Rafal Zaborowski, 'Figures of Crisis: The Delineation of (Un)Deserving Refugees in the German Media', *Sociology* 53 (2018): 534–50, https://doi.org/10.1177/0038038518759460, and Harriet Gray and Anja K. Franck, 'Refugees as/at Risk: The Gendered and Racialized Underpinnings of Securitization in British Media Narratives', *Security Dialogue* 50 (2019): 275–91, https://doi.org/10.1177/0967010619830590.

11. Elisabeth El Refaie, 'Metaphors We Discriminate By: Naturalized Themes in Austrian Newspaper Articles about Asylum Seekers', *Journal of Sociolinguistics* 5 (2001): 352–71, https://doi.org/10.1111/1467-9481.00154, Alexandria J. Innes, 'When the Threatened Become the Threat: The Construction of Asylum Seekers in British Media Narratives', *International Relations* 24 (2010): 456–77, https://doi.org/10.1177/0047117810385882, Nick Lynn and Susan Lea, 'A Phantom Menace and the New Apartheid: The Social Construction of Asylum-Seekers in the United Kingdom', *Discourse and Society* 14 (2003): 425–52, https://doi.org/10.1177/0957926503014004002, and Gerald V. O'Brien, 'Indigestible Foods, Conquering Hordes, and Waste Materials: Metaphors of Immigrants and the Early Immigration Restriction Debate in the United States', *Metaphor and Symbol* 18 (2003): 33–47, https://doi.org/10.1207/s15327868ms1801_3.

12. Esses, Medianu, and Lawson, 'Uncertainty, Threat, and the Role of Media', 519.

13. Idem, 522.

14. Idem, 519.

15. As cited in: Robert Lifton, *The Nazi Doctors: Medical Killing and the Psychology of Genocide* (London: Basic Books, 1988), p. 232.

16. Erving Goffman, *Stigma: Notes on the Management of Spoiled Identity* (London: Penguin, 1963), p. 13.

17. Paul Bloom, *Just Babies: The Origins of Good and Evil* (New York: Broadway Books, 2013), p. 133.

18. Esses, Medianu, and Lawson, 'Uncertainty, Threat, and the Role of Media', 522.

19. Idem, 527.

20. Leyens et al., 'Infra-Humanization', 143.

21. Nick Haslam, 'What Is Dehumanization?' in *Humanness and Dehumanization*, edited by Paul Bain, Jeroen Vaes and Jacques-Philippe Leyens (New York and London: Routledge, 2014), pp. 34–48.

22. Geras, *Solidarity in the Conversation of Humankind*, 97.

23. This argument corresponds to Butler's claim that judgements about who is considered human are fundamental to settling the question of who is entitled to human rights. See: Judith Butler, *Frames of War: When Is Life Grievable?* (London and New York: Verso, 2010), p. 75.

42 Dehumanization in the Global Migration Crisis

24. Since Esses and her colleagues draw from an understanding of dehumanization that does not maintain as stark a distinction between dehumanization and infra-humanization as I do, for their account it is not an issue that 'cheaters' are cast as inferior human beings.

25. This status allegedly allowed for the violent mistreatment, abuse, and torture of prisoners in Guantanamo Bay. See: Erin Chlopak, 'Dealing with the Detainees at Guantanamo Bay: Humanitarian and Human Rights Obligations under the Geneva Conventions', *Human Rights Brief* 9 (2002): 6–9, 13, https://digitalcommons.wcl.american.edu/hrbrief/vol9/iss3/2/.

26. Such calls are presented, for example, by the journalist Scott Atran in *Talking to the Enemy: Violent Extremism, Sacred Values, and What It Means to Be Human* (London: Penguin, 2011).

27. It is also important to note that the connection drawn between asylum seekers and terrorists, no matter how unjustified, may have an effect on the general perception of people claiming asylum. Bauman draws attention to this aspect:

> Overgeneral, unwarranted and even fanciful as the association of terrorists with asylum seekers and 'economic migrants' might have been, it did its job: the figure of the 'asylum seeker', once prompting human compassion and spurring an urge to help, has been sullied and defiled, while the very idea of 'asylum', once a matter of civil and civilized pride, has been reclassified as a dreadful concoction of shameful naivety and criminal irresponsibility.

> Zygmunt Bauman, *Wasted Lives: Modernity and Its Outcasts* (New Jersey: Wiley, 2003), p. 57.

28. See, for example: Athanasia Batziou, 'Framing "Otherness" in Press Photographs: The Case of Immigrants in Greece and Spain', *Journal of Media Practice* 12 (2011): 41–60, https://doi.org/10.1386/jmpr.12.1.41_1, Lynda Mannik, 'Public and Private Photographs of Refugees: The Problem of Representation', *Visual Studies* 27 (2012): 262–76, https://doi.org/10.1080/1472586X.2012.717747, Paul Slovic, Daniel Västfjäll, Arvid Erlandsson, and Robin Gregory, 'Iconic Photographs and the Ebb and Flow of Empathic Response to Humanitarian Disasters', *Proceedings of the National Academy of Sciences of the United States of America* 114 (2017): 640–4, https://doi.org/10.1073/pnas.1613977114, Annabelle C. Wilmott, 'The Politics of Photography: Visual Depictions of Syrian Refugees in U.K. Online Media', *Visual Communication Quarterly* 24 (2017): 67–82, https://doi.org/10.1080/15551393.2017.1307113, Xu Zhang and Lea Hellmueller, 'Visual Framing of the European Refugee Crisis in Der Spiegel and CNN International: Global Journalism in News Photographs', *International Communication Gazette* 79 (2017): 483–510, https://doi.org/10.1177/1748048516688134.

29. Wilmott, 'The Politics of Photography'.

30. Zhang and Hellmueller, 'Visual Framing'.

31. Bleiker et al., 'The Visual Dehumanisation of Refugees'.

32. Idem, 399.

33. Ibid.

34. Liisa Malkki, 'Speechless Emissaries: Refugees, Humanitarianism, and Dehistoricization', *Cultural Anthropology* 11 (1996): 377–404, https://doi.org/10.1525/can.1996.11.3.02a00050.

35. Idem, 388.

36. Giorgio Agamben, *Homo Sacer: Sovereign Power and Bare Life*, translated by Daniel Heller-Roazen (Stanford: Stanford University Press, 1998).

37. Agamben's notion of bare life is frequently used in the field of migration studies to theorize the loss of humanity that can be caused by restrictive asylum regimes and the securitization of immigration. See, for example: Roxanne Doty, 'Bare Life: Border-Crossing Deaths and Spaces of Moral Alibi', *Environment and Planning D: Society and Space* 29 (2011): 599–612, https://doi.org/10.1068/d3110, Nick Dines, Nicola Montagna, and Vincenzo Ruggiero, 'Thinking Lampedusa: Border Construction, the Spectacle of Bare Life and the Productivity of Migrants', *Ethnic and Racial Studies* 38 (2015): 430–45, https://doi.org/10.1080/01419870.2014.936892, and Willem Schinkel, '"Illegal Aliens" and the State: or: Bare Bodies vs. the Zombie', *International Sociology* 24 (2009): 779–806, https://doi.org/10.1177/0268580909343494. For a critical account, see: Patricia Owens, 'Reclaiming "Bare Life"? Against Agamben on Refugees', *International Relations* 23 (2009): 567–82, https://doi.org/10.1177/0047117809350545.
While the notion of bare life is in my view problematic when understood as a description of the actual condition of refugees, asylum seekers, and migrants, it is conducive in denoting particular ways in which refugees, asylum seekers, and migrants may be represented. As a way of representation, the concept of bare life stands for, what Nicholas De Genova calls, 'a political fiction', which is summoned by political authorities to communicate the ultimate, but never fully realized, consequence of a complete exclusion from consideration as a judicial-political subject. See: Nicholas De Genova, 'Bare Life, Labor-Power, Mobility, and Global Space: Toward a Marxian Anthropology?' *The New Centennial Review* 12 (2012): 133, https://doi.org/10.2307/41949805.

38. Malkki, 'Speechless Emissaries', 390.

39. Ruben T. Azevedo, Sophie De Beukelaer, Isla L. Jones, Lou Safra, and Manos Tsakiris, 'When the Lens Is Too Wide: The Political Consequences of the Visual Dehumanization of Refugees', *Humanities and Social Sciences Communications* 8 (2021): 14, https://doi.org/10.1057/s41599-021-00786-x.

40. The centrality of the moral sense of humanity to dehumanization will be set out in more detail in Chapter 2.

41. Frelick, 'Dispatches'.

42. Ibid.

43. Salil Shetty, 'Tackling the Global Refugee Crisis: Sharing, Not Shirking Responsibility', *Amnesty International*, 4 October 2016, https://www.amnesty.org/en/latest/campaigns/2016/10/tackling-the-global-refugee-crisis-sharing-responsibility/.

44. United Nations, 'Refugees, Migrants Branded "Threats", Dehumanized in Campaigns Seeking Political Gain, High Commissioner Tells Third Committee, Appealing for Return to Dignity', *General Assembly Third Committee, Seventy-third Session, 41st Meeting*, 31 October 2018, https://www.un.org/press/en/2017/gashc4247.doc.htm.

45. As cited in: Fiske, 'Human Rights and Refugee Protest', 22.

46. Malone, 'Why Al Jazeera'.

47. I will return to Shetty's example dehumanizing living conditions in certain refugee camps in Chapter 3 where I analyse in more detail when a failure to help people in need amounts to dehumanization.

48. Animalization, objectification, and brutalization can be recognized in various works on the treatment of refugees and migrants, including: Raith Zeher Abid, Shakila Abdul

Manan, and Zuhair Abdul Amir Abdul Rahman, '"A Flood of Syrians Has Slowed to a Trickle": The Use of Metaphors in the Representation of Syrian Refugees in the Online Media News Reports of Host and Non-Host Countries', *Discourse & Communication* 11 (2017): 121–40, https://doi.org/10.1177/1750481317691857, Bridget Anderson, 'The Politics of Pests: Immigration and the Invasive Other', *Social Research: An International Quarterly* 84 (2017): 7–28, doi:10.1353/sor.2017.0003, Ruben Andersson, 'Hunter and Prey: Patrolling Clandestine Migration in the Euro-African Borderlands', *Anthropological Quarterly* 87 (2014): 119–49, https://www.jstor.org/stable/43652723, Bauman, *Wasted Lives*, Bleiker et al., 'The Visual Dehumanisation of Refugees', Calais Writers, *Voices from the 'Jungle': Stories from the Calais Refugee Camp* (London: Pluto Press, 2017), David Cisneros, 'Contaminated Communities: The Metaphor of "Immigrant as Pollutant" in Media Representations of Immigration', *Rhetoric & Public Affairs* 11 (2008): 569–601, doi:10.1353/rap.0.0068, DeBono, '"Less than Human"', Elgot and Taylor, 'Calais Crisis', Esses, Medianu, and Lawson, 'Uncertainty, Threat, and the Role of Media', Esses, Veenvliet, Hodson, and Mihic, 'Justice, Morality, and the Dehumanization of Refugees', Fiske, 'Human Rights and Refugee Protest', Orhun Gündüz, '"Burden on our Shoulders" Rhetoric: Objectification of Syrian Refugees in Turkey through Political and Economic Discourse', *Refugee Review* 3 (2017): 34–45, Hartley and Fleay, '"We Are like Animals"', Paresh Kathrani, 'Object or Subject? The Ongoing "Objectification" of Asylum Seekers', *International Comparative Jurisprudence* 3 (2017): 1–7, https://doi.org/10.13165/j.icj.2017.03.001, Sang H. Kil, Cecilia Menjívar, and Roxanne Doty, 'Securing Borders: Patriotism, Vigilantism and the Brutalization of the US American Public', in *Immigration, Crime and Justice (Sociology of Crime, Law and Deviance, Vol. 13)*, edited by William F. McDonald (Bingley: Emerald Group Publishing Limited, 2009), pp. 297–312, Shantal Marshall and Jessica Shapiro, 'When "Scurry" vs "Hurry" Makes the Difference: Vermin Metaphors, Disgust, and Anti-Immigrant Attitudes', *Journal of Social Issues* 74 (2018): 774–89, https://doi.org/10.1111/josi.12298, O'Brien, 'Indigestible Foods, Conquering Hordes, and Waste Materials', Sydney Morning Herald, 'Think Australia's Treatment of Refugees and Asylum Seekers is OK? Read This. An Open Letter From a Refugee on Nauru to the Leaders of the UN's Summit for Refugees and Migrants', 19 September 2016, http://www.smh.com.au/comment/think-australias-treatment-of-refugees-and-asylum-seekers-is-ok-read-this-20160919-grjjz2.html, Vaughan-Williams, '"We Are Not Animals!"', Wroe, 'Social Workers', and Yinanç, 'Treating Migrants'.

49. Fiske, 'Human Rights and Refugee Protest', 22.
50. Andersson, 'Hunter and Prey'.
51. Anderson, 'The Politics of Pest'.
52. Abid et al., '"A Flood of Syrians"'.
53. Bauman, *Wasted Lives* and O'Brien, 'Indigestible Foods'.
54. Amnesty International, 'Turkey/EU: Refugees Must Not Pay the Price in Political Game', 28 February 2020, https://www.amnesty.org/en/latest/news/2020/02/turkeyeu-refugees-must-not-pay-the-price-in-political-game/.
55. See, for example: DeBono, '"Less than Human"' and Sydney Morning Herald, 'Think Australia's Treatment of Refugees and Asylum Seekers is OK?'
56. Salim's testimony will be discussed in more detail in Chapter 4.

2
Animalization

> The way I was treated in Libya, I never believed people could be treated like that, like animal.
>
> **Musa, asylum seeker from the Gambia**

Introduction

Musa is a Gambian electrician who came to Libya for work and who fled to Italy after civil war broke out in 2014. Reflecting on the difficult times he encountered during his travel to Europe, Musa spoke about how he had to wait for three weeks in the port town of Sabratha before he could embark on a boat. The traffickers held him and the other passengers in overcrowded warehouses, beat them, and gave them food only once a day. When the boat finally arrived, people were forced on it, even when there was no more space. He notes how the human smugglers mistreated the passengers: 'Like animal, they were loaded'.

Musa's account is typical of situations where refugees, asylum seekers, and unwanted migrants are mistreated and abused. His story speaks to the notion of animalization. In studies of dehumanization, animalization is generally understood as the act of denying people human status by viewing, portraying, or treating them like animals.[1] Animalization is an important conceptual lens for analysing dehumanization in the global migration crisis because scholars, journalists, commentators, and refugees and asylum seekers often use or allude to this term to make sense of the challenges that forced migrants face.

Likening people to animals seems a straightforward way of viewing, portraying, or treating them as less than human. Since the human and the animal are often seen as opposites, identifying people with animals may be viewed as an effective way of denying their humanity. At the same time, not all forms of regarding, representing, or treating people like animals necessarily involve considering, portraying, or treating them as less than human. After all, the distinction between humans and animals is not quite as stark as we often wish to

---

Dehumanization in the Global Migration Crisis. Adrienne de Ruiter, Oxford University Press. © Adrienne de Ruiter (2024).
DOI: 10.1093/oso/9780198893400.003.0003

46 Dehumanization in the Global Migration Crisis

believe, and it is therefore conceivable that people may be viewed, portrayed, or treated like animals in ways that do not deny their humanity. This points to the need to examine the relation between dehumanization and animalization more closely and to reflect on when, if ever, perceiving, portraying, or treating people like animals should be considered a form of dehumanization.

The first part of this chapter presents and discusses examples of animalization in the global migration crisis. The chapter then considers the various ways in which refugees, asylum seekers, and unwanted migrants are portrayed like animals, how they are treated like animals, and may be viewed as animals. The final section explains when these practices and processes amount to dehumanization by clarifying how some forms of animalization entail that the victims are viewed, portrayed, or treated as less than human in a moral sense, whereas others do not.

Animalization in the global migration crisis

The conceptual lens of animalization is often used, explicitly or implicitly, in reporting on the global migration crisis. In particular, it shows up frequently in criticisms of allegedly dehumanizing rhetoric and policies. This frame was used, for example, in critical responses to a statement Prime Minister David Cameron made in 2015 where he referred to migrants in Calais as a 'swarm of people' seeking to reach the United Kingdom.[2] This language was criticized by the Refugee Council for being dehumanizing. Harriet Harman, Labour's interim leader, also replied that Cameron 'should remember he is talking about people, not insects'.[3] While this choice of words was definitely not the most sensitive, it is not evident that calling migrants a 'swarm of people' is directly dehumanizing. After all, a swarm can refer not only to a large group of flying insects, but also to a large number of people moving together, as in a 'swarm of tourists'. This case raises the question, furthermore, as to whether people can be dehumanized through a statement that literally calls them people. These reflections suggest a need to carefully consider when likening people to animals constitutes a form of dehumanization.

An example of animalizing rhetoric that evidently amounts to dehumanization can be found in the opinion piece that columnist Katie Hopkins published on 17 April 2015 in *The Sun*.[4] In this column, Hopkins claimed that migrants coming by boat to Europe 'are like cockroaches'. She spelled out the implications of this subhuman status in her statement that rather than providing aid and assistance to people stranded in the Mediterranean, '[w]hat we need are gunships sending these boats back to their own country'. In this case, it does not seem controversial to claim that the use of animalizing depictions constitutes a form of dehumanization since the portrayal of refugees, asylum seekers, and other unwanted migrants as cockroaches serves as a means to deny their right to even basic moral consideration, as illustrated by the argument that gunships should be used to impede them from reaching Europe.

Animalization is recognized not only in galvanizing rhetoric but also in certain policies of border control. In an insightful analysis of animalizing aspects of policies that seek to curb irregular migration, the international security scholar Nick Vaughan-Williams presents the account of a detainee from the Gambia who was interviewed by Amnesty International about the conditions of his detention in a migration processing centre, located in a former zoo, in Tripoli, Libya. The detainee claims that he and the other inmates are treated and depicted as animals: 'They [the guards] don't even enter our room because they say that we smell and have illnesses. They constantly insult us, and call us "You donkey, you dog". When we are moving in their way, they look disgusted and slap us'.[5] A detainee of a facility for migrants awaiting deportation in Rome likens the place in which they are held to a cage where one would keep animals: 'Every cage has two rooms. The cages have barriers almost 5–6m high. We are left there like savage beasts'.[6] Similar stories are recounted by organizations monitoring the situation in other immigration detention centres in Europe. About the detention camp Moria on the island of Lesvos in Greece, Borderline-Europe notes that the worst thing about the treatment of refugees, asylum seekers, and migrants is 'the political normality to lock people up in camps and treat them like animals'.[7]

This type of treatment can be considered a form of animalization not only because people are treated in ways similar to animals, but also due to the fact that subjecting people to degrading conditions of detention may make them resemble and feel like animals in certain ways. The migration scholar Daniela DeBono reports, for example, how an immigrant from Congo felt diminished after having passed more than eighteen months in detention in Malta: 'Detention dehumanizes the human being. The detainee is reduced to the state of an animal. One wakes up, eats, sleeps, wakes up'.[8] Similar experiences are recounted by an Iranian refugee who passed years in immigration detention centres on Nauru, off the coast of Australia:

> After being brought to Nauru we spent almost 24 months in detention, before we were finally found to be genuine refugees. Since then I have not slept even one night without having recurring nightmares of those endless months living in a hot, mouldy tent. We became so alienated from our humanity, we were thoroughly

transformed into a bunch of animals after years of living in the most appalling conditions possible.[9]

The same person notes that the detrimental effects of prolonged detention may stay with people for a long time, stating that 'to this day we are still walking ghosts, utterly broken and hopeless. We are hollowed out and devoid of enthusiasm for life, and we are stuck in an animalistic state of existence because that is what we have become.'[10]

While these testimonies provide powerful allegations against securitization regimes that hold migrants in detention for extensive periods of time and under detrimental conditions, the appeal that detention alienates people from their own humanity is ambivalent. This may be seen reflected in the fact that the testimonies above call out the conditions of detention precisely because they are unfit for human beings, indicating that recognition of human status is not completely lost, even if people under such dire circumstances may come to feel they are more similar to animals than human beings.[11]

This overview indicates that animalization plays a central role in rhetoric and policies that involve refugees, asylum seekers, and other migrants. It also highlights that while animalization and dehumanization seem to be connected, this relation is complex. Although the notion of animalization is central to common ways of thinking about dehumanization, not all ways of viewing, portraying, or treating people like animals appear to be straightforwardly dehumanizing. It is therefore important to examine what it means to portray, treat, and view people as animals and which aspects render animalization dehumanizing.

Another tension that speaks from these stories concerns the way in which the use of the lens of animalization to criticize the mistreatment of people appears to condone the abuse and brutal handling of animals. The philosopher Will Kymlicka emphasizes that appeals against treating humans as animals reinforce the view of a moral hierarchy based on a radical separation between human beings and other animals.[12] Similarly, the philosopher Alice Crary points out that 'animal-indexed forms of dehumanization depend for their power to degrade on representations of animals as morally insignificant beings who invite the callous and even lethal treatment that is urged upon members of specific human groups.'[13] In accounting for animalization, it is therefore important to avoid reinforcing moral bias against animals while taking seriously the claims of victims that the ways that they are treated are inappropriate modes of relating to fellow human beings.

Portraying people like animals

When people think of dehumanization, often the first thing that comes to mind is how the humanity of persons may be denied by identifying them with animals. This is not surprising given that many of the most notorious and paradigmatic cases of dehumanization in history included the use of animal analogies or metaphors to justify atrocities.[14] The radio channel *Radio-Télévision Libre* des *Milles Collines* in Rwanda has become infamous, for example, for calling Tutsis cockroaches in the period leading up to and during the Rwandan genocide.[15] Other examples include Nazi propaganda, which likened the Jews to rats, or the way in which the Stalinist regime identified opponents with vermin.

In the global migration crisis, animalizing depictions of refugees, asylum seekers, and unwanted migrants are commonplace as well. As illustrated by the above discussion of portrayals of displaced people as a 'swarm' or 'cockroaches', these groups are at times portrayed as a pestilence. Another example of this practice can be found in Donald Trump's tweet from 2018 that Democrats want immigrants 'to pour into and infest our Country'.[16] The choice for the term 'infest' tends towards dehumanization since it refers to takeovers by vermin, rodents, or insects.[17]

These examples of ways in which refugees, asylum seekers, and unwanted migrants are portrayed by politicians and other opinion leaders point to the central role that metaphors play in the politics of representation. To understand this role better, we need to consider how metaphors help shape our views of reality. Metaphors are important for our perceptions of the world because they are not simply linguistic or visual constructs that offer a particular depiction of a state of affairs. They structure the way we view, think, understand, evaluate, and feel about people, institutions, and the world more generally.[18] When the pestilence metaphor is used to depict immigrants, for example, this frames immigration as a problem. Just like you do not let rats, cockroaches, or other vermin run loose, the movement of migrants needs to be curtailed, given that failing to check their outbreak will lead to contagion and infestation, sickening the nation. Furthermore, far-reaching measures are justified to end the plague, following this logic, since the interests of vermin are allegedly nothing compared to those of the people these measures seek to protect. Describing immigration through a metaphor that portrays immigrants as vermin thus frames the issue in a particular way, which evokes powerful emotions and suggests what the 'right' way of dealing with this problem is.

Vermin, lovebirds, and chickens

The tendency to portray immigrants as vermin is not new. The social work scholar Gerald V. O'Brien notes, for example, how analogies that likened migrants to animals that were perceived as disgusting, loathsome, and parasitic were used in the debate on immigration restrictions that took place in the United States in the early twentieth century.[19] Although the use of animalistic portrayals was less common back then than depictions that identified immigrants with organisms, objects, natural catastrophes, or that drew from war metaphors, animal metaphors were at times used as well.[20] As examples, O'Brien describes how inhabitants of 'Little Italy', 'Little Ghetto', 'Little Hungary', and other colonies of immigrants in New York were called 'parasites on the oak of national prosperity' who 'should be eradicated'.[21] He also notes how immigrants of allegedly 'inferior quality' were referred to as 'a big swarm of mosquitoes, infested with malaria and yellow fever germs'.[22] These examples show a tendency to liken immigrants to pestilences that expose the local population to the risk of contagion and disease. O'Brien notes that likening people to 'parasites' or 'lower animals' 'capable of infection and contamination' is a strategy regularly used to depict groups that authorities seek to discipline and place under their control.[23]

In an insightful article called 'The Politics of Pests', the migration scholar Bridget Anderson observes that the metaphoric trope of 'the migrant as invasive insect' played an important role in reporting on the 2015 refugee crisis as well.[24] Her analysis helpfully unpacks the associations to which this metaphor is linked, presenting several important insights. First, vermin are perceived as useless. Unlike beasts of burden, vermin have no qualities that can be of service to human beings. Indeed, the negative value attached to vermin is reflected in its etymology, which relates to 'noxious animals' or 'troublesome creatures'.[25] Names given to vermin in Germanic languages still clearly reflect this meaning, such as in the German 'Schädlinge' or 'Ungeziefer', the first term relating to damaging creatures and the second to animals unfit for sacrifice, or in the Dutch 'ongedierte', which refers to bad and unpleasant animals. Second, vermin are associated with filth and dirt, thriving on human waste and appearing in large numbers in times of disarray and chaos. The arrival of vermin thus forebodes bad tidings. Third, vermin invade the home and make it an unhealthy place to live. Vermin cannot, therefore, be left alone without harm coming to us in our houses. Fourth, vermin are perceived not to matter from a moral point of view and can therefore be disposed of without scruples. The English term 'vermin' comes from the Latin *vermis*, meaning 'worm'. Worms, like other animals now included in the vermin category, such as insects and rodents, are generally attributed a low position on the ladder of moral concern, if they are even placed there at all. Anderson thus notes that, since insects are not seen as sentient, many consider it acceptable to exterminate them.[26]

This brief discussion provides relevant insights into the question when animalizing depictions amount to dehumanization. A crucial point that this discussion highlights is that immigrants are likened to animals that are attributed negative characteristics. This raises the question as to whether the use of animal metaphors would also be dehumanizing if they emphasized positive qualities of a person. Here we may think, for example, of cases where we use nicknames for our friends or dote on a person we love. For instance, in British English, the term 'duck' has been used as a term of endearment at least since the time of Shakespeare.[27] It does not seem right to claim that a Brit who lovingly calls his or her partner a 'duck' thereby dehumanizes him or her. Similarly, in various languages, newly married couples are called 'love-birds', after a monogamous parrot genus known for its affectionate and social nature, or 'turtle doves', animals that symbolize loyalty and faithfulness. It would appear odd to claim that when friends and family speak about a couple as 'lovebirds' or 'turtle doves', this should be seen as a form of dehumanization. For an animalizing portrayal to be dehumanizing, the used metaphor should thus highlight the negative, rather than positive, traits of a person or group. In other words, the depiction of the other as an animal should have a derogatory function. If this were the only criterion, however, this would imply that many insults amount to dehumanization. This does not seem correct either. When a person calls someone a 'chicken', for instance, the point is to insult the person by calling them a coward, not to deny their human status.

The discussion of the use of the pestilence metaphor above suggests that dehumanizing forms of animalizing depictions go beyond a mere negative representation of a particular quality of the person who is likened to an animal. In the case of the chicken insult, this depiction applies only to one aspect of the person's identity or behaviour, namely their cowardice, whereas the portrayal of immigrants as vermin discredits their general usefulness to society and presents them as a dangerous source of infestation and pollution. The foregoing analysis also suggests that an important role in this process is played by the emotion of disgust. The animals to which refugees, asylum seekers, and unwanted migrants in the above-mentioned examples are likened, such as cockroaches, parasites, and insects, generally elicit disgust, whereas (living) chickens usually do not. The effects of the arousal of disgust are potentially far-reaching, as social psychologists theorize that this feeling is a strong evolutionary-adapted reaction that urges people to pull back from

52 Dehumanization in the Global Migration Crisis

something that may lead to infestation and prove potentially lethal.[28] The work of the psychologist Paul Bloom indicates, furthermore, that the act of likening people to animals that are considered disgusting may undermine concern for their well-being, as disgust 'makes us indifferent to the suffering of others and has the power to incite cruelty and Dehumanization'.[29]

War propaganda and moral disengagement

It is no coincidence, then, that vermin metaphors are frequently used in war propaganda as well. The philosopher David Livingstone Smith provides some vivid illustrations of the use of this type of metaphor in his book *Less Than Human*. He recounts, for instance, how Japanese soldiers participating in the Rape of Nanking 'called the Chinese "chancorro" ... that meant below human, like bugs or animals'.[30] In a similar way, American propaganda portrayed the Japanese in animalizing ways during the Second World War. Smith observes, for example, how '[t]he "Japs" were considered animals, and were often portrayed as monkeys, apes, or rodents, and sometimes as insects'.[31]

The example of war propaganda can help us grasp more fully the difference between dehumanizing forms of animalistic portrayal and cases like the chicken insult. When I call someone a 'chicken' as a mode of indicating cowardice, I do not thereby imply that it would be acceptable to kill them, beat them up, or fail to provide them with assistance if they would be in danger. On the contrary, when the Japanese called the Chinese 'bugs' or the Americans portrayed the Japanese as rodents, this allegedly served as a psychological mechanism for moral disengagement that was to reduce the restraints that people normally feel in committing grave violence against other human beings.

The author Aldous Huxley proposed an insightful account of this process in a speech, held in 1936, on the way in which dehumanizing propaganda seeks to reduce the natural inhibitions that people generally have against the severe mistreatment of others:

> Most people would hesitate to torture or kill a human being like themselves. But when that human being is spoken of as though he were not a human being, but as the representative of some wicked principle, we lose our scruples. ... All political and nationalist propaganda aims at only one thing; to persuade one set of people that another set of people are not really human and that it is therefore legitimate to rob, swindle, bully, and even murder them.[32]

Huxley thus argues that dehumanizing war propaganda aims at convincing the audience that certain people are not truly human in order to lessen the restraints that people normally feel in committing atrocities against fellow human beings. This effect has also been observed in psychological experiments that demonstrate that dehumanization can function as a mechanism of moral disengagement that renders violent conduct permissible in the eyes of perpetrators.[33]

What distinguishes the use of animal metaphors and analogies in contexts where such depictions foster (violent) schisms between human beings, on the one hand, from animalistic portrayals in more benign settings, on the other, is the fact that the moral status that people hold as human beings is denied. This denial of human status in a moral sense facilitates the perpetration of severe forms of violence and abuse that are (to be) inflicted on the victim, in the case of war propaganda, while in the case of depictions of refugees, asylum seekers, and unwanted migrants as vermin and pestilences, this denial leads to moral disengagement and a lack of concern for the plea of fellow human beings.

Clearly, portrayals of the forcibly displaced differ from depictions of enemies in war. Refugees, asylum seekers, and unwanted migrants are not usually seen as enemies in a literal sense, even though they are at times depicted as invading hordes.[34] In armed conflict, portraying enemies as allegedly contemptable, disgusting, or threatening animals can make strategic sense, as such depictions are prone to lead to moral disengagement, which makes harming, maiming, and killing less difficult from a psychological point of view. Dehumanizing portrayals of refugees, asylum seekers, and unwanted migrants that draw from animal metaphors do not usually serve the same function of allowing for their violent mistreatment, although this does happen as well.[35] These portrayals nonetheless undermine recognition of the moral status that refugees, asylum seekers, and unwanted migrants hold as fellow human beings, thereby making it easier to reject claims for asylum, humanitarian aid, and assistance.

Moral disengagement can thus have different effects. It can undermine the moral scruples that the use of excessive force against fellow human beings generally evokes in people with an ordinary sense of compassion, but it can also diminish people's willingness to help others. This argument is supported by studies about the way in which dehumanizing depictions impact on people's readiness to provide assistance to people in need. In their research on the role that dehumanization plays in lowering the willingness of people to provide help in response to natural disasters, the social psychologist

54 Dehumanization in the Global Migration Crisis

Luca Andrighetto and his colleagues found, for example, that dehumanization diminishes empathy, leading to a reduced preparedness to provide humanitarian assistance to victims.[36]

The foregoing analysis suggests that not all acts of likening people to non-human animals can be considered dehumanizing, given that not all animalistic portrayals challenge the human status of the other in a meaningful sense. What renders such depictions dehumanizing is not the act of likening a person to an animal in itself, but the denial of normative human status that this portrayal in some cases entails. We can therefore conclude that portraying people like animals is dehumanizing when this depiction signals that the persons involved hold a moral status below that of human beings.

Treating people like animals

The humanity of people can also allegedly be denied or undermined by treating them like animals. While this is a popular idea, it is more complex than it appears at first sight to determine what it means precisely to treat people like animals and when such treatment should be considered to be dehumanizing. For one, not all forms of treating people like animals seem to be morally problematic. People are a particular type of animal, and we are therefore in many ways similar to non-human animals. For example, as sentient beings, we are vulnerable to physical suffering. If treating human beings like animals thus meant that we give people food when they are hungry, provide them with water when they are thirsty, and take care of them when they are ill, this clearly would not be dehumanizing. We should thus focus on cases where people are treated like animals in ways where they ought to be treated like human beings.

In the discussion of animalization in the global migration crisis above, examples were provided of detaining migrants in cages, treating them with disregard and disdain, and subjecting them to persistent beatings. Other examples may be found in violence inflicted on refugees, asylum seekers, and unwanted migrants at borders. This point is raised by Tariq, the asylum seeker from Pakistan whose experiences of detention in Bulgaria were mentioned in the previous chapter. He recalled mistreatments that occurred on the border between Turkey and Bulgaria, observing how 'in Bulgaria, there are volunteer refugee hunters who literally shoot people who come from Turkey. You shoot animals, don't you?'[37]

Similar stories about the use of wanton or excessive violence are reported by NGOs. In a report by Médecins Sans Frontières (MSF) from 2015, a young man from Morocco recounted, for example, how Croatian policemen beat him up when he tried to cross the border with Serbia:

> We don't know what is happening, but we can't pass Croatia and here I don't know what is happening. In Croatia the police were very bad. They pointed guns and sent us back and beat us. Look at my foot: The policeman threw me to the floor and just started kicking and kicking. I don't understand. We have the papers from Greece, Macedonia and Serbia but they didn't let us pass and sent us back, like animals.[38]

Gender-based violence also features in testimonies of refugees and asylum seekers about animalizing treatment. A woman from Eritrea told MSF about the abuse to which women were subjected in Tripoli while waiting for a boat to take them from Libya to Europe:

> I stayed three months in Tripoli. I have no words to describe my life there. It's the worst place in the world. They treated us like animals. They separated women from men and every day they took one of us to quench their lust. Who wants to stay in Libya under these conditions? I don't want to be abused again! So we had no choice. It's true, we knew that we could die at sea, but it was our choice.[39]

These testimonies link animalization to abuse. People object against their mistreatment, claiming that they feel treated like animals. It is important to consider what this means precisely because in many of these cases victims are not directly treated as animals. In the case of the story recounted by Tariq, for example, the shooting of people who cross the border between Turkey and Bulgaria on foot demonstrates not only important similarities with the hunting of animals, but also crucial differences. While the hunting element is clearly reminiscent of the (mis)treatment of animals, the use of violence in the case of border patrols may also be seen as a technique of social control, conveying to refugees, asylum seekers, and other migrants the message to stay away from the Bulgarian border. This has no direct equivalent with animal hunting since the use of violence in the latter case is not used as an instrument of communication.[40]

Similarly, in the case of the Moroccan immigrant who was stopped at the border with Croatia, beaten up, and then sent back, this treatment demonstrates some key distinctions with how people would treat animals. For example, if a sheep would try to cross over into a field where it should not go, a farmer would put up a fence. If the sheep managed to get through the

56   Dehumanization in the Global Migration Crisis

fence, the farmer would chase the animal back but would not beat it up before returning it to the meadow. In terms of sexual violence, the relation may contain an interpersonal aspect as well, if rape and abuse is used as a tool of humiliation and submission, even though the equal moral status of victims as persons who have the right to refuse sexual intercourse is evidently denied in forcing them to engage in this activity against their will.[41] Let us therefore look more closely at whether practices like these should be considered dehumanizing forms of animalization.

As if

Our preliminary definition of dehumanization, as set out in the Introduction, held that dehumanizing treatment consists in treating people in ways that signal that they are attributed a moral status below that of human beings. This applies to cases where people are treated like animals because this treatment signals that perpetrators do not regard them as human beings. This would be the case, for example, when people exterminate others in genocide as if they were vermin. In such cases, victims are treated in ways that signal that they are attributed a lower moral status than that of human beings. Treating people like animals in this sense therefore evidently constitutes a form of dehumanization. The situation is more complex, however, when people are not treated like animals but *as if* they were animals. When people are treated as if they were animals, this treatment sends mixed signals regarding the perceived human status of the victim(s).

The philosopher Avishai Margalit develops this point in his cogent account of dehumanization as a special type of humiliation.[42] Reflecting on the way in which the inmates of the Nazi concentration and extermination camps were treated, he argues that '[t]he special cruelty toward the victims in the forced-labor and death camps—especially the humiliations that took place there—happened the way it did because human beings were involved. Animals would not have been abused in the same way.'[43]

Margalit contends that it would not make sense to abuse animals in the same way because, unlike human beings, animals are not vulnerable to transgressions of their semiotic and moral sensibilities. This observation points to the idea that humiliation requires a certain recognition of the victim as someone who at least shares those sensibilities that allow them to experience a sense of symbolic denigration. These sensibilities appear to be distinctively human. The philosopher Kwame Anthony Appiah summarizes this point in his observation that

> [t]he persecutors may liken the objects of their enmity to cockroaches or germs, but they acknowledge their victims' humanity in the very act of humiliating, stigmatizing, reviling, and torturing them. Such treatment—and the voluble justifications the persecutors invariably offer for such treatment—is reserved for creatures we recognize to have intentions and desires and projects.[44]

Indeed, refugees, asylum seekers, and unwanted migrants who report having been subjected to animalistic treatment at times speak about a sense of humiliation they experience in response to their mistreatment. In an interview with *The Guardian* from 2018, an asylum seeker from Honduras recounts, for example, how his family was detained in a migrant holding centre in the Rio Grande Valley of South Texas in the United States where they were subjected to denigrating treatment by the guards: 'There we were, caged up like animals, and they were laughing at us'.[45] A similar connection between humiliation and animalistic treatment is recounted by Abdul, a young Syrian in Beirut, who told me how he was humiliated by local youth while sleeping rough. Boys would come and beat him up. Abdul reflects that 'they treat me inhumanely, like a dog'.

It is important to note that beating up a dog or laughing at a caged up animal with a highly developed sense of social interaction, such as a chimpanzee, would be inhumane as well. Inhumane treatment is marked by an absence of compassion, sympathy, and consideration for others. 'Others' include humans, but also other beings whose traits require consideration in our evaluation of how to treat them. The divide between human beings and other animals is not so wide as to rule out the need to take into account their feelings and experiences. Particularly if we consider the similarities between humans and those animals, which share a high level of sentience or social awareness, their humane treatment will likely not differ much from the proper treatment of human beings. Certain animals, which are similar or close to us, such as chimpanzees or dogs, might even be sensitive to experiences (akin to) humiliation through the development of semiotic or (proto-)moral sensibilities that are close enough to ours to allow for complex interactions to take place.[46]

Still, the element of humiliation, as an element of interpersonal contact between human beings, requires careful attention in our analysis of dehumanization. If treating people *as if* they were animals actually confirms the human status of the victims in certain ways, this raises doubts about how to categorize this treatment in terms of dehumanization. The issue to address here is whether ambivalent cases in which a certain recognition of the human status of the victim appears to coincide with a treatment that seeks

58 Dehumanization in the Global Migration Crisis

to contradict this acknowledgement should also be regarded as instances of dehumanization.

Hunting refugees

Let us consider here in more detail the example of refugee hunting, as recounted by Tariq. Following our preliminary definition, dehumanizing treatment consists in treating people in ways that signal that they are attributed a moral status below that of human beings. There are two ways that potentially could establish that a treatment is dehumanizing. First, there may exist universal criteria for determining whether a practice signals that victims are attributed this lower status. Second, there may exist contingent criteria related to particular cases that indicate that victims are considered less than human in a moral sense.

If there are any universal criteria for determining whether a practice is de facto dehumanizing, this would mean that forms of treatment exist that always entail a denial of the moral status that victims hold as human beings. Examples we might think of here include enslaving or torturing people. Enslavement and torture appear as the most plausible candidates for practices that are de facto dehumanizing because both include treating people in ways that conflict with core beliefs about what minimal recognition of the humanity of others requires in terms of their proper treatment. This is the case for enslavement because this practice effectively takes away people's ownership over their own lives, bodies, and actions. It does not seem possible to enslave people while recognizing them as minimally human in a moral sense because recognition of the moral standing of humans would grant them the final say in how to live their lives, use their bodies, and engage in action. Basic recognition of moral human status thus entails at least a minimal respect for people's autonomy, which does not allow for their enslavement. Torture, at least in some of its guises, similarly transgresses fundamental moral boundaries in interpersonal relations because it involves using people's bodies and minds against them in an effort to break their will.

At this point in the argument, it suffices to introduce the idea that there could be acts that are always dehumanizing without developing it in full detail. I will return to this point in the Chapter 5 to unpack this notion further based on insights into the nature of dehumanization that will be developed over the next chapters. For now, it is important to note that a category of universally dehumanizing practices may exist. The example of the violence used against migrants in border areas does not seem to fit this category, however, as violence occurs in many shapes and guises, which do not all automatically signal that victims are ascribed a moral status below that of human beings. We therefore need to look at the particulars of the situation to determine whether this practice signals that the victims are denied human status in a moral sense.

It is important to consider the meaning attributed to the action by perpetrator(s), victim(s), and onlookers to determine whether this type of practice is dehumanizing. Whether a treatment signals that people are attributed a moral status below that of human beings depends, on my view, on the way the action is perceived by the persons involved. To understand how meanings attributed to an action influence the nature of the action, it will be helpful to consider the work of the cultural anthropologist Clifford Geertz on thick and thin description.[47] Geertz discusses the difference observed by the philosopher Gilbert Ryle between a twitch and a wink, which from the outside might look the same for the observer:

> Consider, he says, two boys rapidly contracting the eyelids of their right eyes. In one, this is an involuntary twitch; in the other, a conspiratorial signal to a friend. The two movements are, as movements, identical; from an I-am-a-camera, 'phenomenalistic' observation of them alone, one could not tell which was twitch and which was wink, or indeed whether both or either was twitch or wink. Yet the difference, however unphotographable, between a twitch and a wink is vast; as anyone unfortunate enough to have had the first taken for the second knows. The winker is communicating, and indeed communicating in a quite precise and special way: (1) deliberately, (2) to someone in particular, (3) to impart a particular message, (4) according to a socially established code, and (5) without cognizance of the rest of the company. As Ryle points out, the winker has done two things, contracted his eyelids and winked, while the twitcher has done only one, contracted his eyelids.[48]

The difference between a twitch and a wink lies in the meaning the wink carries in expressing a message. The nature of the action therefore depends on the meaning attributed to it by the persons involved. Geertz uses this example to demonstrate the relevance of a careful, detailed 'thick' description of action, rather than a 'thin' one, which describes only the contraction of the eyelids. The situation becomes even more complex when Ryle introduces additional variations to the theme, wherein the wink takes on different meanings according to the intention of the winker and the particulars of the social context.

> Suppose, he continues, there is a third boy, who, 'to give malicious amusement to his cronies', parodies the first boy's wink, as amateurish, clumsy, obvious, and

> so on. He, of course, does this in the same way the second boy winked and the first twitched: by contracting his right eyelids. Only this boy is neither winking nor twitching, he is parodying someone else's, as he takes it, laughable, attempt at winking. Here, too, a socially established code exists (he will 'wink' laboriously, over-obviously, perhaps adding a grimace—the usual artifices of the clown); and so also does a message. Only now it is not conspiracy but ridicule that is in the air. If the others think he is actually winking, his whole project misfires as completely, though with somewhat different results, as if they think he is twitching. One can go further: uncertain of his mimicking abilities, the would-be satirist may practice at home before the mirror, in which case he is not twitching, winking, or parodying, but rehearsing; though so far as what a camera, a radical behaviorist, or a believer in protocol sentences would record: he is just rapidly contracting his right eyelids like all the others.[49]

Drawing from Ryle, Geertz points out the various meanings that can be attached to an eye twitching motion, which can turn it into a variety of actions. What is interesting for our analysis here is the idea that the meaning of the action is determined by the way it is perceived by the persons involved in the action. It is important to distinguish, however, between the meaning of the action and what the action signals. For the wink to constitute a form of parody, the winker and the audience need to understand that the twitching motion adheres to social conventions that distinguish a twitch from a wink from a wink-as-parody. The meaning of the twitch is thus determined by the twitcher and the onlooker(s). What the twitching motion *signals*, however, depends on the meaning the twitcher attributes to the eye movement, if any, even if the signal may fail due to not being interpreted in the intended way.

In the case of refugee hunting, the perception of the action of the perpetrator(s) should therefore guide our assessment, in my view, because this treatment could express a dehumanizing signal, even if this would not be picked up by victims or onlookers.[50] It seems likely that in at least some of the cases where people take to the frontier on their own accord to hunt migrants, individuals engaging in this activity fail to recognize the human status of their victims in a moral sense and dehumanize them by signalling this misattribution through their actions. It is important to note, however, that this treatment, in my view, does not necessarily signal that perpetrators attribute to victims a moral status *below* that of human beings. Some refugee hunters might view unwanted migrants, for example, as inferior human beings or recognize their humanity but not their right to enter their country and regard their alleged 'crime' of trying to enter the country as a valid excuse to use severe violence against them.

This argument entails faulty moral reasoning since citizens do not have the right to use violence to keep people from entering their country, and even state authorities are restricted by the human rights of migrants in their use of violence to ward off outsiders. Nonetheless, it is quite conceivable that people can treat others *as if* they were animals and nonetheless fail to treat them in a genuinely dehumanizing way because their actions do not signal that their victims hold a moral status below that of human beings. What occurs in these cases is rather a form of infra-humanization, as discussed in the previous chapter, through which refugees and other migrants crossing the border are treated as lesser human beings. This suggests that while particular ways of treating people *as if* they were animals can amount to dehumanization, not all of them do.

To determine whether treatments that do not belong to the category of de facto dehumanizing treatments are dehumanizing, we thus need to analyse the perceptions of the perpetrator(s) closely. Although this makes it more difficult to determine when dehumanization takes place, it reflects the reality that dehumanization not only concerns the way in which people are treated or portrayed, but also how they are perceived.

Making people resemble animals

Dehumanization as a form of treatment is not only closely tied to dehumanization as a form of perception, but also interacts with dehumanization as a form of portrayal. This is the case because some forms of treating people as if they were animals force them to behave in ways that make them resemble animals. Efforts to treat people like animals oftentimes seek to achieve a visible differentiation of animalized victims from other human beings, which jeopardizes the victim's human status in its normative sense, and may therefore be understood to perform a similar function as portrayals that identify people with animals.

This type of animalizing treatment frequently draws from a denial of basic civility. If civility gives expression to humanity, people may come to appear or perceive of themselves as being more similar to animals and less human when they are hindered from manifesting these qualities. A common way of achieving this effect is by denying people civil means of defecation.[51] Such a denial is recounted by people held in certain immigration detention centres. The human rights organization Pro Asyl notes, for example, that there is no toilet in one of the rooms in the Tychero centre in the Evros region in Greece. The report recounts how '[i]f a detainee of cell three has to urinate, police

62 Dehumanization in the Global Migration Crisis

guards would guard him/her to the fields or he/she had to urinate through the bars into the corridor'.[52] A similar effect of animalistic appearance can be reached when detainees are impeded from washing themselves and keeping up their personal hygiene. This is reflected in the testimony of the person who was detained in Tripoli, Libya, and noted how the guards 'don't even enter our room because they say that we smell and have illnesses'.[53]

Impeding people from demonstrating a basic level of civility thus functions as a marker of difference that negatively impacts on the human status of the persons affected, mediated by disgust. The relation between disgust and these two elements is observed by Bloom, who argues that 'disgust leads you to construe the other as diminished and revolting, lacking humanity'.[54] People thus come to be perceived as more akin to animals than human beings, which in turn may lead to a lessening of concern for their fate.[55] When a treatment leads for onlookers to come to regard people as less than human, in this sense this treatment may be said to be dehumanizing because it achieves the lowering of moral standing to a degree where people are perceived as less than human.

In brief, some but not all forms of treating people like animals amount to dehumanization. Such treatments constitute a form of dehumanization when they signal that victims are attributed a moral status lower than that of human beings. Treating people like animals is also dehumanizing when this treatment leads to a perception of the victim(s), either on the side of the victims themselves or in the eyes of perpetrators or bystanders, as holding a status below that of human beings.[56] Following this logic, treating people as if they were animals may constitute a particular form of portraying them as animals.

Viewing people as animals

A third way in which animalistic dehumanization may be understood is as perceiving of people as animals. The analysis above makes it doubtful, however, that dehumanization often takes the form of genuinely seeing people as animals. After all, many cases of dehumanizing treatments and representations allegedly seek to humiliate the victim. This attempt to humiliate requires recognition of the victim as a human being who should at least share particular sensibilities that make it possible to bring about a sense of humiliation to which dehumanization as a form of mistreatment often, if not always, strives. Such humiliating forms of dehumanization can therefore not coincide with a perception of the victims as non-human animals, even if they are depicted as such, given that this perception would rule out the belief that the victim can be humiliated. While people may thus view others as similar to animals in certain regards, it seems rare for them to consider their victims as nothing more than animals. Furthermore, it seems difficult to perceive of people as animals, given that animals often are evidently dissimilar to human beings.

This logic is reflected in Hopkins's claim that migrants are *like* cockroaches. Even though she engages in blatant and explicit dehumanization, she does not claim that migrants literally are cockroaches, as this would not make much sense. Rather, her point seems to be that migrants have a moral status similar to cockroaches, which entails that we need not be concerned about their fate and may even take active measures to harm them, given that they hold no significant moral status that would rule out any such treatment. This is where the metaphoric use of animalization comes in again.

While it is clear that people do not usually consider the victims they dehumanize to literally be (non-human) animals, it may still be possible that people on rare occasions view others as non-human animals or regard them as human animals. If people are indeed capable of genuinely considering others to be non-human animals, the animal with which dehumanized persons are identified arguably needs to be very similar to human beings to allow for this perception. Here we may consider, for example, the long history of the racist dehumanization of African people in the United States and Europe through which persons were explicitly dehumanized at the hand of portrayals that presented them as apes.[57] While for most audiences that were receptive to such dehumanizing depictions, these representations assumedly led to views of African people as inferior human beings, some may have been persuaded that Africans were literally more similar to apes than to humans and therefore should be seen as animals. This ill-founded belief can allegedly only be upheld because of the relative similarity between apes and human beings. If racists would have depicted Africans as bats, for example, it would have been far less conceivable that large audiences could have been truly convinced that Africans were, naturalistically speaking, bats. When the difference between human beings and the animals with which they are identified becomes too flagrant, the identification can only be understood in a metaphorical sense.

The evolutionary scale

An alternative way in which people may hold dehumanizing views of others draws from a scalar notion of humanity. This idea is used in a fascinating study conducted by the social psychologist Nour Kteily and his colleagues

64 Dehumanization in the Global Migration Crisis

on the blatant dehumanization of members of various ethnic, religious, and national groups. Drawing on a (historically incorrect) visual representation of evolutionary development from apes to humans, their research asked participants in three countries to rank different peoples according to their advancement on an evolutionary scale.[58] The outcomes showed that Americans listed Muslims, Arabs, and Mexican immigrants significantly lower than Americans, Europeans, Swiss, or Japanese.[59] Although these results are shocking, the relative closeness on the scale between the least humanized group and the most humanized group (13.6 percentage points) seems to indicate that Muslims are not viewed as fundamentally different from an evolutionary perspective, but rather as inferior human beings.[60]

Human animals

A further way in which viewing people as animals may be dehumanizing is when people are regarded as human animals. This form of animalization does not require that people are regarded as non-human animals but reduces victims to their mere biological human existence. In the discussion of the work of Malkki and Agamben in the previous chapter, we touched upon this notion. This idea is also expressed by the political theorist Hannah Arendt whose reflections inspired the work of Agamben. Arendt maintains that, to be truly human, people need to be able to express themselves through their action and speech as members of a political community. The humanity of our existence, in her view, thus derives from our acting with and among others. In *The Human Condition*, Arendt thus contends that '[a] life without speech and without action ... is literally dead to the world; it has ceased to be a human life because it is no longer lived among men'.[61]

Arendt is concerned that the loss of a political community entails that stateless people are at risk of losing their humanity. She thus maintains that people who are excluded from community in this way remain tied to humanity in a biological sense only:

> The great danger arising from the existence of people forced to live outside the common world is that they are thrown back, in the midst of civilization, on their natural givenness, on their mere differentiation. They lack that tremendous equalizing of differences, which comes from being citizens of some commonwealth and yet, since they are no longer allowed to partake in the human artifice, they begin to belong to the human race in much the same way as animals belong to a specific animal species.[62]

Without participation in collective action, it becomes difficult to view others as human beings since their similarity loses its political character. People bereft of a community, which can confer on them an identity that ties them to others in bonds of resemblance, thus become characterized by a form of humanity that cannot express itself in any morally meaningful way.

The importance of this form of inclusion in relation to refugees, asylum seekers, and unwanted migrants is illustrated by the human rights scholar Lucy Fiske in a study that focuses on protest enacted by detainees in immigration detention centres on Nauru, off the coast of Australia.[63] Based on Arendt's theory, Fiske argues that detainees are dehumanized when they are deprived of the recognition that they are persons who can engage in speech and act on a basis of equality with other people. She points out that this neglect of people's expressions entails a failure to recognize their individuality, as the identity of detained individuals is reduced to their membership of a social category, namely that of being an 'illegal migrant'.[64] Nonetheless, detainees retain a sense of agency and humanity through the staging of protests that focus on the management of their bodies, which is the last object under their control, for example, through hunger strikes or the sewing of their lips.

Although Fiske's article draws on Arendt's ideas, it is also in tension with them in important ways. Following Arendt, recognition of the status of people as persons who can express their identity through the participation in collective action depends on the protection of their fundamental rights by a political authority that is bound to a national community. On Fiske's account, however, the acts of resistance staged by the detainees of immigration detention centres are understood as practices through which people may regain their human status. This contrasts with Arendt's views since the particular mistreatment the detainees protest arises from the very fact that their fundamental rights are not guaranteed by any national authority. The argument presented by Fiske thus calls into question the centrality of the political community as tied to the nation state found in Arendt, placing in its stead a social, ideological, or moral understanding of community through which detainees may appeal to the solidarity of international human rights advocates or humanitarian sympathizers.

Fiske's account also raises a deeper question as to whether the failure to recognize people's capacity to speak and act on a basis of equality with other people is in itself sufficient to amount to dehumanization. According to our initial characterization of dehumanization, people are viewed as less than human when they are not attributed the moral status of human beings and the moral status that they are ascribed instead, if any, is lower than that of human beings. The question is thus whether failing to recognize people's capacity to speak and act on a basis of equality with other people entails regarding them as less than human. If neurotypical adult human beings are regarded as unable to speak and act, this indeed seems to deny their moral status as human beings since recognition of these capacities is a central part of acknowledging them as moral persons. It is unclear, however, whether the failure to recognize people's capacity to speak and act on a basis of equality with other people should be considered dehumanizing in all cases or rather points to infra-humanization or other forms of discrimination and marginalization. The point of contention centres on what it involves to recognize people's capacity to speak and act *on a basis of equality with other people*. Does this mean that we should allow that they are equally capable of acting and speaking, at least in a minimal sense, or does this entail that their actions and expressions should be taken equally serious to that of other people? If the former, reducing people to mere human animals can indeed be seen as dehumanizing. If the latter, it seems more fitting to describe this view as infra-humanizing, or discriminatory in a more general sense.

The moral dimension

What this discussion of animalistic or animalizing perception illustrates is that people do not often seem to genuinely regard others as animals in a literal sense. To uphold the view that human beings are animals, people should maintain that the dehumanized are closer to certain non-human animals that are nonetheless very similar to human beings, lag behind on a scale of evolutionary development, or are so-called human animals. Each of these perceptions allows for infra-humanization as well as dehumanization. In many of the cases discussed, it seems more likely that people consider victims lesser human beings rather than genuinely less than human. It is important, however, to also consider the moral dimension here. What renders perceptions dehumanizing is usually not a genuine belief that the dehumanized are biologically less than human but the conviction that they hold a moral status below that of human beings. Their moral status is therefore what is at stake.

Animalizing migrants

Let us return to the examples of the various ways in which the notion of animalization is used to comment on the global migration crisis, discussed at the start of this chapter, and consider when animalization should be considered dehumanizing following the insights developed in the chapter. In terms of portraying refugees, asylum seekers, and unwanted migrants as animals, this chapter has argued that animalistic depictions amount to dehumanization when such portrayals signal that the persons involved hold a moral status lower than that of human beings. The difficulty lies in knowing exactly when this point is reached. This is evidently the case when migrants are likened to cockroaches as a rhetorical tool to justify the use of gunships instead of rescue vessels. In this case, the evocation of disgust is used to diminish a sense of moral engagement and reduce the willingness to provide humanitarian aid to people in need, even if this refusal leads to widespread death and suffering. The moral implications of this dehumanizing view are even explicitly spelled out in Hopkins's claim that she does not care about 'pictures of coffins' or 'bodies floating in water'.[65] A more evident example of dehumanization is hard to come by.

It is more difficult to establish whether more ambivalent examples of animalistic portrayal should be considered dehumanizing. When migrants are portrayed as a 'swarm of people', it is not apparent, for instance, that their moral status as human beings is denied. To assess whether this is the case it is helpful to look at the context of this claim. Cameron stated that, 'you have got a swarm of people coming across the Mediterranean, seeking a better life, wanting to come to Britain because Britain has got jobs, it's got a growing economy, it's an incredible place to live'.[66] This depiction does not evidently deny people's human status in a moral sense by likening them to animals, objects, or entities that hold a moral status below that of human beings. Since a 'swarm' can also refer to a group of people moving, as when one speaks of a 'swarm of tourists', and since the claim is made in a sentence that emphasizes specifically human endeavours, such as 'seeking a better life' in a context marked by 'jobs' and 'a growing economy', on my view, this claim fails to be dehumanizing.

How about Donald Trump's tweet that Democrats want illegal immigrants 'to pour into and infest our Country'?[67] This statement draws from a metaphor that establishes a conceptual link between human beings and vermin. 'Infest' is a term with a forceful negative connotation that refers to the spreading of something dangerous or undesired. Like 'swarm', the term 'infest' can also be used for human beings. In this case, 'infestation' refers to the presence, or inflow, of a large number of unwanted people. While this notion can be used to dehumanize, there is greater room for interpretation than there is in cases where people are explicitly likened to cockroaches, rats, or insects and where this portrayal indicates that victims are attributed the equivalent moral status of these animals. When 'infestation' is used to advocate for the extermination of minorities, for example, this clearly is dehumanizing, since people are thereby attributed a moral status below that of human beings. When this term is used to call for stricter migration controls, however, it could also fall under infra-humanization, or discrimination, marginalization, or stigmatization, whereby people are portrayed as inferior, but not necessarily depicted as *less than* human in a moral sense.

Considering Trump's wider rhetoric about illegal migration, this tweet fits within a trend of discourse that animalizes and dehumanizes migrants arriving to the United States via the Mexican border. At an earlier occasion, Trump referred to migrants as 'animals', although this statement was later qualified by emphasizing that the slur was directed at members of the MS-13 gang. Even if the claim supposedly only applied to this group, the statement reflected an evident dehumanizing logic in explicitly stating that these individuals do not qualify as people: 'We have people coming into the country, or trying to come in—and we're stopping a lot of them—but we're taking people out of the country. You wouldn't believe how bad these people are. These aren't people. These are animals.'[68]

Repeated portrayals of a particular group of persons in animalizing ways may contribute to their dehumanization, even if a distinct claim considered in isolation does not reflect an evident dehumanizing logic. This is the case because metaphoric speech structures the way that people understand the world. For followers familiar with Trump's earlier representations of (delinquent) migrants as animals, the claim that 'illegal immigrants' would be allowed by Democrats 'to pour into and infest our Country' may thus reinforce the dehumanization of migrants, even if the notion 'infest' taken on its own does not directly imply a denial of the human moral status of the people who are portrayed as the source of the infestation.

The examples of animalistic treatments in the global migration crisis that this chapter discussed focused on the way in which detained migrants are kept in cages, treated with disregard and disdain, subjected to persistent beatings and sexual forms of abuse, and on the way in which violence is inflicted on refugees, asylum seekers, and unwanted migrants at international borders. To know whether these forms of mistreatment are dehumanizing, we need to consider if they signal that the victims are attributed a moral status below that of human beings or lead to a perception of the victims as less than human. Being detained in cages, for example, could indeed signal that migrants are seen as animals who hold a moral status lower than that of fellow human beings. Determining whether treatments are dehumanizing is often complex, however, because the dividing line between dehumanization and infra-humanization is often hard to draw. This means that it is difficult to tell whether people mistreat others because they perceive of them as less than human or as inferior human beings.

Let us consider some of the examples mentioned throughout the chapter, starting with the testimony of a detainee of an immigration detention facility in Rome: 'Every cage has two rooms. The cages have barriers almost 5–6m high. We are left there like savage beasts.'[69] While this indictment evidently speaks to the animalization of detained migrants, it is more difficult to establish if the treatment should also count as dehumanizing. We can consider first if locking people up is de facto dehumanizing. This does not seem to be the case because there may be legitimate reasons to detain people, setting aside for a moment the question whether this is also the case for migrants. How about locking people up in animal cages? One could argue that locking people up in animal cages would be de facto dehumanizing because it violates dignity and therefore signals that people are attributed a moral status below human beings. From this passage, it is not evident, however, that the migrants are actually detained in animal cages or that the testimony perceives of his cell as an animal cage. What we can tell from this fragment is that this person feels animalized by the treatment received, but the objection against the treatment signals that this sense of animalization does not lead to thoroughly dehumanized perception of the self.[70]

The detainee of the processing centre, located in a former zoo, in Tripoli, Libya, who recounted how he and the other inmates were treated and depicted as animals by the guards presents more details about the treatment received: 'They [the guards] don't even enter our room because they say that we smell and have illnesses. They constantly insult us, and call us "You donkey, you dog". When we are moving in their way, they look disgusted and slap us.'[71]

In this case there is a stronger basis to conclude that this treatment is dehumanizing because the combination of likening the detainees to donkeys and dogs, expressions of disgust, and abuse signals that the guards attribute the inmates a status below that of human beings, more similar to that of a donkey or a dog, which meant that they could be beaten without concern.

A further way in which detention can be dehumanizing is by making migrants lose touch with their own sense of humanity. As noted above, an immigrant from Congo felt diminished after having passed more than eighteen months in detention in Malta: 'Detention dehumanizes the human being. The detainee is reduced to the state of an animal. One wakes up, eats, sleeps, wakes up.'[72] In this chapter, we did not explore this phenomenon in detail because we will return to this form of dehumanization in Chapter 4. It is important to note, however, that if treatment makes people perceive of themselves as holding a moral status below that of human beings, this constitutes another form of dehumanization.

Conclusion

This chapter considered animalization in its guises as representation, treatment, and perception. In terms of representation, we found that depictions of people as animals are not always dehumanizing. Dehumanizing portrayals focus on negative characteristics and encompass the full being of the victim, rather than just a particular aspect of the person. The likening of the person to an animal discredits him or her fully in a moral sense. Our discussion of dehumanizing portrayals also indicated that dehumanization can render violence more palatable and make it easier to turn away from requests for aid.

In terms of treatment, the chapter found that treating people like animals is dehumanizing when people are treated in ways that signal that they are attributed a moral status below that of human beings. Dehumanization as treatment is closely tied to dehumanization as perception because whether this signalling occurs depends on the views held by the perpetrator(s). Animalizing treatments can also be dehumanizing when they lead to a perception of the victims, either on the side of the victims themselves or in the eyes of the perpetrators or bystanders, as holding a status lower than that of human beings. In this sense, treatment can work as an active form of representation through which the perception of onlookers of the victim, or of the victim him- or herself, is altered.

In terms of perception, the chapter argued that it is oftentimes difficult for people to literally believe that dehumanized victims are the animals with which they identify them. While it is clear that people do not usually consider the victims they dehumanize to literally be (non-human) animals, it may still be possible that people on rare occasions view others as non-human animals or regard them as human animals. Usually, however, the likening to an animal works in a metaphoric sense to signal that certain people have a moral status comparable to that of lowly considered animals, which would entail that we need not be concerned about their fate and may even take active measures to harm them, given that they allegedly hold no significant moral status that would rule out any such treatment. People may therefore be genuinely perceived as being less than human (in a moral sense) even if they may not be genuinely seen to be animals (in a literal sense).

The main insight developed in this chapter is then that the moral sense of humanity is central to understanding when animalization turns into dehumanization. Animalization becomes dehumanizing when victims are viewed, portrayed, or treated as *less than* human in a moral sense. In animalization, this reduction to subhuman status often coincides with feelings of contempt, hatred, or disgust. This sets animalization apart from cases of objectification, where a more distanced, indifferent stance generally prevails, as the next chapter will set out.

Notes

1. The notion of animalization is central, for example, to Nick Haslam's account of dehumanization, which distinguishes between two types of denial of human status. Whereas animalization refers to the denial that people have particular uniquely human traits, relating to an Enlightenment understanding of humanness, such as rationality and civility, mechanization corresponds to a denial of traits that are characteristic of human nature, relating to a Romantic sense of humanness, such as empathy and individuality. Dehumanization can thus revolve either around likening people to animals, when they are viewed, portrayed, or treated as irrational, savage or barbarous, or around identifying them with objects or automata, lacking in feeling and personality. See: Haslam, 'Dehumanization: An Integrative Approach'.
2. Elgot and Taylor, 'Calais Crisis'.
3. Ibid.
4. Katie Hopkins, 'Rescue Boats? I'd Use Gunships to Stop Migrants', *The Sun*, 17 April 2015, http://www.gc.soton.ac.uk/files/2015/01/hopkins-17april-2015.pdf.
5. As cited in Vaughan-Williams, '"We Are Not Animals!"', 1.
6. Borderline-Europe, 'At the Limen: The Implementation of the Return Directive in Italy, Cyprus, and Spain', 2013, https://www.borderline-europe.de/sites/default/files/readingtips/at%20the%20limen_12_2013.pdf, p. 25
7. Borderline-Europe, '"That is the Worst: The Political Normality to Lock People Up" Interview with Borderline-Lesvos', 2020, https://www.borderline-europe.de/sites/default/files/readingtips/Interview%20borderline%20lesvos.pdf.
8. DeBono, '"Less than Human"', 71.
9. Sydney Morning Herald, 'Think Australia's Treatment'.
10. Ibid.
11. These dynamics will be analysed in more detail in Chapter 4.
12. Will Kymlicka, 'Human Rights Without Human Supremacism', *Canadian Journal of Philosophy* 48 (2018): 763–92, https://doi.org/10.1080/00455091.2017.1386481.
13. Alice Crary, 'Dehumanization and the Question of Animals', in *The Routledge Handbook of Dehumanization*, edited by Maria Kronfelder (New York: Routledge, 2021), p. 159.
14. For a large sample of examples of this practice, see: Sam Keen, *Faces of the Enemy: Reflections of the Hostile Imagination* (New York: HarperCollins Publishers, 1991).
15. Tirrell, 'Genocidal Language Games', 197.

72 Dehumanization in the Global Migration Crisis

16. David A. Graham, 'Trump Says Democrats Want Immigrants to "Infest" the U.S.', *The Atlantic*, 19 June 2018, https://www.theatlantic.com/politics/archive/2018/06/trump-immigrants-infest/563159/.

17. Ibid.

18. George Lakoff and Mark Johnson, *Metaphors We Live By* (Chicago: University of Chicago Press, 1980).

19. O'Brien, 'Indigestible Foods'.

20. Idem, 42.

21. Idem, 43.

22. Ibid.

23. Ibid.

O'Brien's point about authorities seeking to legitimate measures of discipline and control by likening people to subhuman life forms that allegedly pose a risk to the nation links to David Livingstone Smith's discussion of the 'management' of dehumanized individuals and groups. Smith draws from the work of the anthropologist Mary Douglas to examine five ways in which traditional societies handle 'aberrant forms', which map onto common strategies for dealing with dehumanized people. These strategies consist in elimination of anomalousness, control, avoidance, labelling, and ritual practices. Discipline and control thus appear as key political responses to the disturbing and disruptive presence of those who are considered to fall outside the human category. See: Smith, *Making Monsters*, 270–6 and Mary Douglas, *Purity and Danger: An Analysis of Concepts of Pollution and Taboo* (New York: Routledge, 1966).

24. Anderson, 'The Politics of Pests', 8.

25. 'Vermin', *Online Etymology Dictionary*, https://www.etymonline.com/word/vermin.

26. Anderson, 'The Politics of Pests', 18.

27. 'Sly Fox, Fat Cat: Animals Names for People: Anthropomorphic names for the human animal', *Merriam-Webster*, https://www.merriam-webster.com/words-at-play/anthropomorphic-animal-names-for-humans/duck.

28. Marshall and Shapiro, 'When "Scurry" vs "Hurry"', 776.

29. Bloom, *Just Babies*, 133. The hypothesis that disgust is a facilitating factor in dehumanization is also confirmed in a study by Erin E. Buckels and Paul D. Trapnell, 'Disgust Facilitates Outgroup Dehumanization', *Group Processes & Intergroup Relations* 16 (2013): 771–80, https://doi.org/10.1177/1368430212471738.

30. Smith, *Less than Human*, 18.

31. Ibid.

32. Huxley, as cited in Smith, *Less than Human*, 21.

33. Albert Bandura, Bill Underwood, and Michael Fromson, 'Disinhibition of Aggression through Diffusion of Responsibility and Dehumanization of Victims', *Journal of Research in Personality* 9 (1975): 253–69, https://doi.org/10.1016/0092-6566(75)90001-X.

34. O'Brien, 'Indigestible Foods'.

35. Although it should be noted that violent mistreatment of refugees, asylum seekers, and migrants does occur, for example, in border control. For studies of these forms of violence, see: Andersson, 'Hunter and Prey' and Samantha Sabo, Susan Shaw, Maia Ingram, Nicolette Teufel-Shone et al., 'Everyday Violence, Structural Racism and Mistreatment at the EU-Mexico Border', *Social Science & Medicine* 109 (2014): 66–74, https://doi.org/10.1016/j.socscimed.2014.02.005.

36. Luca Andrighetto, Cristina Baldissarri, Sara Lattanzio, Steve Loughnan, and Chiara Volpato, 'Human-itarian Aid? Two Forms of Dehumanization and Willingness to Help after Natural Disasters', *British Journal of Social Psychology* 53 (2014): 573–84, https://doi.org/10.1111/bjso.12066. The findings of Andrighetto et al. correspond to similar results produced by other social psychologists on the role that dehumanization plays in reducing empathy and caring for the suffering of others. See: Sabina Čehajić, Rupert Brown, and Roberto Gonzalez, 'What Do I Care? Perceived Ingroup Responsibility and Dehumanization as Predictors of Empathy Felt for the Victim Group', *Group Processes & Intergroup Relations* 12 (2009): 715–29, https://doi.org/10.1177/1368430209347727 and Paolo Riva and Luca Andrighetto, '"Everybody Feels a Broken Bone, But Only We Can Feel a Broken Heart": Group Membership Influences the Perception of Targets' Suffering', *European Journal of Social Psychology* 42 (2012): 801–6, https://doi.org/10.1002/ejsp.1918.

37. For journalistic accounts of violence used against migrants and refugees in border zones in Bulgaria and neighbouring countries, see: Felix Bender, 'Why the EU Condones Human Rights Violations of Refugees in Hungary', *Open Democracy*, 15 April 2018, https://www.opendemocracy.net/en/can-europe-make-it/why-eu-condones-human-rights-violations-of-refugees-in-hungary/, Mac William Bishop, 'Bulgarian Vigilantes Patrol Turkey Border to Keep Migrants Out', *NBC News*, 10 March 2017, https://www.nbcnews.com/storyline/europes-border-crisis/bulgarian-vigilantes-patrol-turkey-border-keep-migrants-out-n723481, Matthew Brunwasser, 'Bulgaria's Vigilante Migrant "Hunter"', *BBC News*, 30 March 2016, https://www.bbc.co.uk/news/magazine-35919068, The Economist, 'Bulgaria Tries to Restrain Its Vigilante "Migrant Hunters"', 19 April 2016, https://www.economist.com/europe/2016/04/19/bulgaria-tries-to-restrain-its-vigilante-migrant-hunters, and James Rothwell, 'Afghan Migrant "Shot Dead by Hunting Party" in Serbian Woods', *The Telegraph*, 24 August 2016, https://www.telegraph.co.uk/news/2016/08/24/afghan-migrant-shot-dead-by-hunting-party-in-serbian-woods/.

38. Médecins Sans Frontières, *Obstacle Course to Europe*, 44.

39. Idem, 16.

40. It may be similar perhaps to situations where people use violence against dangerous animals, like tigers, or animals who take life stock, such as foxes or wolves, to try to keep them out of populated areas or the chicken barn.

41. The complex relation between dehumanization and rape will be discussed in more detail in Chapter 5.

42. Margalit, *The Decent Society*.

43. Idem, 112.

44. Kwame Anthony Appiah, *Experiments in Ethics* (Cambridge, Massachusetts: Harvard University Press, 2008), p. 144.

45. Andrew Gumbel, '"They Were Laughing At Us": Immigrants Tell of Cruelty, Illness, and Filth in US Detention', *The Guardian*, 12 September 2018, https://www.theguardian.com/us-news/2018/sep/12/us-immigration-detention-facilities.

46. For fascinating insights into morality among animals, see: Frans de Waal, *The Age of Empathy: Nature's Lessons for a Kinder Society* (New York: Three Rivers Press, 2009).

47. Clifford Geertz, 'Thick Description: Toward an Interpretive Theory of Culture', in *The Interpretation of Cultures: Selected Essays* (New York: Basic Books, 1973), pp. 310–23.

48. Idem, 312.

49. Ibid.

74   Dehumanization in the Global Migration Crisis

50. An alternative here would be to make the perception of the victim leading. To understand what this would mean we can consider the wink-as-parody case. Imagine a scenario where a person winks at a person. This person winks back. Due to the low self-esteem, the first person does not believe that the recipient of the original wink could actually wink back and interprets the return-wink as a form of ridicule. I believe it is problematic to conclude that the second wink was indeed a wink-as-parody if the sender intended it to be a genuine wink.

51. A vivid example of this kind of practice is presented in the memoirs of Primo Levi. Levi recalls how during the transports to Auschwitz not even a bucket was provided for the people in the wagons, forcing them to either defecate in a corner or wait for the scarce stops the trains made. He recounts the humiliating scenes that occurred during these moments:

> The doors were opened another time, but during a stop in an Austrian railroad station. The SS escort did not hide their amusement at the sight of men and women squatting wherever they could, on the platforms and in the middle of the tracks, and the German passengers openly expressed their disgust: people like this deserve their fate, just look how they behave. These are not *Menschen*, human beings, but animals, it's clear as the light of day.

Impeding people from demonstrating a basic level of civility thus functions as a marker of difference that negatively impacts on the human status of the persons affected, mediated by disgust. People come to be perceived as more akin to animals than human beings, which in turn may lead to a lessening of concern for their fate. See: Primo Levi, *The Drowned and the Saved*, translated by Raymond Rosenthal (London: Abacus, 1989), pp. 88–9.

52. Pro Asyl, *Walls of Shame: Accounts from the Inside: The Detention Centers of Evros*, 2012, https://www.proasyl.de/en/material/walls-of-shame-accounts-from-the-inside-the-detention-centres-of-evros/, p. 30.

53. As cited in Vaughan-Williams, '"We Are Not Animals!"', 1.

54. Bloom, *Just Babies*, 140.

55. Čehajić, Brown, and Gonzalez, 'What Do I Care?'

56. Treatments through which victims come to lose touch with their own humanity will be discussed in more detail in Chapter 4.

57. For a historical account of this issue, see: Gustav Jahoda, *Images of Savages: Ancient Roots of Modern Prejudice in Western Culture* (New York: Routledge, 1999). For an account of dehumanization that concentrates on the role of racism, see: Smith, *Making Monsters*.

58. Kteily, Bruneau, Waytz, and Cotterill, 'The Ascent of Man'.

59. Muslims received the lowest score of 77.6 compared to 91.5 for Americans.

60. I draw this conclusion based on the fact that these scores still correspond to images on the 'human' side of the spectrum. This suggests that the participants did not perceive of these groups as more similar to monkeys learning to stand (as displayed as a visual representation on the low side of the spectrum) than to human beings walking up right (as displayed as a visual representation on the high side of the spectrum).

61. Hannah Arendt, *The Human Condition. Second Edition* (Chicago: Chicago University Press, 1999 [1958]), p. 176.

62. Hannah Arendt, *The Origins of Totalitarianism* (New York: Harvest, 1973 [1951]), p. 302.

63. Fiske, 'Human Rights and Refugee Protest'.

64. Ibid.
65. Hopkins, 'Rescue Boats?'
66. Elgot and Taylor, 'Calais Crisis'.
67. Graham, 'Trump Says Democrats'.
68. Ibid.
69. Borderline-Europe, 'At the Limen', 25.
70. This point of dehumanized self-perception will be worked out in more detail in Chapter 4.
71. As cited in Vaughan-Williams, '"We Are Not Animals!"', 1.
72. DeBono, '"Less than Human"', 71.

3
Objectification

> You are of no value.
>
> **Hassan, refugee from Syria**

Introduction

Hassan illegally sells fruit from the back of his cart on the streets of a popular neighbourhood in Beirut.[1] When asked what his life looks like after he fled from Syria, he states that he feels valueless. Hassan explains that it is not easy to live in a foreign country as a forcibly displaced person, but the situation he is in has become untenable. He has to provide for his large family while he is not allowed to work. The decision to clandestinely sell fruit from the back of his cart in an attempt to maintain his wife and children has led to several fines. Even if Hassan and his family would try to leave Lebanon, they would be confronted with fees for forfeiting the payment for a residence permit, which have accumulated to more than two thousand dollars per person. Everyday life is filled with problems and humiliations.[2]

The sense of feeling valueless, as expressed by Hassan, is a common theme in personal stories of refugees and asylum seekers. Forcibly displaced persons at times recount how they feel like they have lost their worth as human beings. This perceived loss of value may speak to their objectification. In studies of dehumanization, objectification is generally understood as the denial of people's human status by viewing, portraying, or treating them as if they were (mere) objects rather than persons.[3]

The global migration crisis involves various ways in which the concerns, needs, and interests of displaced persons are overlooked as they are viewed, portrayed, and treated in objectifying modes. For example, media have depicted displaced persons as waste products, indigestible foods, or poison.[4] In reporting on political negotiations that involve considerations of migration control, refugees, asylum seekers, and unwanted migrants are sometimes referred to as 'bargaining chips' or 'pawns'.[5] Refugees may also be treated in

Dehumanization in the Global Migration Crisis. Adrienne de Ruiter, Oxford University Press. © Adrienne de Ruiter (2024).
DOI: 10.1093/oso/9780198893400.003.0004

78 Dehumanization in the Global Migration Crisis

ways reminiscent of objects through processes that disregard their agency, as they are cast as helpless victims in need of aid or when their needs and rights are not considered to be of any importance.

While certain ways of viewing, portraying, or treating people in objectifying ways may be dehumanizing, the relation between objectification and dehumanization is not straightforward. Not all modes of depicting, treating, and viewing people like objects necessarily seem to entail a denial of human status. This chapter therefore examines the relation between dehumanization and objectification. The first part of this chapter provides examples of objectification from the global migration crisis. The chapter then analyses various ways in which refugees, asylum seekers, and unwanted migrants are portrayed, perceived, and treated in objectifying ways. The final section explains when these practices and processes amount to dehumanization and when they do not.

Objectification in the global migration crisis

Objectification is a theme that can be identified in reporting and scholarship on the migration crisis, although it is less prevalent in the testimonies of refugees and asylums seekers themselves. Scholars have noted that asylum seekers and immigrants are frequently portrayed in objectifying ways. Such portrayals include depictions of them as natural disasters, diseases, waste, and indigestible foods. Examples of portrayals that identify refugees with the elements can be found in an insightful article by Raith Zeher Abid, Shakila Abdul Manan, and Zuhair Abdul Amir Abdul Rahman about the use of water metaphors, like 'flood' and 'surge', in reporting on Syrian refugees in Egyptian, Jordanian, Lebanese, and Turkish online media.[6] Their analysis concludes that in portraying (the arrival of) these people as a natural disaster, these metaphors detach 'any human aspect that Syrian refugees have' and thereby render them 'indistinguishable and as dehumanized entities'.[7]

While it is evident that the use of this type of metaphor diminishes view of the individuality and humanity of refugees, it is not apparent that all such portrayals amount to dehumanization. Metaphors like 'influx', 'flow', 'flood', and 'surge' at least implicitly identify refugees with water, an entity that may be considered threatening when it arrives suddenly and in great quantities, but these terms can also be used to refer to the movement or arrival of other entities. 'Influx' designates not only the inflow of water, for example, but also the entry of a large number of people or objects. 'Flow' can refer to the steady

Objectification **79**

movement of gas, liquids, or electricity, yet also of people. 'Flood' is more strongly connected to water, although it can also be used to speak about the arrival of overwhelming amounts of something. 'Surge' entails a sudden and strong movement, which originates from a crowd or the tide. While it is conceivable that at least some of these metaphors may be used to dehumanize people, this does not necessarily seem to be the case for all.

Refugees, asylum seekers, and unwanted migrants may also be portrayed in objectifying ways through depictions that take away from their moral human status as persons. Scholars have noted that refugees are objectified when they are presented not as identifiable individuals, but as members of a category that overdetermines their identity. Refugees are often cast as a generic figure who is defined by need and victimhood. What requires protection in refugees frequently appears as nothing more than their mere and bare humanity.[8] Yet, as we noted in the previous chapters, the relation between such minimalist depictions of humanity and dehumanization is complex.

In terms of treating refugees, asylum seekers, and unwanted migrants in objectifying ways, there is the issue of handling displaced persons as 'bargaining chips' or 'pawns' in international politics, mentioned above. Treating the forcibly displaced and other unwanted migrants as pawns or bargaining chips displays an instrumentalist logic as the value of people is reduced to their undesirableness, which works as a compelling force that helps persuade or dissuade political actors from taking particular decisions. It can be argued that refugees, asylum seekers, and unwanted migrants are thus objectified because they are treated like mere objects, rather than as human beings with rights, interests, and needs that ought to be taken into account. This also suggests that such treatments may be regarded as dehumanizing because displaced persons are treated in ways in which their status as human beings seemingly does not matter.

It is not evident, however, that treating people like bargaining chips or pawns is necessarily dehumanizing. Here we might think, for example, of political prisoners who are used in negotiations for an exchange of detainees. In this case, people are used like bargaining chips or pawns to reach a certain objective. Nonetheless, the individuals who are used in this way do not seem to be dehumanized, as this exchange actually takes their concerns into consideration. An important difference lies in the fact that a political prisoner would in all likelihood want to be exchanged, whereas refugees, asylum seekers, and unwanted migrants do not wish to be used in foreign policy negotiations, since the outcome of this bargaining process is likely to impede on their interests. The example of the political prisoner exchange indicates

80 Dehumanization in the Global Migration Crisis

that treating people like pawns or bargaining chips may not amount to dehumanization when negotiators in this process demonstrate at least minimal concern for the interests, needs, and rights of the so-called 'pawns' or 'bargaining chips'. What it means to treat people like objects in a dehumanizing way thus requires further reflection.

Viewing people as objects is complex as well. It seems that we usually speak about objectification as something that happens when people fail to take the humanity of others into consideration. It is thus marked by a certain absence (of consideration of this human aspect) rather than some positive element (a literal view of people as objects). People generally do not genuinely see others as inanimate objects but relate to them in ways that are more similar to the ways in which human beings relate to things rather than persons. To understand what this means, in the global migration crisis and more generally, it is thus important to consider in what ways people can hold objectifying views of others.

This overview suggests that objectification plays a role in various portrayals and policies that deal with refugees, asylum seekers, and unwanted migrants. It also highlights that while connections seem to exist between objectification and dehumanization, this relation is complex. Not all ways of viewing, portraying, or treating people like objects appear to be straightforwardly dehumanizing. It is therefore important to examine what it means to portray, treat, and view people like objects and which aspects of objectification, if any, render such depictions, treatments, and perceptions dehumanizing.

Portraying people like objects

The first form of objectification that may dehumanize people involves portraying them as objects. As in the case of animalization, such objectifying depictions generally draw from metaphors. Scholars have found that refugees, asylum seekers, and other unwanted migrants are at times represented as waste, indigestible foods, polluting factors, poisons, or natural disasters. Gerald V. O'Brien, the scholar of social work whose study on the use of metaphors in the American immigration restrictions debate of the early twentieth century was discussed in the previous chapter also identifies various object-related metaphors that were used in this period.[9] In fact, O'Brien notes that metaphors related to objectification were more common in this debate than metaphors that identified immigrants with animals.[10] Among the various metaphors identified are the immigrant as indigestible food, poison, and garbage.

Indigestible food, poison, and waste

O'Brien explains that at the time of the immigration restrictions debate the political community was often represented as a body. This physiognomic analogy readily suggested metaphors to link newcomers to indigestible food products, poisons, and polluting agents. Participants in the debate wondered, for example, whether the rapid intake of immigrants, particularly from Eastern and Southern Europe, would not lead to problems as 'the food is strange and alien, or does it possibly contain poisons against which we have no antidote'?[11] Concerns were also raised about the potential 'pollution' of the nation that could be caused by the accommodation of immigrants. Newcomers were depicted as a 'stream of impurity', a 'tide of pollution', and a 'turgid stream of undesirable and unassimilable human "ofscourings"'.[12]

Other metaphors identified arrivals with garbage or raw material. Immigrants were likened to waste as advocates of restrictive measures claimed that the United States was becoming a '"dumping ground" of the refuse material of the Old World' with Europe ditching its 'human refuse at our doors' and using America 'as a human garbage can'.[13] Slightly less derisive, yet similarly objectifying analogies cast immigrants as 'assimilable material' or 'raw material' that could be used for making profit.[14]

These examples show that most of the metaphors that likened immigrants to objects or inanimate entities in this debate cast their arrival and presence in a negative light. It is interesting to note that the type of objects and entities with which immigrants were likened were generally negatively valued. Poison is dangerous and presents severe risks to the health of the population. The depiction of immigrants as polluting agents brings to mind not only a threat to 'purity' but also to the well-being of the nation. The identification with waste shows the lack of value attributed to immigrants.[15] The depiction as material that can be used for the economy is more neutral in terms of ascribing specific characteristics to immigrants, yet this neutrality derives precisely from the fact that, following this representation, they have no defining features. Objectification in this case takes the shape of portraying people as pliable material that can be used for any purpose.

As in the case of animalistic depictions, portrayals of people as objects or entities need not necessarily have negative overtones. For example, it is common in many languages to refer to loved ones as 'treasures'.[16] The term in the English language that comes closest here is probably 'gem' or 'jewel'. Imagine how the meaning of the rhetoric would change if immigrants in the examples above where not cast as poisons, impurities, waste, or raw material, but as treasures, gems, or jewels. Rather than being represented as a threat and a

82 Dehumanization in the Global Migration Crisis

nuisance, undesirable, or at best something that may be practical because it can be used, immigrants would be portrayed as desirable, coveted, and valuable. Whereas the depiction of immigrants as poison, impurities, and waste dictates a logic of restrictive countermeasures that require an antidote, purification, or for unwanted residue to be kept out of sight, if it cannot be eliminated, the portrayal of immigrants as treasure entails an imperative to encourage their arrival, look after them, and appreciate their presence. For objectifying portrayals to be considered dehumanizing, it thus seems necessary, as in the case of animalizing depictions, that the objects to which persons are likened are valued negatively, or at least neutrally.

From floods to flows

Objectifying metaphors are also used in contemporary debates on the migration crisis. As noted above, Abid, Manan, and Rahman identify the frequent use of water-related metaphors in Middle Eastern news outlets as one example of this type of objectifying portrayal.[17] The use of metaphors that liken refugees to water could in principle be neutral in terms of value orientation because water can be positively valued (as a resource that is necessary to sustain life) or negatively valued (as a force with great destructive power). Whether water-related metaphors should be seen as dehumanizing depends, then, at least in part, on the role that is assigned to it. The potentially destructive force of water clearly shines through in terms like 'flood' and 'surge', but is absent from notions such as 'influx' and 'flow', which relate to calmer, more continuous movements. To consider whether it is dehumanizing to represent refugees, asylum seekers, and other migrants as a flood or a surge, it will be helpful to consider aspects that were raised previously in the discussion of animalization.

The key factor that distinguished animal metaphors that dehumanize from those that do not, as discussed in the previous chapter, was the denial of the moral status that people hold as human beings, which leads to moral disengagement and a lack of concern for their fate. If newspapers report on 'a flood of people' or 'a surge of asylum seekers', this language is alarmist. The terms 'flood' and 'surge' bring to mind an overly large quantity of something arriving suddenly. While it paints the arrival of refugees, asylum seekers, and other migrants in a negative light, this terminology does not directly deny the moral status that they hold as human beings. Similarly to Cameron's 'swarm' statement, these depictions do not deny people's human status in a moral sense by likening them to animals, objects, or entities that hold a moral status below that of human beings. Rather, 'flood' and 'surge' describe the type of movement with which refugees, asylum seekers, and other migrants arrive.

This reading goes against Abid, Manan, and Rahman's conclusion that such metaphors render Syrian refugees 'indistinguishable and as dehumanized entities'.[18] The authors regard this type of depictions as dehumanizing because it 'represents Syrian refugees as an unwelcome disaster as well as detaches any human aspect that Syrian refugees have'.[19] For Abid, Manan, and Rahman, dehumanization thus derives from the way in which these representations allegedly strip Syrian refugees of their personal and human traits. While I agree with their claim that some of these metaphors, most notably 'flood', portray Syrian refugees as a calamity, I do not think it correct to conclude that the use of water-related terminology to describe the movements of people is in itself sufficient to symbolically detach them of all their human aspects, as Abid, Manan, and Rahman suggest. These terms are used to describe their collective migration. The concerted motion is what is allegedly threatening and raises concern in this case. In my view, more is needed to dehumanize refugees.

The story is quite different for the examples mentioned above of immigrants being portrayed as poison, polluting factors, or waste. Depicting people in these ways constitutes a form of dehumanization because these representations liken them to objects or entities that hold a moral status below that of human beings and disengage moral concern. Poison has qualities that render it particularly suitable for the purposes of dehumanization. First, it is dangerous and potentially lethal. Second, it is often not easily recognizable as perilous and may therefore not be identified as a danger until it is too late. The combination of these two factors makes likening people to poison a convenient instrument for their dehumanization. The moral status of poison, if any is explicitly attributed, is negative because poison kills or makes people ill. When people are likened to poison they are therefore attributed a moral status lower than that of human beings. Furthermore, this depiction is an effective means of stimulating moral disengagement, even in cases where the dehumanized may appear innocent, because it suggests that their destructive potential may not be visible at the surface. Poison, furthermore, needs to be disposed of before it can do harm. This portrayal thus justifies forms of treatment that otherwise would not be deemed acceptable ways of treating fellow human beings.

Depictions of people as polluting factors elicit disgust. As explained in the previous chapter, disgust and dehumanization are closely linked as disgust may incite dehumanization.[20] Waste can evoke disgust, most notably when it contains perishable goods that have gone bad. Even in cases where garbage

84   Dehumanization in the Global Migration Crisis

is not viewed as disgusting, depicting people as waste can be dehumanizing because it attributes them a moral status below that of human beings as entities that are worthless and useless. The portrayal of people as waste indicates that we need not be concerned about them, as their value is based on their (in)ability to contribute in any meaningful sense. Their designation as waste highlights their lack of worth in the eyes of the people who liken them to refuse. Like garbage, these people can be discarded without concern.

The 'refugee' category

Besides depictions that liken refugees, asylum seekers, and unwanted migrants to concrete objects and entities, dehumanizing forms of objectification may also be at play in portrayals that deny people's moral status as human beings by identifying them with a category of 'raw' and 'bare' humanity, similar to the accounts of Arendt, Agamben, and Malkki discussed in the previous chapters. Malkki goes in this direction, for example, when she claims that the 'refugee' is often considered a generic figure, which stands for a liminal figure in the order of nation states.[21] She explains that refugees fit with the cultural anthropologist Victor Turner's famous description of 'liminal personae' as '"naked unaccommodated man" or "undifferentiated raw material"'.[22] Malkki concludes that 'the term "refugees" denotes an objectified, undifferentiated mass that is meaningful primarily as an aberration of categories'.[23] The refugee is thus defined foremost as a disruption to the international system of nation states.

Social psychologist Kesi Mahendran and her colleagues contend that the refugee category derives from bureaucratic distinctions that come to determine the way in which people are perceived. These authors explain that 'the form of dehumanization of people fleeing conflict involves a psychologized elaboration of the bureaucratic refugee category into a way of being'.[24] The objectification involved here concerns abstracting away from the individuality of refugees through a process in which refugeehood is not considered a temporary or contingent status, but a mode of existence. This categorical identity is furthermore saturated with negative meaning. At best, the refugee category depicts a helpless victim in need of assistance. At worst, the figure of the refugee is linked to chaos and disorder.[25] Either way, lacking the protection of a political order, the refugee is often seen as a burden on the environment.[26]

Given the liminal position of the refugee, it could be argued that refugees are not so much cast as objects, but rather as *abjects*, following a distinction suggested by psychoanalyst and linguist Julia Kristeva. Kristeva describes

Objectification **85**

the abject as involving 'what disturbs identity, system, order. What does not respect borders, positions, rules'.[27] The psychologist Guglielmo Schininá discusses how abjectification plays a role in our engagement with refugees through the discomfort that many people feel in addressing the unsettling of order that the displaced person symbolizes:

> In reality, a migrant's presence makes us question our very symbolic and social order because migration displays all the horrors that, as a society, we have tried to exclude in order for us to persist (poverty, war, injustice, pandemics). The existence of migrants traumatizes us by reminding us that these horrors still exist.[28]

This negative value attached to the generic figure of the forced migrant may help account for the unwillingness of many forcibly displaced people to identify with this category. Suha, a Syrian woman who filed with her family for asylum in Germany, notes, for example, how hard it is to see herself as a refugee: 'It is a burden. It is difficult to accept. It feels shameful. We are capable people. We are open. We can work. Historically it was the word for weak people'.[29] In a fairly similar way, Hanan, a young Syrian woman who fled from Aleppo to Europe, links the refugee experience to a sense of humiliation when she claims that 'to be a refugee means to be humble'.

Similarly to the discussion of the notion of 'bare' and 'naked' humanity in the first chapter, I consider problematic the idea that dehumanization is at play in cases of objectification through which people are cast as less human. Refugees may indeed be dehumanized through objectifying depictions that signal the attribution of a moral status below that of human beings. Yet, the humble liminal figure described is not evidently expelled from the moral community of humanity altogether. In fact, the appeal to humanitarian assistance draws precisely from our human communality, even if the refugee is cast as a pitiable human being. Rather, this kind of portrayals of refugees as weak and dependent human beings entail their infra-humanization.

Against my reading, it could be argued that something else is at stake in cases of objectifying representations. The way in which refugees are cast as objects, rather than subjects, denies their agency and thereby depicts them as less than human. It is not simply that the humanity of refugees and other forcibly displaced persons is not fully acknowledged in portraying them as human in a minimal sense. It is rather that the denial of agency expressed through this representation entails a denial of moral human status in itself. On this understanding, to recognize the moral standing of human beings involves at least minimal recognition of their status as subjects who can act, rather than objects who can only be acted upon. I believe this to be true. The point of contention is whether, and when, this denial of subjectivity occurs.

86 Dehumanization in the Global Migration Crisis

Many of the tensions that surround the archetypical refugee depiction, in my view, centre on the question how lacking in agency this figure actually is. The representation of the refugee as a purely responsive victim is already dispelled by the very acts that are required for becoming a refugee. To become a refugee, at a minimum, one has to take note of the detrimental developments in one's country, assess that the situation has become untenable, make a decision to leave, collect one's belongings, depart from one's house, and make it over an international border. The idea that at the moment of reaching a place of refuge, these very same persons turn into helpless bundles of humanity is untenable in light of the ordeals they have gone through to become refugees in the first place.[30] These facts do not rule out that refugees may be depicted as nothing more than objects without agency and thereby be dehumanized, yet may help to account for the fact that such portrayals are not that common. Debilitating portrayals of refugees, on my reading, generally tend to be infrahumanizing, rather than dehumanizing since most of these representations cast them as weak, dependent human beings but do not portray them as less than human.

The analysis above accentuates that not all portrayals of displaced persons that represent them in objectifying ways can be considered dehumanizing, given that not all of these portrayals challenge the human status they hold in a moral sense. What renders such depictions dehumanizing is not the act of likening a person to an object in itself, but the denial of normative human status that this portrayal in some cases entails. In the generic refugee figure, infra-humanization is more centrally at work, I claim, through which refugees are cast as deplorable, lesser human beings without excluding them from the moral category of humanity altogether. In cases where refugees, asylum seekers, or unwanted migrants are portrayed as diseases, poisons, or waste, on the other hand, these depictions deny their moral human status. By attributing the displaced no moral status, or one that is lower than that of human beings, these representations dehumanize.

Treating people like things

The global migration crisis also exposes various ways in which refugees, asylum seekers, and migrants are treated in objectifying ways. Reports claim that people on the move are used in international negotiations as 'bargaining chips' and 'pawns'—or more alarmist, as 'weapons'.[31] Strategies of 'warehousing' refugees in camps allude to the image of forcibly displaced persons being stored away like objects.[32] Another way in which displaced persons may be treated like (mere) things is when failures to provide assistance signal that their plight is not considered a matter of concern. The philosopher Derek Parfit explains that treating someone like a mere thing entails treating a person as 'something that has no importance, like a stone or heap of rags lying by the road'.[33] The failure to help people in need can thus be seen as an indicator that they are treated like things. Treatments through which people are used as sheer instruments to obtain money or other benefits, as may be seen reflected in the exploitation, extortion, and abuse of refugees, asylum seekers, and other migrants in detention centres and prisoner camps, as found in Libya, offer further examples of objectifying treatment.[34]

This range of cases suggests that treating people like things holds various meanings. Let us therefore consider first what it means to treat people in objectifying ways. A helpful starting point for this analysis can be found in the typology of seven ways of treating people as things, proposed by the philosopher Martha Nussbaum.[35] Nussbaum identifies instrumentality, denial of autonomy, inertness, fungibility, violability, ownership, and denial of subjectivity as key forms of objectification.[36] Instrumentality refers to treating people as an instrument to obtain one's own ends. A denial of autonomy involves treating people in ways that deny their ability to make decisions for themselves. Inertness entails that persons are treated as if they lack agency. Fungibility has to do with interchangeability and revolves around the idea that persons are replaceable. Violability entails that persons are treated as if they have no right to physical and mental integrity and can therefore be violated. Ownership signifies that people are treated like possessions. A denial of subjectivity occurs when people are treated in ways that disregard their experiences and feelings as irrelevant. Nussbaum's typology of seven forms of objectification can help structure our analysis of the objectifying treatment of the forcibly displaced.

Bargaining chips and pawns

In cases where refugees, asylum seekers, and unwanted migrants are used as 'bargaining chips' or 'pawns' for international negotiations, instrumentality is central, as people are treated as a means to obtain certain ends. Nussbaum notes that instrumentalization is not always morally objectionable because it is possible to use people as instruments without harming them, with their consent, and within the context of a relationship that is not based solely on the advantages gained by using them for a particular purpose. She thus claims that 'what is problematic is not instrumentalization per se, but treating people

88 Dehumanization in the Global Migration Crisis

primarily or merely as an instrument'.[37] When people are treated *primarily* as an instrument, this entails that their usefulness for the goal at hand overrules other considerations regarding how they are treated. If people are treated *merely* as an instrument, their usefulness is the only thing that counts. When displaced persons are used as instruments to reach agreements that satisfy ulterior objectives, which overlook their rights, interests, and needs, this thus constitutes a morally problematic form of instrumentalization as people are used merely as instruments in ways to which they would not consent and that harm their interests.

This type of instrumentalization would be dehumanizing, following our preliminary definition of dehumanization, if people are treated in ways that signals that they are attributed a lower moral status than that of human beings. It could be argued that this is the case when people are used as bargaining chips because the value of the persons concerned is reduced to the compelling force of their perceived undesirableness. If people are treated in ways that signal that they are seen as nothing more than a burden, this would indeed be dehumanizing. It is difficult to tell, however, whether the displaced are indeed seen in this way. After all, people quite frequently regard others as undesirable burdens (in certain limited ways) without this ruling out that they also recognize the moral status they hold as fellow human beings. The fact that refugees, asylum seekers, and unwanted migrants can be used as bargaining chips and pawns in this type of negotiations in fact seems to demonstrate at least a minimal level of recognition of the moral status that these groups hold as human beings, on at least one side of the table. After all, if the displaced would truly be seen as having a moral status similar to that of mere undesirable objects, their fate could hold no weight in the bargaining process to begin with.

Warehousing refugees

With regard to containment strategies that accommodate refugees for extensive periods in camps without the right to work or the freedom to move, the key aspects of objectification are inertness, fungibility, and denial of subjectivity.[38] Inertness plays a key role here because the agency of refugees is discounted and restricted by limiting their ability to participate in society. Fungibility is involved too. By sidelining refugees and disallowing them to develop and use their personal skills and talents outside the confines of the camp, this strategy may give rise to perceptions of refugees living in camps as lacking in individuality and being more or less interchangeable. The warehousing strategy also entails a denial of subjectivity because the experiences and feelings of refugees are made subordinate to concerns about the estimated costs involved, in both financial and symbolic terms, of integrating them in society.

Claiming that refugees are treated as mere objects through containment policies seems problematic, though, because protection is provided based on humanitarian concerns, thereby acknowledging the status of the forcibly displaced as human beings. It is also relevant to note that warehousing strategies are used to impede refugees from enacting their human capacities to work, travel, and engage in other fundamental freedoms. Restrictions on the right to work and the freedom to move are put in place precisely to limit the freedom that refugees have to build up a life in new places, thereby acknowledging their human capacity to do so. In other words, it only makes sense to 'contain' agents with a will of their own, since inanimate objects can simply be stored without concern that they will inadvertently show up somewhere else. The idea that refugees are dehumanized in objectifying ways when they are warehoused in camps therefore seems problematic, although there are important, yet different, reasons to object to the containment strategies that are used all over the world to respond to forced migration.[39]

Failing to care

When considering what it means to treat people like things, we may be tempted to look for examples of active mistreatment. It seems important, however, to also consider how objectification might be expressed through failures to act. If Parfit is right in claiming that treating someone like a mere thing entails treating a person as something of no importance, omissions to act in the face of preventable harm and suffering may provide relevant insights into what it means to treat people like things as well. In fact, it could well be that objectification is often expressed through the failure to treat a person as being of even minimal importance.

Here we might think, for example, of the statement by Salil Shetty, Secretary General of Amnesty International, as discussed in the first chapter, that 'people who have fled war are now enduring dehumanizing living conditions and dying of entirely treatable diseases. They escaped bombs to die of infections, diarrhoea or pneumonia.'[40] Shetty's appeal calls attention to the fact that the squalid conditions in certain refugee camps present severe risks to the health and well-being of refugees through the unsanitary environment in which they live. Given that people in refugee camps fall under international protection, the fact that their lives are not adequately protected from health risks that could be easily addressed becomes even more startling. It seems difficult to account for the omission to provide adequate healthcare and basic sanitary conditions, but through a failure by the international community to care sufficiently for the predicament of inhabitants of refugee camps.

This points to the idea that refugees living under these conditions may thereby also be dehumanized. After all, if the moral status of refugees as fellow human beings were appreciated, the international community would not allow them to die from afflictions that could be prevented at little cost. If we draw from our working definition of dehumanizing treatment, allowing such conditions to endure is dehumanizing, given that allowing people who fall under international protection to die of diseases that could be easily prevented or cured entails treating them in ways that signal that they are attributed a moral status below that of human beings.

The challenge here lies in establishing when failures to help people in need constitute a case of failing to treat them as even minimally important in a moral sense and when such omissions derive from an inability to help. Evidently, not every failure to help persons in need should be seen as a case of objectifying dehumanization through which persons are treated as mere things. Many people are in need and not everyone is capable of helping some, let alone all of them. The willingness to help and the perceptions that potential helper(s) hold of the person(s) in need appear to be central here. To get a clearer idea of what it means for omissions to signal the attribution of a moral status lower than human beings, it is therefore important to consider what it means to regard people like objects.

Torture and abuse in prison camps

Refugees, asylum seekers, and migrants also experience objectifying treatment on the route to finding a place of refuge. People who have made the sea travel from Libya to Europe told me about the mistreatment to which they were subjected along the way. Musa, the Gambian engineer whose recollections of the violations and abuses that took place in the migrant warehouses in Sabratha were discussed at the start of the previous chapter, also reflected on practices that speak to objectification during his travel. He recalls how the ordeal that he and his companions had to endure did not end once they managed to depart from the Libyan coast. While on the boat, Musa and his fellow travellers were held at gunpoint by a gang that tried to steal their belongings. Recalling the distressing situation, he observed that 'it was very crazy. All the way to reach here it was. There was a group firing at us while there was a

Objectification **91**

group trying to help us off the boat. They don't care about you. They try to get things from you. If they can't get anything, they just leave you.'

Musa's story can be read as a case of objectifying treatment, I believe, because the gang used the migrants on the boat as a means to obtain money and valuables without concern for their rights or interests, as shown by the fact that they were shooting at them to compel them to hand over their belongings. This speaks to the aspects of violability and instrumentality. Similar accounts are provided about prison camps that have been set up in Libya to exploit and extort migrants.[41] Amadou, an asylum seeker from Guinea-Bissau, spoke to me of the abuse and torture he endured in prison camps in Sabha and Tripoli where human traffickers sought to extort money from prisoners and their relatives. He recalls how people who were unable to raise the requested amount were killed or left to die: 'They asked us money. There are many who die. There are many prisons. They are all the same thing: they mistreat people for money.'

Similar testimonies are provided by other survivors who speak about a vast system of bondage, slavery, abuse, and extortion in which not only gangs and militias, but also employees from official immigration detention centres and the Libyan coast guard are allegedly implicated.[42] The stories of Musa and Amadou recount severe forms of objectification. Whether these cases amount to dehumanization depends on whether these forms of treatment signal that the victims are attributed a moral status below that of human beings. The problem in making this assessment is that the instrumentality that characterizes the described interactions does not necessarily require that the human status of people in a moral sense is overlooked. As the philosopher Kate Manne insightfully argues, there is a tendency in the academic literature on dehumanization to maintain that severe forms of mistreatment are only possible once the victims have been denied human status.[43] This overlooks the fact that human interactions can just as well be characterized by hostility and aggression as care and concern.

The answer to the question whether these acts of objectifying mistreatment involve dehumanization, in my view, depends on the attitudes, perceptions, and viewpoints of the people who are responsible for the violations and the consequences that these violations have for the way the victims are perceived by others as well as themselves. Think, for example, about the situation on the boat that Musa described, where a band of armed robbers tried to steal the belongings of the passengers. It is very well possible that the band failed to recognize the moral status of the people on the boat as fellow human beings given that the robbers shot at them and allegedly would just leave them behind, if nothing more could be taken from them. Clearly, this form of mistreatment amounts to inhumane treatment given its lack of

92 Dehumanization in the Global Migration Crisis

compassion, sympathy, and consideration. It is not certain, however, that the robbers necessarily failed to recognize the humanity of the passengers, in the sense that they did not attribute them even minimal moral human status. After all, it could also be that the robbers viewed their actions as permissible, for example, based on the conviction that the hopeless political situation in Libya left little room for people to act in considerate and compassionate ways towards strangers. In this case, the question whether dehumanization was involved depends on the views that the robbers held. Given that it is at least conceivable that forms of racism and discrimination, falling short of dehumanization, inspired the hostile attitude towards the passengers on the boat and served to justify their inhumane treatment, this form of abuse does not necessarily seem to require the dehumanization of the victim(s).

The situation in the torture camps in Libya, described by Amadou, is different, in my view. The kind of mistreatment that occurred there falls under that exceptional category of acts that are always dehumanizing because they are inconceivable without the prior dehumanization of the victims. This is the case because it is only possible to torture a person to death in an attempt to extort money, if that person is no longer perceived a fellow human being in a normative sense. This treatment combines elements of torture and enslavement, which were identified in the previous chapter as the most likely candidates for practices that should be considered de facto dehumanizing. Torture is dehumanizing because it involves the use of people's bodies and minds in an effort to break their will and thereby expresses utter disregard for the moral standing of human beings.[44] The deprivation of freedom as a means of extortion is dehumanizing, as well to those people who are unable to pay ransom because they are forced in a position of slavery.[45] Consider, for example, an alternative scenario where no torture would be inflicted on the people who are kept in the Libyan prison camps. People would not be beaten. Women would not be raped. Yet, they would not be allowed to leave unless they have paid a large sum of money. If nothing more could be taken from them, people would be killed or left to die. This situation would still be dehumanizing because the people who are held in this way and who are unable to buy their way out are forced in a position of utter powerlessness that characterizes slavery. Basic recognition of the moral human status of victims entails at least minimal respect for their autonomy, which does not permit this kind of treatment.[46]

In conclusion, some but not all forms of treating people like objects amount to dehumanization. Objectifying treatments constitute a form of dehumanization when victims are treated in ways that signal that they are attributed a lower moral status than that of human beings. This occurs when people mistreat others because they hold them to be less than human in a moral sense.

Viewing people like objects

While people may portray and treat others like things, it appears more difficult, if not impossible, to view others literally as things. Consider what it would mean to truly view a person as an inanimate object. I cannot walk into a café and accidentally mistake the bartender for an umbrella, for example, although it would probably be possible to walk into a clothes shop and take the vendor for a mannequin. In this case, however, the confusion would arise from the fact that a mannequin is modelled after a human being and a human being therefore also looks like a mannequin. Even then, the confusion is unlikely to last long, for any attempt at interaction would give away the difference between the vendor and the mannequin.

The curious case of Dr P.

To grasp what it means to view people literally as objects it will be helpful to consider the extraordinary story of Dr P. whose impairment inspired the title for the book *The Man Who Mistook His Wife for a Hat* by the neurologist Oliver Sacks.[47] Due to a brain tumour, which caused him to suffer from visual agnosia, Dr P. was unable to see human faces and was only able to recognize certain people by their distinctive characteristics. Sacks describes this tragic inability of the professor to see the people in his life:

> By and large, he recognised nobody: neither his family, nor his colleagues, nor his pupils, nor himself. He recognised a portrait of Einstein because he picked up the characteristic hair and moustache; and the same thing happened with one or two other people. 'Ach, Paul!' he said, when shown a portrait of his brother. 'That square jaw, those big teeth—I would know Paul anywhere!' But was it Paul he recognised, or one or two of his features, on the basis of which he could make a reasonable guess as to the subject's identity? In the absence of obvious 'markers', he was utterly lost.[48]

Sacks continues by commenting on the strange way in which Dr P. tried to recognize people, not by regarding their faces as *faces* but rather as containers of information, which might contain a clue for who or what it was he

94 Dehumanization in the Global Migration Crisis

was looking at. This unusual way of approaching human faces, according to Sacks, accounted for a certain indifference and objectification in Dr P.'s ways:

> But it was not merely the cognition, the *gnosis*, at fault; there was something radically wrong with the whole way he proceeded. For he approached these faces— even of those near and dear—as if they were abstract puzzles or tests. He did not relate to them, he did not behold. No face was familiar to him, seen as a 'thou', being just identified as a set of features, an 'it'. Thus, there was formal, but no trace of personal, gnosis. And with this went his indifference, or blindness, to expression. A face, to us, is a person looking out—we see, as it were, the person through his *persona*, his face. But for Dr P. there was no *persona* in this sense—no outward *persona*, and no person within.[49]

The inability to recognize people's faces coincided with an inability to consistently recognize people as people. Sacks thus recounts how Dr P. confused his wife's head with a hat, trying to place it on his head after his first meeting with the neurologist:

> He also appeared to have decided that the examination was over and started to look around for his hat. He reached out his hand and took hold of his wife's head, tried to lift it off, to put it on. He had apparently mistaken his wife for a hat! His wife looked as if she was used to such things.[50]

The case of Dr P. suggests that viewing people literally as objects is quite unusual. His story is mentioned by the philosopher Avishai Margalit in a discussion of what it means to view people as objects. Margalit notes that people are unable to see human beings literally as objects with the exception of some highly unusual cases. This is so because we cannot choose to see people other than human: 'I see human beings in their human aspect not as an act of choice or decision, but because I cannot see otherwise.'[51] Viewing people in objectifying ways thus entails that we relate to them *as if* they were mere objects, but it does not mean that we 'actually believe that the people involved are things.'[52] In my view, Margalit is right in being sceptical about the possibility of literally seeing people as mere objects. What is involved is rather perceiving of them as if they were mere things.

Its and Thous

The question is, then, what it means for people to regard others in objectifying ways in this more abstract sense. Here it may be helpful to draw on the insights of the philosopher Martin Buber. Drawing from Hegel's argument in *The Phenomenology of Spirit* on the development of self-consciousness,[53] Buber contends that people can have two different attitudes to the world.[54] We can either experience it, which means that we relate to the objects and persons we encounter as things that we can use and possess, or we can participate in the world by standing in a relation to the beings we meet. In the first case, we constitute ourselves as an 'I' that stands against an 'It', whereas in the second case, we take on the position of an 'I' as being with a 'Thou' (or 'You' as we would say nowadays), who is similar to my 'I'.

The valuable insight that Buber provides is that people do not necessarily relate to other humans as persons with whom we stand in a relation, but often make them into objects that we merely experience. Although humans naturally long for confirmation from others, this process of acknowledgement is an uncertain one, making it easier to remain within the reliable sphere of experience, where everything and everyone presents itself simply as an object to us.[55] It often proves difficult to uphold a genuine relation with other people because this depends on the acceptance of their radical otherness, which entails that we are 'limited by man, cast upon [our] own finitude, partialness, [and] need of completion'.[56]

The distinction that Buber draws between relating to entities in the world as 'Its' and 'Thous' is compelling. Not only does his account speak to situations where we treat other minds as 'Its', human beings also at times have the tendency to treat things like 'Thous'. Yet, for our account of dehumanization, it seems that Buber's account can only help us along so far. His theory focuses on something different from recognition of the moral status of the persons we encounter. What is at stake in his account is what it entails to truly allow others to be Other. Yet, dehumanization does not necessarily occur when we do not leave space for others to approach us in this way. The restraining desire for sameness—and the resulting psychological need for reduction—is a problem in interpersonal relations, yet does not automatically entail an exclusion from a shared moral category of humanity. A lot goes wrong in human interactions, but not all that goes wrong should be seen as dehumanization.

Reification

An alternative account of what it means to relate to people as objects in a more figurative sense, and one that fits more closely with the analysis this book undertakes, has been developed by the philosopher Axel Honneth. Dehumanization, following his account, consists in a particular form of reification through which people forget to recognize the humanity of others.[57] Honneth maintains that people naturally tend to perceive each other's humanity, yet may fail to acknowledge the humanity of others when social interactions are impaired through underlying issues. These issues can be caused by biases or ideology, or arise when we need something from others and thereby lose sight of their needs and interests. When interactions are distorted through reification, as Honneth explains, '[w]e may indeed be capable in a cognitive sense of perceiving the full spectrum of human expressions, but we lack, so to speak, the feeling of connection that would be necessary for us to be affected by the expressions we perceive'.[58] What is missing from relations where people regard others as mere objects is this automatic sense of connection through which humans ordinarily respond to the expressions of others. Like a psychopath, we are no longer affected by the expressions of the other, even if we are still capable of registering them.[59]

Dehumanization, then, does not necessarily require that perpetrators express strong feelings of hatred, contempt, or disgust but can also involve indifference and disregard. This is what makes dehumanization particularly difficult to recognize in cases of objectification. Since indifference and disregard are not necessarily expressed as hatred, anger, and contempt are, it can be hard to tell when objectifying treatments signal dehumanization, or rather infra-humanization, or other forms of discrimination.

People thus generally do not literally view others as objects but rather engage in objectifying forms of engagement with them when they relate to them in a way that is more befitting for objects rather than fellow human beings. What is at stake in objectification is, then, a certain failure of moral engagement. Unlike animalization, which generally involves strong feelings of disgust, hatred, and contempt, objectification is often marked by an absence of emotion.[60] When people are objectified, there is something missing. It is characterized by a lack of connection as the subjectivity of the victim(s) does not resonate with the perpetrator(s).

Objectifying migrants

It is time to return to the examples of the various ways in which the notion of objectification is used to comment on the global migration crisis, discussed throughout this chapter, and consider when these should be regarded dehumanizing following the insights developed in the chapter. In terms of objectifying representations, I argued that for these to be considered dehumanizing, portrayals should deny the moral human status of the person(s) depicted and attribute them a lower moral status, if any. When newspapers report an 'influx of refugees', for example, this should not be taken to be dehumanizing, as this term does not entail a negative evaluation of the moral status of refugees. 'Influx' can also be used, for instance, to describe the arrival of a large amount of money, something which is generally seen as positive. 'Flood' is the term with the strongest negative overtone, yet still does not amount to the kind of denial of moral status, entailed in portrayals that cast refugees, asylum seekers, or unwanted migrants as indigestible food, poison, or waste.

The generic refugee category also contains dehumanizing tendencies in the sense that it undermines the moral status refugees hold as subjects and casts them as weak, pitiable victims who impose a burden on their environment. Through these portrayals, the image of a pejorative deplorable humanity is set up. Refugees are thereby not excluded from the human category, however, but attributed a low and marginal position within it. Infra-humanization is therefore at play.

Treating refugees, asylum seekers, and other unwanted migrants as pawns or bargaining chips amounts to dehumanization if they are thereby treated merely as instruments. When people are instrumentalized in a way in which their concerns, needs, interests, and rights are not taken into account, this should be considered dehumanizing because this treatment signals that they are perceived as holding a moral status below that of human beings as they are treated as mere means to obtain some further end. It is not necessarily the case that people who are treated like pawns or bargaining chips in nego-tiations are dehumanized, however, as the example of prisoner exchanges from the start of this chapter illustrated. Treating people as instruments is not dehumanizing when their concerns, needs, interests, and rights are taken into account.

Warehousing refugees, at least on the surface, may also seem an example of objectifying treatment since goods, not people, are stored in warehouses. The reason why containment strategies should be considered objectifying is not because these policies are reminiscent of the handling of products, however, but due to the effects this strategy of setting people apart and limiting their freedoms has on refugees, which reduces their ability to exercise their human agency. Still, the fact that camps are set up to protect refugees, even if this environment generally fails to offer the conditions for a thriving human life, demonstrates at least minimal concern for the forcibly displaced. Concern for the bare humanity of refugees, although an absolute minimum, still reflects inclusion in the moral category of humanity.

Things look different for situations, as described by Shetty, where refugees die of entirely treatable diseases, infections, diarrhoea, or pneumonia. These conditions vividly illustrate Parfit's point that treating people as things entails treating them as something that holds no (moral) importance. These cases

98 Dehumanization in the Global Migration Crisis

amount to dehumanization. For if the moral status of refugees as fellow human beings were acknowledged, the international community would not allow conditions to endure under which people who fall under their protection die from afflictions that could be prevented at little cost.

Indifference and disinterest can also lead people to turn a blind eye to the mistreatment of refugees, asylum seekers, and unwanted migrants, as occurs in prison and detention camps, such as in Libya. Whether acts of extortion, abuse, and mistreatment amount to dehumanization depends on the attitudes, perceptions, and viewpoints of the people who are responsible for the violations and the consequences that these violations have for the way the victims are perceived by others as well as themselves. The exception to this rule is found in cases of torture and enslavement, as these acts always exclude minimal recognition of the moral status of the victim as a human being.

Conclusion

This chapter considered various ways in which refugees, asylum seekers, and unwanted migrants may be said to be objectified in the global migration crisis. The key insight of this chapter is that objectification is foremost marked by an absence. It is characterized by a lack of connection, as the subjectivity of the victim(s) does not resonate with the perpetrator(s). People generally cannot literally see other human beings as things. What is not necessarily acknowledged, however, is the moral status people hold as human beings.

Objectification becomes dehumanizing when objectifying perceptions, representations, or treatments entail that the moral status attributed to victims, if any, is lower than that of human beings. In cases of representation, the likening to an object works in a metaphoric sense to signal that the victim holds no inner life, and is more similar to a thing without agency, rather than a living, thinking, and feeling subject. This kind of portrayal justifies indifference to the well-being of the victims as there is nothing 'there' to be concerned about.

With treatment, objectification tends towards disregard for the interests, needs, and viewpoints of the persons involved. This is reflected in cases of inhumane treatment where the perpetrators recognize nothing of moral importance in their victims that would count against their abuse. Yet, objectification also characterizes failures to act on behalf of victims when these omissions result from indifference to their suffering. Such disregard for the concerns, experiences, and interests of displaced persons is reflected in situations where their basic rights are not guaranteed and the international community looks away when even small efforts could save lives, increase well-being, and allow for more dignified living conditions.

Containing refugees in camps away from the public eye may contribute to their objectification. Conditions in camps that keep refugees from participating in society, pursuing education or work, and enjoying basic freedoms that allow them to orchestrate their own life, more generally, can also be considered objectifying in undermining people's agency. Some regard these restraints to living one's life as a fully human life as dehumanizing. On my view, these limitations generally involve infra-humanization, since people are treated and cast as lesser human beings, but not necessarily excluded from the moral category of humanity altogether. While the lives of people contained in refugee camps are diminished by these conditions, they do not appear to have completely lost its human dimension.

Still, it cannot be ruled out that people may be pushed to a point where even minimal recognition of the human aspects of their life and existence are beyond reach. The next chapter will consider if it is possible for people to lose touch with their own sense of humanity through severe mistreatment and abuse or through living for prolonged periods under harrowing conditions. By considering the notion of brutalization, the following chapter will analyse how refugees, asylum seekers, and migrants may come to feel alienated from their own humanity or reduced to a subhuman condition through the ways in which they are treated.

Notes

1. According to the UNHCR, over a million Syrian refugees were registered in Lebanon in 2016, which corresponds to almost 25% of the Lebanese population of 4.4 million. Since the Lebanese government has prohibited the registration of Syrian refugees after 6 May 2015, the actual number of Syrians living in Lebanon is estimated to be higher and to exceed, at least, 1.5 million. Obtaining exact information about the number of Syrian refugees living in Lebanon is further complicated, by the fact that the Lebanese authorities consider the Syrians 'displaced persons' rather than 'refugees', which reflects the government's stance that the presence of Syrians in Lebanon should be considered of a temporary nature. See: Maja Janmyr, 'Precarity in Exile: The Legal Status of Syrian refugees in Lebanon', *Refugee Survey Quarterly* 35 (2016): 58–78, https://doi.org/10.1093/rsq/hdw016, Maja Janmyr, 'UNHCR and the Syrian Refugee Response: Negotiating Status and Registration in Lebanon', *International Journal of Human Rights* 22 (2018): 393–419, https://doi.org/10.1080/13642987.2017.1371140, Maja Janmyr and Lama Mourad, 'Modes of Ordering: Labelling, Classification and Categorization in Lebanon's Refugee Response', *Journal of Refugee Studies* 31 (2018): 544–65, https://doi.org/10.1093/jrs/fex042.

100 Dehumanization in the Global Migration Crisis

2. A report by the Norwegian Refugee Council on the living conditions of Syrians in Lebanon presents similar stories about precariousness resulting from obstacles to obtaining and renewing legal papers. See: Racha el Daoi, 'Syrian Refugees Deprived of Basic Human Rights', *Norwegian Refugee Council*, 10 December 2017, https://www.nrc.no/syrian-refugees-deprived-of-basic-human-rights.

3. The notion of objectification is central to Haslam's account of dehumanization, which distinguishes between animalization and mechanization. Mechanization, which identifying people with objects or automata, lacking in feeling and personality, relates to what I call objectification. See: Haslam, 'Dehumanization: An Integrative Approach'.

4. Cisneros, 'Contaminated Communities' and O'Brien, 'Indigestible Foods, Conquering Hordes, and Waste Materials'.

5. Euromed Rights, 'Refugees Must Not Be Used as Bargaining Chips!', 3 March 2020, https://euromedrights.org/publication/refugees-must-not-be-used-as-bargaining-chips/, Ben Rawlence, 'Refugees Shouldn't Be Bargaining Chips', *The New York Times*, 17 May 2016, https://www.nytimes.com/2016/05/17/opinion/refugees-shouldnt-be-bargaining-chips.html, and Cihan Tuğal, 'Syrian Refugees in Turkey Are Pawns in a Geopolitical Game', *The Guardian*, 15 February 2016, https://www.theguardian.com/commentisfree/2016/feb/15/refugees-turkey-government-eu-crisis-europe.

6. Abid, Manan, and Rahman '"A flood of Syrians"'.

7. Idem, 137–8.

8. Malkki, 'Speechless Emissaries'.

9. O'Brien, 'Indigestible Foods, Conquering Hordes, and Waste Materials'.

10. Idem, 42.

11. Idem, 37.

12. Idem, 38.

13. Ibid.

14. Idem, 39.

15. Bauman theorizes refugees as waste in a more abstract sense of the term. Following his reflections, the displaced are the waste of globalization (p. 58). The recognition of human waste entails there are 'wasted humans' in the world who are cast as 'excessive' and 'redundant'. This category is made up of 'the population of those who either could not or were not wished to be recognized or allowed to stay' (p. 5). These people are cast to the side as '[w]e dispose of leftovers in the most radical and effective way: we make them invisible by not looking and unthinkable by not thinking' (p. 27). See: Bauman, *Wasted Lives*.

16. In the languages most central for my affective life (Dutch and Italian) key terms of endearment refer to treasure: *schat* in Dutch and *tesoro* in Italian.

17. Abid, Manan, and Rahman '"A Flood of Syrians"'.

18. Idem, 137–8.

19. Idem, 137–8.

20. Bloom, *Just Babies*, 133.

21. Lisa Malkki, 'National Geographic: The Rooting of Peoples and the Territorialization of National Identity among Scholars and Refugees', *Cultural Anthropology* (1992): 33–4, https://doi.org/10.1525/can.1992.7.1.02a00030.

22. Idem, 34. See: Victor Turner, *The Forest of Symbols: Aspects of Ndembu Ritual* (New York.: Cornell University Press, 1967), pp. 98–9.

23. Malkki, 'National Geographic', 34.

24. Kesi Mahendran, Nicola Magnusson, Caroline Howarth, and Sarah Scuzzarello, 'Reification and the Refugee: Using a Counterposing Dialogical Analysis to Unlock a Frozen Category', *Journal of Social and Political Psychology* 7 (2019): 582, https://doi.org/10.5964/jspp.v7i1.656.

25. The idea that the refugee category can portray members as helpless victims or disturbing agents of chaos and disorder hints at a duality in objectification, which mirrors a duality in dehumanization. David Livingstone Smith highlights this duality in distinguishing between what he calls 'enfeebling dehumanization' and 'demonizing dehumanization' (see: *Making Monsters*, 251). Whereas demonizing dehumanization casts the dehumanized as 'horrifying', 'dangerous', 'sinister', and 'malevolent', enfeebling dehumanization presents the dehumanized as weak, deficient, and powerless.

26. Liudmila Arcimaviciene and Sercan Hamza Baglama, 'Migration, Metaphor and Myth in Media Representations: The Ideological Dichotomy of "Them" and "Us"', *SAGE Open* 8 (2018), https://doi.org/10.1177/2158244018768657.

27. Julia Kristeva, *Powers of Horror: An Essay on Abjection* (New York: Columbia University Press, 1984), p. 4.

28. Guiglielmo Schininá, 'Objectification and Abjectification of Migrants: Reflections to Help Guide Psychosocial Workers', *Intervention* 15 (2017): 103, http://doi.org/10.1097/WTF.0000000000000146.

29. Suha's claim also resonates with Hannah Arendt's observation that the meaning of the term 'refugee' changed during the interbellum as the predominant basis for a claim for asylum shifted from individuals' political acts and opinions to their identity as members of a prosecuted ethnic or religious minority:

> A refugee used to be a person driven to seek refuge because of some act committed or some political opinion held. Well, it is true we have had to seek refuge; but we committed no acts and most us never dreamt of having any radical opinion. With us the meaning of the term 'refugee' has changed. Now 'refugees' are those of us who have been so unfortunate as to arrive in a new country without means and have to be helped by Refugee Committees.

Arendt points out that historically refugees were the victims of political persecution, who arrived in small numbers in countries where they applied for asylum. After the First World War, however, nationalist politics began to produce large numbers of people who were denaturalized and expelled based on their ethnic or religious identity. The profile of stateless people and refugees thereby changed—from members of the political and cultural elite to mass movements that included people from all layers of society. With this change in profile came about a change in the way refugees were generally perceived. Given that these 'new' refugees were in need of support to reconstruct their lives in the countries that granted them asylum, they oftentimes came to be viewed as a burden.
See: Hannah Arendt, 'We Refugees', in *Altogether Elsewhere: Writers on Exile*, edited by Marc Robinson (London: Faber & Faber, 1994), p. 110.

30. It should be noted, however, that the current refugee regime with its emphasis on keeping people safe in camps where they often spend many years of their lives does contribute to crippling their ability to act and form a life for themselves. For a critical appraisal of this regime, see: Serena Parekh, *Refugees and the Ethics of Forced Displacement* (Milton Park: Taylor & Francis, 2016) and Serena Parekh, *No Refuge: Ethics and the Global Refugee Crisis* (Oxford: Oxford University Press: 2020).

102 Dehumanization in the Global Migration Crisis

31. See, for example: Kelly M. Greenhill, *Weapons of Mass Migration: Forced Displacement, Coercion, and Foreign Policy* (Ithaca, New York: Cornell University Press, 2016). For a critical analysis of the use of this terminology, see: Lev Marder, 'Refugees Are Not Weapons: The "Weapons of Mass Migration" Metaphor and Its Implications', *International Studies Review* 20 (2018): 576–88, https://doi.org/10.1093/isr/vix055.

32. For critical views on the policies of warehousing refugees, see, for example: Merril Smith (ed.), 'Warehousing Refugees: A Denial of Rights, a Waste of Humanity', *World Refugee Survey* 38 (2004): 38–56, https://www.refugees.org/wp-content/uploads/2021/06/Warehousing_Refugees_A_Denial_of_Rights-English.pdf and U.S. Committee for Refugees and Immigrants, *Lives in Storage: Refugee Warehousing and the Overlooked Humanitarian Crisis*, December 2019, https://reliefweb.int/sites/reliefweb.int/files/resources/USCRI-Warehousing-Dec2019-v4.pdf.

33. Derek Parfit, '*As* a Means and *Merely* as a Means', in *On What Matters: Volume One* (Oxford: Oxford University Press, 2011), p. 227.

34. Office of the United Nations High Commissioner for Human Rights, *Detained and Dehumanised: Report on Human Rights Abuses against Migrants in Libya*, 13 December 2016, http://www.ohchr.org/Documents/Countries/LY/DetainedAndDehumanised_en.pdf.

35. Martha C. Nussbaum, 'Objectification', *Philosophy & Public Affairs*, 24 (1995): 249–91, https://doi.org/10.1111/j.1088-4963.1995.tb00032.x.

36. Idem, 257.

37. Idem, 255.

38. For a critical account of the moral implications of the containment strategy, see: Parekh, *Refugees and the Ethics of Forced Displacement*.

39. Parekh's work presents an insightful critique of the current way in which the international community treats refugees. See: Parekh, *Refugees and the Ethics of Forced Displacement* and Parekh, *No Refuge*.

40. Shetty, 'Tackling the Global Refugee Crisis'.

41. Stories about detention camps in Libya where migrants are extorted and tortured are recounted, for example, by human rights organization, such as Amnesty International, and by asylum seekers and migrants making their way to Europe. See e.g.: Amnesty International, *Libya's Dark Web of Collusion: Abuses against Europe-Bound Refugees and Migrants*, 11 December 2017, https://www.amnesty.org/en/documents/mde19/7561/2017/en/. Similar stories are recounted about Sudan and Egypt. See, for example: Human Rights Watch, '*I Wanted to Lie Down and Die': Trafficking and torture of Eritreans in Sudan and Egypt*, 11 February 2014, https://www.hrw.org/report/2014/02/11/i-wanted-lie-down-and-die/trafficking-and-torture-eritreans-sudan-and-egypt.

    For testimonies, see, for example: Calais Writers, *Voices from the 'Jungle'*, 82–6. Milkesa from Ethiopia recounts, for instance, about how he was kept for several weeks in the desert before he managed to escape: 'The smugglers detained me for more than three weeks in the Nubian desert, asking me to pay \$15,000 as a ransom or to lose one my kidneys as compensation' (p. 86).

42. See, for example: Amnesty International, *Libya's Dark Web of Collusion*, Ruth Sherlock and Lama Al-Arian, 'Migrants Captured in Libya Say They End Up Sold as Slaves', *NPR*, 21 March 2018, https://www.npr.org/sections/parallels/2018/03/21/595497429/migrants-passing-through-libya-could-end-up-being-sold-as-slaves, and *Voices from the 'Jungle'*, 82–5.

43. Manne, *Down Girl*, 134–5.
44. This point will be discussed in more detail in Chapter 5.
45. Sherlock and Al-Arian, 'Migrants Captured in Libya'.
46. Ibid.
47. Oliver Sacks, *The Man Who Mistook His Wife for a Hat, and Other Clinical Tales* (New York: Touchstone, 1998 [1985]).
48. Idem, 12–13.
49. Idem, 12–13.
50. Idem, 11.
51. Margalit, *The Decent Society*, 95.
52. Idem, 91.
53. Georg Wilhelm Friedrich Hegel, 'Lordship and Bondage', in *The Phenomenology of Spirit*, translated by Arnold Miller (Oxford: Oxford University Press, 1977 [1807]), pp. 110–19.
54. Martin Buber, 'From *I and Thou*', in *The Martin Buber Reader: Essential Writings*, edited by Asher Biemann (New York: Palgrave MacMillan, 2002), pp. 181–84.
55. Buber, 'From *I and Thou*', 185–6.
56. Martin Buber, 'Distance and Relation (1950)', in *The Martin Buber Reader: Essential writings*, edited by Asher Biemann (New York: Palgrave MacMillan, 2002), p. 211.
57. Honneth, *Reification*.
58. Idem, 57–8.
59. The psychologist Jonathan Haidt observes, for example, that psychopaths 'feel no compassion, guilt, shame, or even embarrassment' and 'seem to live in a world of objects, some of which happen to walk around on two legs'. See: Jonathan Haidt, *The Righteous Mind: Why Good People Are Divided by Politics and Religion* (London: Penguin, 2013), p. 72.
60. An exception here is objectification that takes the form of portraying people as waste or polluting factors, which evokes disgust, or as poison, which elicits fear.

4
Brutalization

I try to feel like a person.

Ammar, refugee from Syria

Introduction

Ammar is a teacher who fled from Aleppo to evade military service after his father died. Without his father's protection, he found that no member of his family or circle of acquaintances was willing to use their influence to get him an exemption from joining the army. It became increasingly difficult for him to move around and avoid the many checkpoints in his town. He realized that living in hiding was becoming too dangerous when two of his cousins did not return home after unknown men took them. Ammar decided to go to Turkey and made his way to Europe, where he filed for asylum in Germany. He explains that it is difficult for him to feel like a person after his experiences in Syria, living in a system that, in his words, seeks 'to destroy the people'. While he notices that people in Germany treat him with respect, it is still difficult for him to feel at ease. He is lonely and misses people who genuinely care about him. He also struggles with letting go of the fear he has felt for so long.

Ammar's story testifies of the effects of living through experiences that violate one's sense of personhood and humanity. His testimony speaks to the notion of brutalization. In studies of dehumanization, brutalization is understood as a process through which people lose touch with their own sense of humanity or become less humane through severe forms of mistreatment or deprivation.[1] Brutalization is an important conceptual lens for analysing dehumanization in the global migration crisis because refugees and asylum seekers at times recount feeling alienated from their own sense of humanity or feeling reduced to a subhuman condition through the ways in which they are treated.

Dehumanization in the Global Migration Crisis. Adrienne de Ruiter, Oxford University Press. © Adrienne de Ruiter (2024).
DOI: 10.1093/oso/9780198893400.003.0005

The first part of this chapter considers the meaning of brutalization and discusses examples from the global migration crisis. The chapter then turns to testimonies of Auschwitz survivors to examine whether people can come to fully disregard their own humanity. This extreme case serves to illustrate the point that complete alienation from one's own humanity is uncommon and seems to occur only under extraordinary circumstances. The chapter considers brutal conditions in particular immigration detention centres and the devastating impact this has on the self-perception of the detained. The final section sets out when brutalizing acts of mistreatment and deprivation amount to dehumanization.

The chapter presents a warning against buying into the logic of dehumanizers who hold that victims can truly be made less than human through brutalizing treatment. In most cases of brutalization, victims are not turned into something less than human but impeded from enjoying or expressing their full range of human qualities. Only when the human spirit is utterly broken is it possible to claim that brutalization dehumanizes people in the sense that they come to fail to recognize their own humanity. Nonetheless, brutalization can serve as a form of dehumanizing representation since brutalizing treatment can portray people as less than human. Brutalization thus amounts to dehumanization when it serves as a performative act of representation that portrays the victim(s) as less than human.

Brutalization in the global migration crisis

Brutalization is a notion that requires a bit of introduction. Following dictionary definition, it holds a dual meaning.[2] First, it refers to a process of making people brutal, unfeeling, or inhuman. Second, it refers to treating brutally. 'Brutal' has several senses as well. Most central to its meaning is the link to bestiality and traits typical of beasts.[3] Brutal is not only used to refer to bestial characteristics, related to savage, unreasoning, and ruthless conduct, however, but also to cruelty, even if cruelty is a uniquely human characteristic.[4] The notion of brutalization thus reflects certain tensions, incongruities, and paradoxes in the conceptual distinction between the human and the animal.

The first sense of brutalization is relevant to our study of dehumanization in the global migration crisis as making people 'inhuman' may constitute a way to dehumanize them. Following our preliminary definition, dehumanization revolves around acts of viewing, portraying, or treating people as less than human in a moral sense. If people can be made brutal, unfeeling, or inhuman through particular forms of treatment or deprivation, this entails that their ability to engage in moral interactions is severely undermined. These processes go beyond viewing, portraying, or treating people as less than human, in a moral sense, by seeking to bring about a reality where victims are impeded from partaking in unaffected interpersonal relations. This may bring about a sensation in victims, and onlookers, that the brutalized no longer are (fully) human and hold a moral status below that of human beings.

The second sense of brutalization as treating brutally can also potentially be dehumanizing, as it may involve treating people in ways that signal that they are regarded as less than human in a moral sense. While treating people brutally may also constitute a form of dehumanization, this seems akin to treating people in dehumanizing ways by treating them like animals or objects. The more interesting question for this chapter is then whether people can actually be made inhuman through brutalizing treatment. The chapter therefore concentrates on this issue.

Sometimes people are treated brutally in an attempt to make them brutal, unfeeling, or inhuman. This is reflected, for example, in the training of torturers, who are at times treated in brutal ways in order to allow them to treat others brutally.[5] Logically, the two senses are distinct, however, as people may treat others brutally because they hate or despise them without caring about the effects this treatment has on them. Brutal treatment therefore does not necessarily aim at making the victim brutal, unfeeling, or inhuman. Furthermore, it may also be possible, at least theoretically, to make someone brutal, unfeeling, or inhuman without treating them brutally. Imagine a scenario where a chip is invented that can be inserted painlessly in the brain, which switches off impulses towards compassion and empathy. Unless we consider the implementation of the chip brutal in itself because of the effects it produces, it seems the process through which the person is rendered brutal in this hypothetical case may be considered quite sophisticated and refined.

This brief discussion suggests that brutalization and animalization are closely related. In the chapter on animalization, a few examples of brutalization were already mentioned. We may recall the case of the immigrant from the Congo who felt diminished after having passed more than eighteen months in detention in Malta. He stated that 'detention dehumanizes the human being. The detainee is reduced to the state of an animal. One wakes up, eats, sleeps, wakes up'.[6] The Iranian refugee who passed years in immigration detention centres on Nauru and whose testimony was also mentioned in Chapter 2 similarly alludes to brutalization, affirming that due to the detrimental conditions of confinement, 'we became so alienated from our humanity, we were thoroughly transformed into a bunch of animals after years of living in the most appalling conditions possible'.[7] Our concern

108 Dehumanization in the Global Migration Crisis

in this chapter is not with the comparison that is drawn with animals but with the undermining of the sense of humanity, as the Iranian refugee expresses: 'to this day we are still walking ghosts, utterly broken and hopeless'.

As the reference to 'walking ghosts' illustrates, the sense of a loss of humanity that brutalizing treatment and deprivation may bring about need not necessarily involve a comparison or analogy with animals. Salim, the Iraqi refugee who now lives in Italy, in a similar vein compares himself to an entity that exists in a state between life and death in recounting the difficulties he experiences in making contact with people. He describes how his inability to build relations with others in his new country makes him feel 'like a zombie'.

Some refugees and asylum seeker literally report not feeling human. Benjamin, an asylum seeker detained on Nauru, explains that he does not have any plans for the future 'because I am still feeling that I am captured. I'm still feeling that I'm not a human'.[8] Mehdi, another refugee who was living in the Nauru detention centre for a prolonged period of time recounts the impact the destitute conditions had on his state of being: 'I had subconsciously distanced myself from feeling joy and happiness. After six years of continuous despair, it was as if I was dead inside'.[9]

These testimonies raise complex questions about what it means for refugees and asylum seekers to feel human. The sense of alienation described in these accounts illustrates the profound impact that brutalizing treatment and deprivation can have on the self-perception of the person involved. Still, these testimonies are characterized by a certain ambivalence. In calling out the hardships that caused them to flee, the detrimental conditions under which they are detained, and the difficulties they encounter in their new environment, an appeal for recognition of shared humanity can still be recognized. It is therefore important to consider in more detail what it means for people to lose sight of their own humanity.

Another relevant issue concerns the brutalization not of the forcibly displaced, but of people in countries that securitize migration. Several scholars have argued that dehumanizing and desensitizing media portrayals of migrants and the criminalization of undocumented migration may diminish compassion, empathy, and understanding for the plea of refugees, asylum seekers, and other migrants among the general public.[10] The justice scholar Sang H. Kil and the sociologist Cecilia Menjívar argue, for example, that militarized policies at the US–Mexico border and the representation of migrants as criminals brutalize the American public by encouraging hostility towards immigrants.[11] In a study of vigilante border troupes, Kil, Menjívar, and the political scientist Roxanne Doty similarly contend that the normalization of state violence against migrants encourages public violence by setting a normative culture where human rights violations and abuse of migrants is considered permissible.[12]

Brutalization can occur in more subtle ways as well. In a study on the perceptions of refugees among advocacy workers, the social psychologist Lauren E. Wroe writes about a campaigner for a charity organization in the United Kingdom who recounts how persons she worked with internalized the brutalizing logic of the immigration system. The campaigner described how a lawyer realized that this had happened to him 'when somebody once told him she'd been raped and his first response was "oh good I can use that".[13]

These studies draw attention to the brutalization of vigilante border guards, refugee attorneys, and the general audience in countries where migration issues are securitized and criminalized. This highlights how brutalizing mechanisms may not only affect persons who are subjected to severe forms of mistreatment and destitution, but can also take the shape of more subtle ideological processes. While it makes sense to speak in these cases of brutalization as a process through which people are rendered more brutal, unfeeling, or inhuman, these appear less intrusive than the above-mentioned cases of refugees and asylum seekers who experience profound difficulties in finding meaning in their lives, restoring trust in others, and engaging in social relations. To get a clear focus of what is involved in brutalization, it is therefore important to first consider more closely these extreme processes, which impede recognition of people's sense of their own humanity.

Breaking humans

Brutalization involves a process through which humans are in a certain sense mentally or morally 'broken'. Through brutalization people may come to feel that they have lost their humanity and no longer belong to the world. The testimonies above provide powerful allegations against the ways in which refugees, asylum seekers, and unwanted migrants are at times treated. It is not evident, however, that the brutalization described in these cases also amounts to dehumanization, understood as a psychological process through which victims come to fail to recognize their own moral human status.[14] After all, in denouncing these conditions, refugees and asylum seekers who report feeling alienated from their own sense of humanity, simultaneously affirm their moral human status in their appeal that these conditions are inappropriate for human beings. This suggests that while these conditions make people feel *less* human, they do not instil in them a genuine belief that they are morally *less than* human.

Dehumanization in the Global Migration Crisis

Dehumanization, experienced as alienation from one's own moral human status, would take away the possibility to object to the inhumane conditions under which one is held or the deprivation entailed in one's treatment on the basis of an appeal to shared humanity. What it means for human rights violations and abuses to produce this type of dehumanization may be understood, to some extent, when we consider testimonies by survivors of the Nazi concentration and extermination camps.[15]

Alienation in Auschwitz

People who have been detained in Nazi concentration and extermination camps describe the mistreatments that occurred there and the detrimental effects these had on the inmates. In his recollections of Auschwitz, Primo Levi reflects upon the fate of people in the camp who were unable to withstand the Nazi attempts to break their will, speaking about

> an anonymous mass, continually renewed and always identical, of non-men who march and labour in silence, the divine spark dead in them, already too empty to really suffer. One hesitates to call them living: one hesitates to call their death death, in the face of which they have no fear, as they are too tired to understand.[16]

In a similar way, Jean Améry describes the prisoner in Auschwitz who had given up and who was given up by his comrades as someone who 'no longer had room in his consciousness for the contrasts good or bad, noble or base, intellectual or unintellectual. He was a staggering corpse, a bundle of physical functions in its last convulsions'.[17] Améry speaks in this sense of a person who through hunger or exhaustion is 'in the actual sense of the word dehumanized'.[18]

The testimonies by Levi and Améry suggest that severe forms of abuse and mistreatment may lead to a distinct form of dehumanization by impeding people from recognizing their own humanity through extreme exhaustion and hunger. Nonetheless, as both point out, the perspective of those who were driven to this point is beyond our epistemological reach. Levi states that the ones who were able to testify about their experiences in the camps were not the 'true witnesses' but people 'who by their prevarications or abilities or good luck did not touch bottom. Those who did so, those who saw the Gorgon, have not returned to tell about it or have returned mute'.[19] He stresses that the inmates who reached this point were unable to recount their experiences as their social death had begun before their physical death:

Brutalization   111

When the destruction was terminated, the work accomplished was not told by anyone, just as no one ever returned to recount his own death. Even if they had paper and pen, the submerged would not have testified because their death had begun before that of their body. Weeks and months before being snuffed out, they had already lost the ability to observe, to remember, to compare and express themselves. We speak in their stead, by proxy.[20]

Given the limits of witnessing in this case, it may be more conducive to focus instead on what survivors say about their own experiences in the camps. Améry presents a view in support of this approach, highlighting the divide that exists between those who persevered and those who had to give up:

I can proceed only from my own situation, the situation of an inmate who went hungry, but did not starve to death, who was beaten, but not totally destroyed, who had wounds, but not deadly ones, who thus objectively still possessed that sub-stratum on which, in principle, the human spirit can stand and exist. But it always stood of weak legs, and it stood the test badly, that is the whole sad truth.[21]

The accounts of survivors who testified of their experiences communicate ambivalence towards their own human status, similarly to the abovementioned refugee testimonies. While testimonies report a sense of being reduced to an animal level, they also speak about moments of reflection that contradict this reduction. A sense of animalization is recounted, for example, in a passage where Levi reflects on the psychological burden of remembering life in the camps:

Coming out of the darkness, one suffered because of the reacquired consciousness of having been diminished. Not by our will, cowardice, or fault, yet nevertheless we had lived for months and years at an animal level: our days had been encumbered from dawn to dusk by hunger, fatigue, cold, and fear, and any space for reflection, reasoning, experiencing, emotions was wiped out. We endured filth, promiscuity, and destitution, suffering much less than we would have suffered from such things in normal life, because our moral yardstick had changed. ... We had not only forgotten our country and our culture, but also our family, our past, the future we had imagined for ourselves, because, like animals, we were confined to the present moment.[22]

This testimony vividly describes the brutalization that occurred to the inmates of Auschwitz, as their capacity for reflection, reasoning, and experiencing emotions was severely limited by imposed hunger, exhaustion,

112   Dehumanization in the Global Migration Crisis

and fear. Immediately following this passage, Levi notes, however, how the inmates occasionally became aware of their condition:

> Only at rare intervals did we come out of this condition of levelling, during the very few Sundays of rest, the fleeting minutes before falling asleep, or the fury of the air raids, but these were painful moments precisely because they gave us the opportunity to measure our diminishment from the outside.[23]

Descriptions of temporary lapses of the ability to exercise one's capacity to reflect, reason, and feel are also described by Elie Wiesel, who was deported to Auschwitz when he was fifteen years old. He recounts how during the first night in Birkenau the brutal environment already had detrimental effects on new arrivals: 'We were incapable of thinking. Our senses were numbed, everything was fading into a fog. We no longer clung to anything. The instincts of self-preservation, of self-defense, of pride, had all deserted us.'[24] In a similar vein to Levi's, this passage is directly followed by a deeper reflection that illustrates that the fog that came over detainees was not permanent: 'In one terrifying moment of lucidity, I thought of us as damned souls wandering through the void, souls condemned to wander through space until the end of time, seeking redemption, seeking oblivion, without any hope of finding either'.[25]

The fact that the recounted incapacity to contemplate is juxtaposed with a terrifying moment of lucidity indicates that the loss of faculties was not total. When it comes to the capacity to feel and care, Wiesel's testimony presents a detailed and gripping description of how the conditions in Auschwitz affected personal relations. Fear for the potentially lethal violence of the SS undermined the bond with his father, as he did not stand up for him when he was hit by the camp guards. Wiesel also recounts how he lost his father during the evacuation of the camp and the ensuing travels westwards during the final stages of the war and noticed in himself the shameful hope not to find his father again so he would not have to worry about him anymore. At the same time, it was his father who gave him a reason to continue living, attesting to the emotional attachment that continued to exist between them even under the direst of circumstances.

Wiesel's recollection of the night of his father's death speaks particularly clearly to the brutalization that camp life had brought about in him. He was unable to heed his father's call to get close to him in his dying moments out of fear to be struck by the SS. Yet, the feeling of guilt and remorse point to the continued connection to his father: 'I shall never forgive myself. Nor shall I ever forgive the world for having pushed me against the wall, for having turned me into a stranger, for having awakened in me the basest, most primitive instincts. His last word had been my name. A summons. And I had not responded'.[26]

The image that comes forward from these testimonies is that mistreatment and destitution can severely affect the sense of humanity of victims. Although extreme forms of forced destitution and mistreatment can make people feel less (than) human, it is not necessarily the case that people truly become alienated from their own humanity. As Améry pointed out, the 'substratum on which, in principle, the human spirit can stand and exist' was still there, even if it was only weakly so. The comparison between the survivors and the 'submerged', as Levi calls them, points to crucial differences in the totalizing effects of brutalization, where certain inmates still found within themselves resources to resist the attempts to break their will. These victims, it seems, were not turned into something less than human but impeded from enjoying or expressing their full range of human qualities. Only when the human spirit is utterly broken does it seem possible to claim that brutalization dehumanizes people in the sense that they come to fail to recognize their own humanity.

The stories of survivors attest to the remarkable resilience of the human mind in the face of attempts to destroy its capacity to think, feel, and judge. Nonetheless, the sense of humanity is severely affected by prolonged exposure to such brutalizing conditions. In spite of affirming his human spirit, Améry recounts how he and other inmates 'emerged from the camp stripped, robbed, emptied out, disoriented—and it was a long time before we were able even to learn the ordinary language of freedom'.[27]

Kafka, zombies, and ghosts

A similar ambivalence towards their own human status can be recognized in the testimonies of certain refugees and asylum seekers. In an interview with the United Nations, Mouhamad, a Syrian refugee in Greece, states, for example, that '[m]y fear, is to wake up one day transformed—as in Kafka's book—into a huge insect, willing to accept anything to survive'.[28] Mouhamad uses the literary metaphor of changing into 'a huge insect' to express his anxiety about losing his humanity, understood in a moral sense. This statement draws from the notions of brutalization and animalization to make sense of the fears and tensions that mark the refugee condition in our current world order. Yet the fear of losing sight of his moral principles speaks to an evident awareness of his own humanity.

114   Dehumanization in the Global Migration Crisis

Even if the meaning of the term originates from the human-beast distinction, brutalization can also relate to ways of treating and regarding persons that are one step removed from animals, such as monsters. This logic is reflected by Salim, who describes that he feels like a zombie. He explains that he finds it difficult to make contact with people because they keep their distance from him: 'If I want to contact with people, they act like I'm a zombie. They don't treat me like a human being'. Salim explains that he feels that people often fear him because he comes from Iraq and people associate Iraqis with militants and terrorists, even though many of the asylum seekers and refugees who have come from Iraq were actually among the principal victims of the so-called Islamic State. Because he does not speak the Italian language well, he cannot convey the message that there is no need to be afraid of him. Like a zombie, he is unable to engage with people, given that their fear and his own problems in communicating rule out the possibility of contact.

The choice of the figure of the zombie to describe himself is striking, as scholars have commonly used this prism in relation to refugees.[29] Legal scholars Penny Crofts and Anthea Vogl argue, for example, that the convergence of the refugee and zombie figure derives from concerns about the transgression of borders, both geographical and metaphysical, and the inability to contain movement and (perceived) threats.[30] In the monstrous universe of the undead, zombies stand in particular for the risk of invasion and defilement. They are usually represented as moving hordes, without identifiable features, coming to befoul and destroy the human world. Crofts and Vogl, as well as other scholars, thus note that media representations that portray particular parts of the world, such as Europe, the United States, or Australia, as under siege from a mass of outsiders whose arrival would allegedly jeopardize the local way of life echoes fears evoked by zombies.[31]

According to the cultural studies scholar Jon Stratton, the most frightening aspect of zombies is 'the liminal condition of death-in-life'.[32] Stratton connects this state between life and death to Agamben's notion of 'bare life', which was introduced in Chapter 1. According to Agamben, human life can be rendered 'bare' by its reduction from an ordinary human life with political, social, and religious meaning (*bios*) to a (virtually) naked biological existence (*zoë*), which is excluded from any sociopolitical and legal order.[33] Zombies are mere bodies without an inner human life. Their 'lives' are therefore literally rendered bare, as there is nothing they care about other than satisfying their urges for killing or turning humans into zombies.

In the case of refugees and other forcibly displaced persons, 'bare life' stands for a condition devoid of possibilities to live one's life as a human life.

Stratton cites in this regard the work of the visual culture scholar Anthony Downey on the politics of aesthetics:

> Lives lived on the margins of social, political, cultural, economic and geographical borders are lives half lived. Denied access to legal, economic and political redress, these lives exist in a limbo-like state that is largely preoccupied with acquiring and sustaining the essentials of life. The refugee, the political prisoner, the disappeared, the victim of torture, the dispossessed—all have been excluded, to different degrees, from the fraternity of the social sphere, appeal to the safety net of the nation-state and recourse to international law. They have been outlawed, so to speak, placed beyond recourse to law and yet still in a precarious relationship to law itself.[34]

The connection drawn between zombies, on the one hand, and refugees, asylum seekers, and other displaced persons, on the other, can thus be understood as signalling the meaning of bare life 'in its modern form'.[35] These conditions can lead to an existential condition, as we explored above, in which people come so close to death, through exhaustion and hunger, that they come to resemble the figure of the zombie, in being devoid of distinctively human reflection and impulses.[36]

To return to Salim's testimony, it is important to note that he links the description of himself as a zombie to his inability to interact and engage with people in a meaningful way. He relates his feeling like a zombie to his linguistic abilities: 'I don't speak the language well. ... I see every door closing. This means that I'm like a zombie'. In stating that he feels like a zombie, Salim, in my view, thus says something about his relations with others, more so than about his perception of himself. He expresses a sense of loneliness and isolation. The figure of the zombie is used as a metaphor to describe the distance and disconnect he feels from other people, as he notes that they tend to be afraid of him because of his background and appearance. While the lack of meaningful social contact affects his sense of humanity, it does not appear to lead to the kind of existential condition, in which people lose touch with their own human sense, described above. The fact that Salim reiterates that he does not speak the language well enough supports this reading, as it emphasizes a feeling of isolation rather than a denial of humanity.[37]

The testimony by the Iranian refugee who felt like a 'walking ghost' after his incarceration on Nauru touches on this existential condition in which people experience their existence as a less than human-like state. Ghosts, like zombies, pertain to the realm of the dead, yet continue to exercise a

116 Dehumanization in the Global Migration Crisis

presence among the living. Ghosts may be seen as the mirror image of zombies. While zombies have a bodily presence but no meaningful soul or mind, ghosts represent the continued existence after death of spirit without physical embodiment. People tend to be frightened by ghosts, although they are not always represented in a negative light or as threatening, given that ghosts can also help and guide people, according to some portrayals.

In an ethnographic study, the anthropologist Heath Cabot considers the relation between the figures of the refugee and the ghost in light of silenced subjects and the limits of representation.[38] Her analysis starts out with the discussion of a campaign set up by the UNHCR in Greece in 2008, which aimed to draw attention to the predicaments of refugees. In a television spot, viewers were told:

> There are ghosts around us. At one time they had life. They had their home. Their own people. But afterward everything was lost. And all that remained was the agony. Because they want to return to the life that belongs to them. ... These ghosts are called refugees. And they are around us. People like us. But hunted. Frightened from expulsions and wars. Are you afraid to look them in the eye?[39]

Cabot considers that there are several reasons why refugees may be portrayed as ghosts, as they have lost their previous life, are forced to continuously moving along without rest, and might scare people. This portrayal exemplifies the stereotype of the refugee as a 'hunted, frightened ghost'.[40] While the campaign intended to raise awareness of the plea of refugees, it casts them as vulnerable victims in line with the spectacle of 'raw' or 'bare humanity', discussed in Chapter 1, which Liisa Malkki criticized for not bringing in the names, opinions, or histories of the persons depicted.[41]

The link drawn here between ghosts and refugees zooms in on a particular diminished state that may be brought about by refugeehood. Having had to flee one's home, people have lost their (previous) life and need to start a new existence elsewhere. The experiences that caused them to flee and that brought them to the place they have arrived now may make it harder to start anew and find rest in their new environment. Since refugees remind people of the detrimental consequences of forced displacement, as caused by the breakdown of social and political order or the threat of authorities, they may furthermore arouse a sense of discomfort and fear, even if there are no personal reasons for arousing distrust or unease.

The testimony of the Iranian refugee alludes to something deeper, however, in claiming that detainees from the centre on Nauru 'are like walking ghosts, utterly broken and hopeless'. It is not merely that restarting a life under the conditions of refugeehood is particularly trying, but that trust in the world is shattered by the inhumane treatment imposed in the detention centre. This testimony suggests that exposure to prolonged periods of harsh and unjust treatment may undermine the sense of presence in one's own lived experience. It is helpful to note here that ghosts appear as 'apparitions of lived experience'.[42] The experiences of living under the harsh conditions of the security regime in Nauru may be said to 'break' something in (some) detainees, who are no longer able to live fully as human beings. Like ghosts, the experience is one of helplessness, separated from a human world on which one can no longer actively exert an influence. Ghosts are simultaneously still present and withdrawn from the world. Lingering in the shadows, their existence is no longer fully felt, either by others or themselves.

Inhumane detention conditions

To understand what gives rise to these feelings of broken existence, it is important to consider in more detail the conditions under which people are held in immigration detention centres. In the previous chapter, the mistreatment and abuse inflicted on refugees, asylum seekers, and (forced) migrants in detention camps in Libya was discussed. It would be a mistake to assume that this kind of conditions only pertains in countries plagued by severe crises of governance, as abundant stories of brutalization recounted by (former) detainees of detention centres on Nauru and Manus testify. Nauru (and formerly Manus) is used as a site for off-shore detention of asylum seekers and migrants seeking to reach Australia by boat. The Manus Regional Processing Centre on Papua New Guinea was formally closed in November 2017 after a ruling from the PNG Supreme Court that the carceral conditions in the centre were unconstitutional.[43] The men detained in the centre were moved to an 'open' centre in Papua New Guinea, although critics maintain that this transfer extends their prison-like conditions under a new guise.[44]

The conditions in Australia's offshore detention centres are notorious and the Australian policy of dealing with unregulated sea migration has been widely criticized by human rights advocates, other nations, and international organizations.[45] The United Nations found Australia in violation of the Convention against Torture due to the inhumane conditions under which people were held on Manus Island.[46] Conditions in the camps on Nauru and Manus have been characterized by prevalent physical and sexual violence, high levels of self-harm and suicide, pervasive mental health issues, and a lack of adequate access to health care.[47] In 2014, Peter Young, the former director

118   Dehumanization in the Global Migration Crisis

of mental health services, stated that the detention environment was 'inherently toxic'.[48] The International Criminal Court's prosecutor concluded that the conditions in the offshore detention camps amount to 'cruel, inhuman, or degrading treatment' and violate international law, although no further legal action was taken to investigate the contraventions.[49]

Myriads of (former) detainees attest to the devastating impact that incarceration in the Nauru or Manus detention centres has had on their lives. Some refugees and asylum seekers literally report feeling out of touch with their own sense of humanity due to the conditions under which they were or are held. Benjamin, an asylum seeker detained on Nauru, states: 'I am still feeling that I am captured. I'm still feeling that I'm not a human'.[50] He recounts that the most difficult aspect of detention is realizing that nobody cares about you. When he spoke with a psychologist about the hardships he was facing, she told him just to cope with it. On sharing with her his intention to commit suicide, she laughed and allegedly said: 'Go, do what you want to do'.[51] Mehdi, a refugee who was also held on Nauru, recounts that he could not feel positive emotions, due to the anguish he has experienced for so long: 'After six years of continuous despair, it was as if I was dead inside'.[52]

The poet and writer Behrouz Boochani who was detained on Manus reflects on the struggle people face every day to not let their desolate environment determine their outlook on life: '[I]n every situation the imprisoned lives and spirits have to reconfigure themselves in the face of death; they avoid projecting the malevolent dimension of their existence as the most dominant'.[53] Boochani describes the defiant attitude that detainees found within themselves as a resource to resist the systemic political forces that sought to break their spirit:

> [T]he detention centre wanted to manufacture a particular kind of refugee with a particular kind of response. However, the refugees were able to regain their identity, regain their rights, regain their dignity. In fact, what has occurred is essentially a new form of identification, which asserts that we are human beings.[54]

The emphasis on this *new* form of identification, which is established through regaining one's identity, rights, and dignity, implies that these markers of personhood were at one point lost. Boochani's testimony thus suggests that one's sense of humanity, identity, and dignity, as well as one's rights, may be temporarily out of reach. Still, the ever present possibility of defiance shines through: 'In opposition to a system of discipline and the mechanization of their bodies, the detained did not surrender. In reality, they proved that the human being is not a creature that can be entirely and completely consumed by politics.'[55]

The image that springs from these lines is one of a continual struggle where human identity, rights, and dignity may be temporarily or partially suppressed through a politics of destitution and oppression in an environment where almost total control is exercised over the lives and bodies of the detained, although not necessarily their minds. Through opposition, the renewed assertion of their human identity and personhood presents itself as a constant possibility. A similar notion of partial alienation speaks from Mehdi's account of how difficult it is to continue his life after Nauru: 'I am like a worm, half of which has been crushed. I am separating the healthy half from the crushed half, which is a difficult thing to do.'[56]

These testimonies attest to the strength and resilience of human subjectivity, and its tendency to resist its subjugation and erasure even under the direst of circumstances. The fact that certain people can testify of the predicaments they have gone through does not entail, however, that all can resist in the ways described above. People who oppose the conditions in the camps are in a condition where resistance is still available to them as a line of action, even if not always easily so. The fact that some persons are able to withstand the pressures exercised on them within the setting of the detention camp does not necessarily entail that all can.

Particular attention is required in this regard for the lot of children held in detention. The policy of separating children from their parents, as practiced in detention centres at the US–Mexico border under the Trump regime, is a particularly concerning example of punitive politics that deprives refugees, asylum seekers, and unwanted migrants of fundamental rights and is due to last a profound mark on the children involved.[57] Lawyers who visited a facility in Texas in June 2019 reported the inhumane conditions under which over 300 children were detained without adequate food, water, and sanitation and with older children trying to take care of younger ones.[58] Dolly Sevier, one of the paediatricians who examined the children at the border patrol detention centre when the scandal came to light, reported that all the children she saw showed signs of trauma, with inappropriate levels of subdued behaviour for their age.[59]

These accounts present a warning against assuming that severe mistreatment of refugees, asylum seekers, and other migrants happens only in remote parts of the world. If the fate of displaced persons is not considered sufficiently morally relevant to warrant public attention inhumane conditions may persist in all parts of the world. It is therefore essential to consider

120 Dehumanization in the Global Migration Crisis

how general perceptions of the (forcibly) displaced may contribute to the brutalization of societies.

Brutal audiences

Brutalization may not only touch refugees, asylum seekers, and other migrants, but also the general public in countries that securitize and criminalize certain forms of migration. Several scholars have argued that dehumanizing and desensitizing media portrayals of (forced) migrants and harsh political rhetoric and policies may diminish compassion, empathy, and understanding for the plea of refugees, asylum seekers, and other migrants among the population. Social justice and development scholar Helen Hintjens comments, for example, on the decisions by EU member states to end support for search and rescue missions on the Mediterranean and to implement measures to destroy smuggler boats in 2015. She claims that 'those who had already experienced brutalization, starvation, torture and rape, were being treated with brutality instead of humanitarian compassion.'[60] The turn in the political stance of EU member states from a humanitarian response to a focus on securitization and criminalization both reflects and reinforces a change in perspective on the plea of the (forcibly) displaced.

The idea that the political stance of the government may have a brutalizing effect on the general public is developed more explicitly in the work by Kil and Menjívar, who claim that the militarized policies at the US–Mexico border and the representation of migrants as criminals brutalize the American public by encouraging hostility towards immigrants.[61] In another piece, Kil, Menjívar, and Roxanne Doty contend that the normalization of state violence in border policies sets a normative culture where the violent and abusive treatment of migrants is considered permissible.[62] These insights echo the idea that dehumanization of others may lead to the dehumanization of oneself. Martin Buber expresses this view when he notes that 'the person who dehumanizes others experiences less emotion, less empathy, and fewer personal feelings, and thus dehumanizes himself or herself as well.'[63] Less emotion, less empathy, and fewer personal feelings are also shown in the refugee lawyer who responded to a client's story of being raped by asserting its instrumental use to the case.[64]

On accounts that fail to draw sharp distinctions between dehumanization and infra-humanization, it makes sense to conclude that the brutalization of the public in countries where migration is securitized and criminalized can lead to their dehumanization. On my account, experiencing less emotion, less empathy, and fewer personal feelings does not amount to dehumanization, however. Dehumanization is something more extreme than demonstrating less compassion for others as a consequence of perceiving of them as lesser human beings. It is not about showing less empathy, but about feeling no empathy at all. Emotions and personal feelings, furthermore, can very well be involved in dehumanization, although in a negative sense, as the chapter on animalization illustrated. While continued exposure to frames of criminalization and securitization in the depiction of refugees, asylum seekers, and other (forced) migrants is unlikely to do our engagement with and empathy for these groups any good, the notion of dehumanization is devalued if we claim that these processes dehumanize the general public. In most cases, this framing leads to marginalization, stigmatization, and infra-humanization. This falls short of dehumanization, for as long as limited forms of engagement are still present, which recognize the plea of refugees, asylum seekers, and other migrants as a factor of some moral concern.

Brutalizing migrants

Let us return to the examples of the various ways in which the notion of brutalization is used to comment on the global migration crisis, discussed at the start of this chapter, and consider when brutalization should be considered dehumanizing drawing on the insights developed. The chapter began with examples of asylum seekers and other migrants who (have) lived in detention for prolonged periods of time and who object against the harsh conditions to which they have been subjected. These conditions alienate people from their own sense of humanity, as reflected in the accounts of the Iranian refugee who describes himself as a 'walking ghost', Benjamin who claims he feels that he is 'not a human', and Mehdi who describes feeling 'dead inside'.

In cases where people object to the detrimental conditions under which they have been detained, an appeal for recognition of shared humanity still rings through. While conditions in which one feels reduced to a subhuman condition make it hard to continue to recognize one's own humanity, the accusation that this treatment does not befit human beings speaks to a lingering sense of shared humanity. This idea is expressed clearly in Boochani's claim that 'the human being is not a creature that can be entirely and completely consumed by politics'.[65]

Nonetheless, it is important to note the ambivalence present in the recognition of one's own humanity. This ambivalence speaks, for example, from Mehdi's vivid and tragic description of his struggle to continue on with his life after his experiences on Nauru: 'I am like a worm, half of which has been crushed. I am separating the healthy half from the crushed half, which is a difficult thing to do.'[66] These words suggest that the dehumanizing effects of brutalization might be partial. While not all recognition of humanity is lost, people may be deprived of distinct elements that render their life a fully human life through experiencing severe abuse and destitution. Some elements of one's human identity may consequently be lost through the hardships endured, which may also undermine people's own sense of the moral status they hold as a human being. People may well feel less human, for example, because they feel their emotions have come to a halt, they are reduced to animals, or go through life like wandering spirits.

The testimony by Boochani implies that dehumanization might take on a temporal character as he claims that the refugees in the Nauru detention centre were able to 'regain their identity, regain their rights, regain their dignity' and through this regained sense of self and moral status find a 'new form of identification, which asserts that we are human beings.'[67] Still, also here, I believe that regaining a sense of identity, rights, dignity, and asserting one's humanity through this recovered sense of self should not too easily be equated with recognizing anew one's humanity. If the recognition of one's own humanity would be completely lost, it seems that no foundation would be left for regaining one's identity, rights, and dignity.

The dehumanizing character of brutalization as a process through which people come to fail to recognize their own humanity therefore presents itself as ambivalent and complex. In many cases, people who are subjected to brutalizing treatment seem to continue to identify as human, at least in some significant ways that hold moral importance. The torment of the experience, at least in part, derives from the humiliation involved in being reduced and having one's mind worked on in ways that seek to bring about a lowering of one's inner life, feelings, and thoughts. Human subjectivity, so it seems, can be 'broken' only in exceptional cases.

If people cannot usually be rendered less than human through brutalizing treatment, what is the appeal of this kind of abuse for perpetrators? It seems that brutalization often contains an expressive, almost ritualistic, character that may help account for at least some of its prevalence. Brutalization seems, at least in part, to be about putting victims in their place and thereby portraying them, both towards themselves and others, as what they are perceived to be by the perpetrators. The response of detention, enacted in the offshore facilities devised by Australia to keep asylum seekers and other migrants from irregular entry, is telling in this sense as a response to the freedom enacted by persons intending to make their way to Australia. Restraining the body under dire and straining circumstances may then be read as a way to castigate the mind, which seeks to violate the rules set by the authorities that seek to exercise control over their territory.

It may be concluded, then, that forms of treatment through which people are brutalized, are dehumanizing when victims are treated in ways that signal that they are attributed a lower moral status than that of human beings. It is also possible for some of these treatments to be viewed as a form of active representation, which leads to a perception of the victim(s), either on the side of the victims themselves or in the eyes of perpetrators or bystanders, as holding a status lower than that of human beings. In many, if not most, cases where such practices lead to victims feeling alienated from their own sense of humanity, however, people allegedly come to view themselves as *less* human rather than *less than* human.

Conclusion

This chapter considered brutalization as a form of dehumanization. Brutalization can refer either to rendering people brutal, unfeeling, or inhuman or to treating people in brutal ways. The analysis here focused on the first sense, as treating people brutally overlaps with animalization and objectification, which were analysed in the previous chapters. Still, it is important to note that brutalizing forms of treatment that signal that victims are attributed a moral status below that of human beings amount to dehumanization, even if they do not necessarily succeed at turning people literally into something less than human or alter the perceptions of onlookers or victims, convincing them that victims hold a moral status below that of human beings.

The discussion of examples from the global migration crisis showed that it is uncommon for brutalizing treatment to genuinely alienate people from their own sense of humanity. Based on survivor testimonies of Auschwitz, the chapter argued that it seems indeed possible to bring people to the point where they become completely indifferent to everything, including their own humanity, through extreme forms of mistreatment and deprivation. The human mind is generally resilient, however, and dehumanization, as the complete disavowal of one's own sense of humanity, appears to be exceptionally uncommon. What brutalizing treatment does often tend to bring about, however, is a weakening of the sense of one's humanity and belonging in the world. Refugees, asylum seekers, and other (forced) migrants who have lived through this type of unsettling experience describe themselves, for example,

124 Dehumanization in the Global Migration Crisis

in terms of zombies and ghosts, alluding to the emptied out and voided nature of their being, having lost trust in the social world and in their connections with others.

The main insight developed in this chapter is that brutalization in many cases is not well described in terms of dehumanization, understood as a process through which people are made in a more or less literal sense less than human, even if it may constitute a form of dehumanizing treatment and representation, given that people are treated in ways that signal that they are attributed a moral status below that of human beings. The chapter heeded a warning against buying into the logic of perpetrators who hold that victims can truly be made less than human through brutalizing treatment. Generally, victims are not turned into something less than human but thwarted in enjoying or expressing their full range of human qualities. Only when the human spirit is utterly broken is it possible to claim that brutalization dehumanizes people in the sense that they come to fail to recognize their own humanity. Still, brutalizing treatment can be dehumanizing because it expresses that victims are attributed a moral status below that of human beings, or alters the perceptions of onlookers or victims, convincing them that victims hold a moral status below that of human beings.

This chapter completes our analysis of animalization, objectification, and brutalization in the global migration crisis. It is now time to turn to the task of presenting a comprehensive account of dehumanization based on the insights developed in the chapters so far. The next chapter will take on this challenge in arguing that dehumanization may be understood to consist in a particular blindness for the significance of the human subjectivity of victims as a moral factor that should be taken into consideration in decisions on how to treat them.

Notes

1. The notion of brutalization features, for example, in the work of the linguist Karen Stollznow. She identifies brutalization as one of the senses of dehumanization and describes it as 'severe treatment or the conditioning of personality and emotions, so that an affected person appears compassionless, emotionally unresponsive and is therefore seeming "less human"'. See: Stollznow, 'Dehumanization in Language and Thought', 181. Several authors note that people who dehumanize others may thereby dehumanize themselves through processes of brutalization. The philosopher Martin Buber describes, for example, how 'the person who dehumanizes others experiences less emotion, less empathy, and fewer personal feelings, and thus dehumanizes himself or herself as well'. See: Martin Buber, *Hasidism and Modern Man* (New York: Horizon Press, 1958), p. 12.

2. 'Brutalize', *Merriam-Webster Online*, https://www.merriam-webster.com/dictionary/brutalize.
3. 'Brutal', *Online Etymology Dictionary*, https://www.etymonline.com/search?q=brutal.
4. The literary scholar Tzvetan Todorov notes, for example, related to this point that 'torture and extermination have not even the remotest equivalent in the animal kingdom'. See: Tzvetan Todorov, *Facing the Extreme: Moral Life in the Concentration Camps*, translated by Arthur Denner and Abigail Pollak (New York: Henry Holt and Company, 1996), p. 123.
5. See, for example: Janice T. Gibson and Mika Haritos-Fatouras, 'The Education of a Torturer', *Psychology Today* 20 (1986): 50–8 and Alette Smeulers and Fred Grünfeld, 'Training and Education of Perpetrators', in *International Crimes and Other Gross Human Rights Violations* (Leiden: Martinus Nijhoff Publishers, 2011), pp. 267–94.
6. DeBono, '"Less than Human"', 71.
7. Sydney Morning Herald, 'Think Australia's Treatment'.
8. Benjamin, an asylum seeker, 'Detained on Nauru: "This Is the Most Painful Part of my Story—When You Realise No One Cares"', *The Guardian*, 24 March 2017, https://www.theguardian.com/world/australia-books-blog/2017/mar/24/detained-on-nauru-this-is-the-most-painful-part-of-my-story-when-you-realise-no-one-cares.
9. Mehdi, 'I Am Leaving Australia's Torture Chambers after Nine Years—But What I Have is the Worst Kind of Freedom', *The Guardian*, 4 March 2022, https://www.theguardian.com/commentisfree/2022/mar/04/i-am-leaving-australias-torture-chambers-after-nine-years-but-what-i-have-is-the-worst-kind-of-freedom.
10. Sang H. Kil and Cecilia Menjívar, 'The War on the Border: Criminalizing Immigrants and Militarizing the US-Mexico Border', in *Immigration and Crime: Race, Ethnicity, and Violence*, edited by Ramiro Martinez Jr. and Abel Valenzuela Jr. (New York: New York University Press, 2006), pp. 164–88, Kil, Menjívar, and Doty, 'Securing Borders', and Lauren E. Wroe, '"It Really Is about Telling People Who Asylum Seekers Are, Because We Are Human like Anybody Else": Negotiating Victimhood in Refugee Advocacy Work', *Discourse & Society* 29 (2018): 324–43.
11. Kil and Menjívar, 'The War on the Border'.
12. Kil, Menjívar, and Doty, 'Securing Borders', 299.
13. Wroe, 'It Really Is about'.
14. It is important to note that treating people in ways that seek to make them resemble animals may nonetheless constitute a form of treatment that is an inadmissible way of treating human beings and that signals the attribution of a moral status below that of human beings. It would therefore constitute a form of dehumanization, even if it would not lead to a genuine failure on the side of the victim to recognize his or her own humanity.
15. The analysis of testimony of survivors from the Nazi concentration and extermination camps is not meant to suggest that the treatment of refugees and asylum seekers should be put on a par with the one of inmates of the labour and death camps. The idea here is that the case of Auschwitz can bring into sharper focus what it might entail to lose touch with one's own humanity due to the extreme conditions of mistreatment and deprivation that occurred there. The debate to which extent the conditions in detention centres resemble those in concentration camps is controversial and complex. I will not go into this issue here as it diverts from the main points this chapter seeks to develop.
16. Levi, *The Drowned and the Saved*, 90.

126 Dehumanization in the Global Migration Crisis

17. Jean Améry, *At the Mind's Limits: Contemplations by a Survivor on Auschwitz and Its Realities*, translated by Sidney Rosenfeld and Stella Rosenfeld (Bloomington: Indiana University Press, 1980 [1966]), p. 9.
18. Ibid.
19. Levi, *The Drowned and the Saved*, 64.
20. Ibid.
21. Améry, *At the Mind's Limits*, 9.
22. Levi, *The Drowned and the Saved*, 56–7.
23. Idem, 57.
24. Elie Wiesel, *Night*, translated by Marion Wiesel (London: Penguin, 2008), p. 36.
25. Ibid.
26. Idem, xii.
27. Améry, *At the Mind's Limits*, 20.
28. UNHCR, 'Mouhamad's Journey, Greece', *Refugee Stories*, 2014, http://stories.unhcr.org/mouhamads-story-greece-p60137.html.
29. Penny Crofts and Anthea Vogl, 'Dehumanized and Demonized Refugees, Zombies and World War Z', *Law and Humanities* 13 (2019): 29–51, https://doi.org/10.1080/17521483.2019.1572290, Schinkel, '"Illegal Aliens" and the State', and Jon Stratton, 'Zombie Trouble: Zombie Texts, Bare Life and Displaced People', *European Journal of Cultural Studies* 14 (2011): 265–81, https://doi.org/10.1177/1367549411400103.
30. Croft and Vogl, 'Dehumanized and Demonized'.
31. Ibid.
32. Stratton, 'Zombie Trouble', 278.
33. Agamben, *Homo Sacer*.
34. Anthony Downey, 'Zones of Indistinction: Giorgio Agamben's Bare Life and the Politics of Aesthetics', *Third Text* 223 (2009): 109, https://doi.org/10.1080/09528820902840581.
35. Stratton, 'Zombie Trouble', 267.
36. Ibid.
37. A seemingly similar story of social disconnect is recounted by Ali who comes from Iran and stayed in the Calais refugee camp. He recounts how on Sunday volunteers came to the 'Jungle' who said hello to him and looked at him with pity. This reaction upset him: 'I can't find peace except by fighting against these reactions. Because I don't understand their language?' Ali continues by noting that the problem goes beyond his incapacity to speak the languages of the volunteers: 'But the problem is not the language. The problem is the prison I have built for myself. I don't even understand the Iranian language anymore. Everything I knew before I got here has changed' (Calais Writers, *Voices from the 'Jungle'*, 128). Ali speaks in a similar vein about issues in entering into contact where the language plays a role, yet is not central to the problem. Rather, it is that something has changed within him, unsettling the structures and orders he used to previously understand the world.
38. Heath Cabot, '"Refugee Voices": Tragedy, Ghosts and the Anthropology of Not Knowing', *Journal of Contemporary Ethnography* 45 (2016): 645–72, https://doi.org/10.1177/0891241615625567.
39. Idem, 2. The translation from the Greek comes from Cabot's text.
40. Idem, 3.
41. Malkki, 'Speechless Emissaries', 388.

42. Cabot, 'Refugee Voices', 4.
43. Maria Giannacopoulos and Claire Loughnan, '"Closure" at Manus Island and Carceral Expansion in the Open Air Prison', *Globalizations* 17 (2020): 1118–35, https://doi.org/10.1080/14747731.2019.1679549.
44. Ibid.
45. Amnesty International, '"Island of Despair": Australia's "Processing" of Refugees on Nauru', 17 October 2016, https://www.amnesty.org.au/island-of-despair-nauru-refugee-report-2016/, Ben Doherty, 'UN Countries Line Up to Criticise Australia's Human Rights Record', *The Guardian*, 9 November 2015, https://www.theguardian.com/law/2015/nov/10/un-countries-line-up-to-criticise-australias-human-rights-record, and United Nations, *Report of the Special Rapporteur on Torture and Other Cruel, Inhuman or Degrading Treatment or Punishment, Juan E. Méndez: Addendum*, 5 March 2015, https://digitallibrary.un.org/record/793910.
46. Ben Doherty and Daniel Hurst, 'UN Accuses Australia of Systematically Violating Torture Convention', *The Guardian*, 10 March 2015, https://www.theguardian.com/australia-news/2015/mar/09/un-reports-australias-immigration-detention-breaches-torture-convention.
47. Ben Doherty, 'International Criminal Court Told Australia's Detention Regime Could Be a Crime against Humanity', *The Guardian*, 13 February 2017, https://www.theguardian.com/australia-news/2017/feb/13/international-criminal-court-told-australias-detention-regime-could-be-a-against-humanity.
48. David Marr and Oliver Laughland, 'Australia's Detention Regime Sets Out to Make Asylum Seekers Suffer, Says Chief Immigration Psychiatrist', *The Guardian*, 4 August 2014, https://www.theguardian.com/world/2014/aug/05/-sp-australias-detention-regime-sets-out-to-make-asylum-seekers-suffer-says-chief-immigration-psychiatrist.
49. Ben Doherty, 'Australia's Offshore Detention Is Unlawful, Says International Criminal Court Prosecutor', *The Guardian*, 15 February 2020, https://www.theguardian.com/australia-news/2020/feb/15/australias-offshore-detention-is-unlawful-says-international-criminal-court-prosecutor.
50. Benjamin, 'Detained on Nauru'.
51. Ibid.
52. Mehdi, 'I Am Leaving'.
53. Behrouz Boochani, *A Letter from Manus Island* (Adamstown, Borderstream Books, 2018), p. 23.
54. Idem, 17.
55. Idem, 19.
56. Mehdi, 'I Am Leaving'.
57. Caitlin Dickerson, '"There Is a Stench": Soiled Clothes and No Baths for Migrant Children at a Texas Center', *The New York Times*, 21 June 2019, https://www.nytimes.com/2019/06/21/us/migrant-children-border-soap.html?module=inline, Martha Mendoza and Garance Burke, 'US Gov't Moves Children after AP Exposes Bad Treatment', *Associated Press*, 25 June 2019, https://apnews.com/article/border-patrols-az-state-wire-tx-state-wire-michael-pence-caribbean-a7a9acc4c6a546829a258e008d10d705, and Grace Tatter and Meghna Chakrabarti, '"Torture Facilities": Eyewitnesses Describe Poor Conditions at Texas Detention Centers for Migrant Children', *WBUR*, 25 June 2019, https://www.wbur.org/onpoint/2019/06/25/texas-border-control-facilities-migrant-children.

128 Dehumanization in the Global Migration Crisis

58. Dickerson, '"There Is a Stench"'.
59. Tatter and Chakrabarti, '"Torture Facilities"'.
60. Helen Hintjens, 'Failed Securitisation Moves During the 2015 "Migration Crisis"', *International Migration* 57 (2019): 190, https://doi.org/10.1111/imig.12588.
61. Kil and Menjívar, 'The War on the Border'.
62. Kil, Menjívar, and Doty, 'Securing Borders', 299.
63. Buber, *Hasidism and Modern Man*, 12.
64. Wroe, 'It Really Is about'.
65. Idem, 19.
66. Mehdi, 'I Am Leaving'.
67. Boochani, *A Letter from Manus Island*, 17.

5
Dehumanization

They look at us as if we're nothing.

Hassan, refugee from Syria

Introduction

Hassan, the Syrian refugee who sells fruit on the streets of Beirut, tells about the negative experiences he has had as a refugee. He recounts how some of the people he meets look at him and other Syrians as if they were nothing. Looking at someone as if they were nothing means depreciating them, failing to recognize the status they hold as persons. In certain ways, looking at people as if they were nothing goes beyond regarding them as less and inferior, or treating them as mere means to one's ends. It signals a form of utter indifference, which expresses itself not in a genuine blindness, but in a humiliating look that symbolizes contempt and disregard.

Hassan's testimony speaks to central themes in the account of dehumanization that this book develops. The previous chapters set out that dehumanization involves a denial of moral human status. This chapter clarifies what kind of moral exclusion is distinctive of dehumanization. Dehumanization, according to this account, consists in a particular form of moral exclusion that is characterized by neglect of or contempt for the moral status of human beings, which expresses itself in blindness for the significance of the human subjectivity of victims as a moral factor that should be taken into consideration in decisions on how to treat them. This means that when persons are dehumanized, their experiences, particularly in terms of suffering, no longer matter in the eyes of the dehumanizer(s), or at least not as a moral reason that counts against their mistreatment. Those who are dehumanized are thereby not simply attributed a lower moral standing than persons whom we include in our inner moral circle(s) but excluded from the moral category of humanity altogether. Dehumanization therefore constitutes a uniquely radical form of exclusion.

Dehumanization in the Global Migration Crisis. Adrienne de Ruiter, Oxford University Press. © Adrienne de Ruiter (2024).
DOI: 10.1093/oso/9780198893400.003.0006

The first part of this chapter introduces this view of dehumanization. The second part discusses the strengths and downsides of this perspective compared to other prominent accounts of dehumanization in social psychology and philosophy. The final section considers various forms of moral exclusion of refugees, asylum seekers, and unwanted migrants and illustrates how this view of dehumanization elucidates when people are dehumanized in the global migration crisis.

Denying the moral relevance of human subjectivity

The analysis in the previous chapters showed that dehumanization involves a denial of the moral status of human beings. What renders animalization dehumanizing is not the denial of biological humanity that appears to be central to it, so I argued, but the denial of moral standing that is expressed through this denial of biological human status. A denial of moral human standing is also key to dehumanizing forms of objectification because the act of treating people as objects signals that they are deemed to hold no inner life and are considered more similar to objects without agency rather than living, thinking, and feeling subjects. By denying the inner life of people their moral standing is reduced to that of inanimate objects, which can be treated with indifference or used as mere instruments. Brutalization, understood as the process of making people brutal, unfeeling, or inhuman, involves dehumanization when severe forms of destitution or abuse cause victims to lose touch with their own sense of humanity or when brutalizing treatments serve as performative acts that portray victims as less than human in a moral sense. Dehumanization, therefore, always involves a certain denial of moral human standing.

The subjectivity of victims is implicated in all these instances of dehumanization. Human subjectivity is denied when perpetrators relate to victims as non-human animals or inanimate objects. It is also involved when perpetrators want to inflict suffering on their victims. In such cases, the suffering of victims is seen as a reason that counts in favour rather than against their mistreatment. Whereas recognition of human subjectivity under ordinary circumstances gives reason to restrain from causing (wanton) suffering, it is considered a ground for doing so in cases of brutalization. When dehumanization is at play, perpetrators thus either feel unconcerned about the suffering of their victims or regard it as something that it would be good to inflict.

Dehumanization, on my view, then involves particular unusual ways of engaging with and responding to the human subjectivity of victims. It is important to reflect on what human subjectivity entails here. I understand this term to denote the distinct ways in which people experience the world, as mediated through their bodily, emotional, symbolic, and moral sensibilities. Humans are social and embodied beings who interpret the world.[1] These aspects of human existence entail that people are vulnerable to suffering from physical, psychological, and symbolic harms. In cases of dehumanization, the human subjectivity of victims is overlooked or used against them in ways that distort ordinary moral relations, as their capacity to suffer due to vulnerabilities inherent in the human condition is regarded not as a reason to protect and care for them, or at least not to inflict avoidable harm on them, but as something that can be wielded against them.

The notion of human subjectivity relates to the aspects of experience and agency, which the philosopher Edouard Machery claims are central to ascribing moral standing.[2] Agency refers to the capacity to engage in rational forms of action and planning, while experience involves the ability to feel pain and pleasure. Dehumanization, following Machery, consists in depriving people of moral standing by denying them agency or experience, or both, which leads to moral indifference: 'When something is deprived of moral standing, its interests tend to have no moral significance when others decide what to do.'[3]

Without moral standing someone or something cannot be morally wronged. The view of dehumanization I propose, understood as a denial of the moral significance of human subjectivity, captures these insights in a unified way since human subjectivity entails both the embodied and social aspects that Machery assigns to the category of experience and the more cognitive, symbolic, and moral dimensions represented by the category of agency. Bringing these aspects together under one notion, namely that of human subjectivity, highlights the various ways in which human suffering can arise through physical, psychological, and symbolic vulnerabilities that are inherent in the human condition. By defining dehumanization as a denial of the moral relevance of human subjectivity, furthermore, my view can account for cases where perpetrators engage with victims in ways that reveal recognition of certain aspects of their human agency without ascribing appropriate moral value to it.

What it means for people to fail to regard the subjective experiences of victims as holding positive moral weight is illustrated by the philosopher Eve

132 Dehumanization in the Global Migration Crisis

Garrard, who analyses the distinction between acts that are wrongful and those that are evil. She observes how in a wrongful act of killing,

> the wrongdoer sees that, say, the suffering of his victim tells against his killing her. But for him, the attractions of the wrongful act—the increase of power, the material gain, the removal of a threat to him, outweigh (wrongly, of course) the importance of her suffering. So he goes ahead and, a little reluctantly, kills her anyway.[4]

In the case of evil acts, different dynamics are at play. Garrard contends that in an evil act of killing, '[the victim's] suffering counts for nothing. It isn't outweighed by the advantages to [the evildoer] of killing her—for him there is nothing to be outweighed'.[5]

The distinction that Garrard draws between wrongful and evil acts of killing offers relevant insights for understanding dehumanization. Dehumanization, on my view, is characterized by disregard for the fact that the victim is a human being whose subjective experiences, particularly in terms of suffering, should be a matter of at least minimal concern. Dehumanization, then, involves a certain ignorance of or contempt for the moral status of human beings, which expresses itself in blindness for the significance of the human subjectivity of victims as a moral factor that should be taken into account in decisions on how to treat them.[6]

There are two ways that this failure to ascribe positive moral value to the human subjectivity of people can come about. The first is to fail to see that victims hold any human subjectivity. The second is to fail to recognize that this subjectivity matters when we consider how to treat others, in counting as a reason against making them suffer. The view of dehumanization I present thus draws inspiration from Garrard's work on the distinction between wrong- and evil-doing but departs from it in important ways by considering that dehumanization does not require that the suffering of victims counts for nothing. It is also possible for dehumanizers to recognize the suffering of their victims but consider it as giving (further) reason to mistreat them. When perpetrators consider the suffering of their victims as something that makes their mistreatment more, rather than less, enticing, this entails that the moral significance of the victims' human subjectivity is disregarded, given that attributing even minimal moral value to the subjectivity of victims would entail that their suffering is recognized as something that should count against, rather than in favour of harming them.

The moral significance of people's human subjectivity is thus overlooked or ignored when they are dehumanized. Perpetrators who engage in dehumanization thereby forget that their victims have an inner life of feelings, thoughts, and experiences, which should hold at least some positive moral weight in deliberations on how to treat them. The moral status of victims is thus denied when perpetrators fail to consider their subjective experiences as reasons that count against their mistreatment, if only in a minimal sense.

Dehumanization as a denial of moral status

This view of dehumanization has a number of strengths. First, it offers a perspective that sharply distinguishes dehumanization from infra-humanization by focusing on what it entails for people's moral human standing to be fully denied, rather than undermined in a more limited sense. Second, the focus on the denial of the moral significance of human subjectivity allows us to account for forms of dehumanization that involve various emotions ranging from indifference to hate. Third, this view provides an answer to growing scepticism about the use of dehumanization as an explanatory factor in mass violence, voiced by critics who observe that perpetrators who allegedly engage in dehumanization frequently interact with victims in ways that seemingly acknowledge their uniquely human traits. By including two sides to dehumanization, consisting in the denial of human subjectivity itself and the denial of the moral relevance of this subjectivity, this view is able to make sense of forms of dehumanization that consist in blindness for the human subjectivity of victims, involve a failure to ascribe moral value to the subjective experiences of victims, or regard the human subjectivity of the victims as a factor that counts in favour of their mistreatment.

Recognizing people as minimally human

The perspective of dehumanization presented in this book concentrates on what it means for people's moral human status to be fully denied, rather than undermined in a more limited sense. In this way, my account differs from that of main currents in social psychology and philosophy, which tend to draw less stark distinctions between dehumanization and infra-humanization. Most authors maintain that dehumanization consists in denying people's humanity, either in blatant or more subtle ways, and regard it as a spectrum concept, which also includes relating to people as inferior human beings.[7] On my understanding, it is important to maintain a sharp conceptual distinction between dehumanization, through which victims are viewed, portrayed, or treated as less than human, and infra-humanization, through which victims

134   Dehumanization in the Global Migration Crisis

are viewed, portrayed, or treated as less human, to avoid losing sight of what is distinctive of dehumanization as a form of moral exclusion.

As I set out in Chapter 1, dehumanization does not simply lower the position victims hold among fellow human beings, but excludes them from this moral category altogether. Someone who is dehumanized is no longer considered normatively human and thereby loses the moral protection that this label provides. By blurring the boundaries between fully denying people's moral human status and relating to them as inferior human beings the distinct nature and wrong of dehumanization is obscured. As a consequence, it becomes harder to see why dehumanization entails a uniquely radical form of moral exclusion and why it requires an adamant response. If we confuse dehumanization and infra-humanization, our responses may be less effective, furthermore, as cases in which victims are viewed as inferior human beings require different counteraction than cases where they are regarded as less than human.

The conviction that it is important to delimit our understanding of dehumanization to practices or processes which involve viewing, portraying, or treating people as less than human, and not just less human, marks an important difference between my perspective and that of other authors who similarly regard dehumanization as a denial of moral status.[8] My work draws, for example, from that of the social psychologist Herbert Kelman, who presents an insightful account of dehumanization in the context of state-sanctioned massacres.[9] Kelman maintains that dehumanization takes place whenever we fail to perceive of persons as being (fully) human, i.e., when we do not sufficiently attribute them individual identity or affirm that they belong to the same community of individuals as we do.[10] His view, like mine, considers dehumanization a particular denial of moral status, as he explains that, when people are dehumanized, 'principles of morality no longer apply to them and moral restraints against killing are more readily overcome.'[11]

What is particularly appealing in Kelman's work, according to me, is the clarity with which he sets out how people may come to be excluded from moral consideration and the detrimental consequences that may follow from this. By pointing out the distinction between dehumanization as a denial of individuality, on the one hand, and community, on the other, Kelman provides valuable insights into the different forms that dehumanization can take. In cases of genocide, for example, people are killed because of their identity as a group member. Individual differences fade from sight as the collective marker becomes central to defining what (rather than who) the person is. At the same time, however, this reduction of persons to a single aspect of their identity also works to exclude them from a community shared with others, which helps explain how dehumanization can produce a loss of a sense of moral obligation that facilitates the perpetration of atrocities.

Yet, an issue with this account, in my view, is that it sets unrealistically high criteria for moral inclusion. This perspective sets the standard for perceiving someone as human too high because it focuses on what it means to recognize a person as fully human, instead of as minimally human. Kelman asserts, for example, that attributing 'community' to others implies that we experience their death as 'a personal loss'.[12] This implies that when people are not profoundly saddened by the death of a fellow human being, this would be dehumanizing.[13] By setting the threshold for recognizing people's humanity this high, it becomes virtually impossible to avoid dehumanization. After all, when do we experience the death of a stranger as a personal loss?

Strangers do not usually engage with each other in emotional bonds to the extent where the death of one would have a strong affective impact on others. While Kelman's account offers an ambitious standard for affective engagement, it thus does not realistically reflect the lack of engagement that characterizes ordinary relations between strangers. A more limited understanding of what it means to fail to recognize people's moral human status is therefore called for. What is required to account for dehumanization is not a view based on what it entails to regard people as fully human, but as minimally so.

The account I present does just that by defining dehumanization as blindness for the moral significance of the human subjectivity of people. This blindness entails that people's human subjectivity is not even minimally valued. Dehumanization therefore does not involve a failure to experience the death of a fellow human being as a 'personal loss', but rather a failure to consider this death as relevant at all in a moral sense.[10] There is thus no need to be strongly moved by the death of each and every human being, although there is a need to at least regret their death as a loss to them and/or those close to them. Furthermore, considering the moral value of human subjectivity more closely, death may not even always be experienced as a painful loss for the person who passes away and their loved ones. If the deceased was suffering from intolerable and irremediable pain, for instance, concern for their subjectivity and its moral value could also entail that we welcome their death as an end to their agony, even if the loss of their life still marks a loss.

Since Kelman's work on dehumanization is centred on state-sanctioned massacres, a setting where death comes about abruptly and violently, cases where death may bring relief after prolonged illness or impairment are not central to his concerns. His work offers a powerful indictment against the processes of moral disengagement at play in genocide and war. Still, the focus on recognizing people's full humanity asks too much from people in requiring them to care deeply for all human beings in order to avoid dehumanizing them. In concentrating on what it entails to fail to regard people as minimally human in a moral sense, the view of dehumanization this book proposes draws clear distinctions with infra-humanization and avoids viewing dehumanization as the rule rather than the exception in human interactions.

From indifference to hate

Another strength of the perspective I propose is that it can make sense of forms of dehumanization that are inspired by various emotions, ranging from indifference to hate. Indifference, as I explained in Chapter 3, is central to Axel Honneth's account of dehumanization as a form of reification.[14] Honneth claims that people tend to automatically recognize each other's humanity and only fail to do so when social interactions are distorted. This can happen, for example, through propaganda and ideological manipulation or when people become overly focused on achieving particular aims and thereby come to see other persons as mere instruments to reach their objectives. What is missing in these cases, according to Honneth, is 'the feeling of connection that would be necessary for us to be affected by the expressions we perceive.'[15] Like a psychopath, people who dehumanize others may register their expressions and emotions, but fail to be moved by them in appropriate ways.

In my view, Honneth is correct in claiming that manifestations of dehumanization that take the form of reification involve a failure to adequately engage with the pleas of others. His perspective highlights the importance of a minimal level of affective involvement for maintaining morally guided interpersonal relations. Yet, dehumanization does not necessarily express itself as reification. By centring his account on the failure to emotionally engage with victims, Honneth rules out forms of dehumanization in which perpetrators are emotionally invested.[16]

The perspective I propose can account for various dehumanizing practices, which may draw from a lack of affective engagement or a strong emotional involvement with victims. Differently to Honneth, my account is focused not on reification—through which perpetrators come to be insensitive for the affective appeal of the expressions of their victims—but highlights the failure to attribute positive moral value to the human subjectivity of victims. The fact that people can fail to ascribe this positive moral value in two ways entails that dehumanization can express itself as a form of indifference or as a process in which perpetrators are (heavily) emotionally involved. When perpetrators fail to see that their victims hold any human subjectivity, their engagement with them will be devoid of affective engagement, as Honneth describes. When perpetrators recognize their human subjectivity but not its moral value, dehumanization can coincide with hate, contempt, and other negative feelings towards the victims. On my account, the moral exclusion that characterizes dehumanization can thus be reflected in a reified attitude through which the perpetrator regards the victim as a mere object or through a strained interpersonal relation marked by hate and enmity.

Recognizing human subjectivity without recognizing its moral value

The dual nature of my account of dehumanization also offers a response to critics who question the use of this concept as an explanatory factor to elucidate the occurrence of (mass) atrocities. In recent years, a growing number of scholars have expressed scepticism about the idea that dehumanization is required to account for allegedly inhumane forms of violence, abuse, and cruelty.[17] Several authors have raised concerns that the concept of dehumanization is overused because perpetrators in many cases do not seem to overlook the humanity of their victims, but rather to engage with it in disturbing ways. Kate Manne argues, for instance, that acts of violence in mass atrocities 'often betray the fact that their victims must seem human, all too human, to the perpetrators. We notice this when we remember to pay attention to man's inhumanity to women, in particular—who are often brutally raped en masse during genocide'.[18]

In a similar vein, the social psychologist Johannes Lang contends that scholars working on genocide and mass killings tend to rely on the concept of dehumanization to account for mass violence without considering the distinct ways in which perpetrators engage with their victims that reveal a certain recognition of their humanity. Reflecting on the situation in the Nazi concentration and extermination camps, Lang observes, for instance, that 'it was precisely the human, or intersubjective, qualities of the violent interaction that provided the violence with much of its meaning'.[19]

The philosopher Harriet Over presents another critique of the often held belief that the human status of victims needs to be denied to impair inhibitions that people normally feel against harming others in extreme and violent ways, such as through genocide or torture. Like Manne and Lang, she

138 Dehumanization in the Global Migration Crisis

emphasizes that perpetrators of dehumanization often engage with victims in ways that seemingly acknowledge their humanity. She calls on proponents of the thesis that dehumanization is required to explain the occurrence of mass violence, cruelty, and abuse to account for cases 'in which target groups are described in terms of uniquely human attributes, mental states, and emotions'.[20]

The view of dehumanization I present can do so, even though I do not hold that dehumanization is always needed to account for violence and mistreatment. By distinguishing between the failure to recognize human subjectivity and the failure to recognize the moral value of this subjectivity, my account is able to accommodate for cases where perpetrators engage with their victims in ways that demonstrate recognition of their uniquely human attributes, mental states, and emotions. After all, the fact that human subjectivity is recognized does not automatically entail that it is morally valued as well. When perpetrators consider that their victims use their human subjectivity in ways that are seen as harmful or threatening, are considered depraved and immoral, or otherwise evoke strong negative responses, they may fail to attribute positive moral value to this subjectivity.[21] If this negative valuation is joined with a sense of the need to punish people for their transgressions, this opens the way to brutalization. It is important then to define dehumanization as the denial of the moral relevance of human subjectivity, rather than the denial of human subjectivity itself, because the denial of moral relevance is what characterizes dehumanization in its various guises.

Entering the mind of the perpetrator

While the view presented here has considerable strengths, it admittedly does not make it particularly easy to determine when dehumanization occurs. Following my account, dehumanization is characterized by complete disregard for the moral significance of the human subjectivity of the victim(s). This entails that whether a portrayal, treatment, or perception is dehumanizing generally depends on the attitudes, beliefs, and viewpoints held by the perpetrator(s). To know whether dehumanization takes place thus seems to require knowing their minds. Since perpetrators, at least in certain cases, may be unwilling to openly share their views of the victims, it may be difficult to assess when dehumanization takes place.

Other accounts of dehumanization direct attention to the mistreatment of victims and provide guidelines for establishing when dehumanization occurs that are less dependent on the perspective of the perpetrator(s).

The philosopher Mari Mikkola, for example, presents a view of dehumanization as an affront to fundamental human interests, needs, and rights, which foregrounds the harm done to the victim(s).[22] According to Mikkola, dehumanization consists in a morally injurious and indefensible setback to legitimate human interests. These legitimate human interests are characterized as interests that are basic to the well-being of human beings and include, among others, interests in being healthy and alive, being able to have meaningful social contact with others, at least minimal means of subsistence, and a certain level of freedom from coercion and interference.[23] Mikkola argues that setbacks to such legitimate human interests count as dehumanizing when they are indefensible and morally injurious. Setbacks are indefensible when they are inexcusable or unjustifiable and they are morally injurious if they fail to recognize people's value, which is the case, for example, when they are based on sexist attitudes.[24] As examples of acts and practices that are dehumanizing, she mentions, for instance, rape and denying education to women.

Mikkola's focus on the wrong and harm done to victims emphasizes the central importance of the affront that dehumanization poses to them. While it is indeed crucial to recognize how dehumanization affects the victims, I believe it risky to make this central to our efforts to understand dehumanization. This lens makes it likely that we see dehumanization in practices that could better be described as infra-humanization and fail to recognize it in situations where blindness or contempt for the moral status that victims hold as humans is not expressed through action. People may set back legitimate human interests in indefensible and morally injurious ways while still attributing some moral value to the human subjectivity of the persons who are harmed by their actions. Especially if we consider infra-humanization as distinct from dehumanization, it follows that people can harm the interests of others in indefensible and morally injurious ways through forms of discrimination through which others are perceived as inferior human beings without necessarily casting them out from the moral category of humanity altogether.

Another issue concerns the fact that people may fail to recognize the moral relevance of the human subjectivity of others without translating these perceptions into action. Victims can be dehumanized not only when they are treated in particular ways, but also by being denied a particular form of respect through the attitude that perpetrators take towards them. This speaks to a distinction that the philosopher Anna Galeotti draws between respect and rights. She notes that a claim to respect transcends claims for a particular form of treatment, observing that 'what is claimed is not a precise thing, but an attitude, an acknowledging attitude which escapes definition and precise

140 Dehumanization in the Global Migration Crisis

behaviour'.[25] The issue is, then, that people can be dehumanized not only when they are treated in certain ways, but also by being denied a particular form of respect through the attitude that people take towards them. The perception of the perpetrator(s) thus needs to be central to determining when dehumanization occurs, on my view, to avoid including cases where perpetrators do recognize the moral relevance of their victims' human subjectivity, although in a limited sense, and to avoid excluding cases where people fail to recognize the moral relevance of the human subjectivity of their victims, but do not act upon these views.

Mikkola could potentially accommodate for these points by arguing that a morally injurious and indefensible setback to legitimate human interests could take the form of (passively experienced) disrespect as well as (actively expressed) mistreatment. It may not be necessary that this setback presents itself in crystallized form as misconduct towards the victim. Furthermore, it could be argued that the specification that setbacks are morally injurious if they fail to recognize people's value signals the central relevance of recognition of the moral status of the victim(s) for her account. Our views might therefore actually be closer than first appears from my discussion. Still, her views on recognition of people's value require more than the acknowledgement of the minimal moral relevance of people's human subjectivity, as becomes clear from her examples of rape and the denial of education to women.

Concerning the example of rape, I believe this not always to be dehumanizing because there seem to exist cases of rape in which the human subjectivity of victims is not completely overlooked or attributed no positive moral weight at all. In analogy to Garrard's reflections on wrong and evil acts of killing, a distinction could be made between different cases of rape. In some, 'the wrongdoer sees that, say the suffering of his victim tells against his [raping] her. But for him the attractions of the wrongful act—[the sexual pleasure, the feeling of domination], outweigh (wrongly, of course) the importance of her suffering. So he goes ahead and [rapes her]'.[26] In other cases of rape, the victim's 'suffering counts for nothing. It isn't outweighed by the advantages to [the rapist of raping her]—for him there is nothing to be outweighed'. Or, adding the dimension of brutalization, the victim's suffering may actually count in favour of the act of rape, making the abuse disturbingly more enticing—for example, when rape is used as a means to humiliate or punish the victim.

Rape, in my view, evidently speaks against viewing others as fully human. If people would appreciate the full moral weight of the human subjectivity of the other, they would not transgress that person's physical, psychological, and emotional boundaries in this intrusive way. Perpetrators could not rape their victims if they would attribute to their subjectivity the value it merits. This does not entail, however, that they necessarily fail to recognize human subjectivity in their victims or do not attribute any positive moral relevance to it. I wish to stress that this line of argument in no way means to minimize the wrongs and harms of rape. It only aims to illustrate that dehumanization may not always constitute the right frame to interpret the dynamics at play in rape.

The denial of education to women, in my view, is an example that is helpful to illustrate the difference between infra-humanization and dehumanization. Women may be denied education because they are seen as lesser, inferior human beings whose minds better not be burdened by putting too many ideas in their heads. If the question of a denial of education literally comes up, it seems likely that infra-humanization, rather than dehumanization, is at stake because the consideration to let girls be educated reveals an underlying recognition of their capacity to learn from schooling in a way that would not come up for creatures that are considered less than human. Especially if a denial of schooling is based on the alleged need to protect women's frail minds, it seems not that a denial of human subjectivity is at stake, but a denial of the quality of that human subjectivity. The notion of protection entails that women's subjectivity is valued, although less so than that of men. A denial of education thus often appears to follow from the infra-humanization of women.

To determine whether dehumanization occurs, I deem it necessary to focus on the attitudes, beliefs, and viewpoints of the perpetrator(s), even if these may not always be easy to discern. While it is not possible to enter the mind of the perpetrator(s), we may be able to tell something about their perceptions by paying close attention to their expressions and actions. After all, people do tend to reflect their views of others in the ways they talk about and act towards them, even if they do not necessarily come out in explicitly admitting to their dehumanization. Complete disregard for the moral significance of the human subjectivity of victims may thus be seen reflected in particular forms of misrepresentation and mistreatment.

The clearest example of the outward manifestation of dehumanization can allegedly be found in the infliction of gratuitous violence. In cases in which wanton suffering is imposed on people, it is evident that there are no reasons that can outweigh the suffering of the victim(s), precisely because the violence is gratuitous. The only reason to impose such violence would be the gratification the perpetrator(s) get(s) out of it, which in itself signals complete disregard for the moral significance of the human subjectivity of the victim(s).

In cases where it is more difficult to determine whether perpetrators fail to attribute any moral relevance to the human subjectivity of their victims, or rather fail to ascribe it sufficient importance for it to outweigh the reasons they have for engaging in their mistreatment, it is helpful to consider the ways that perpetrators speak about their victims and represent their actions. Portrayals that seek to persuade the audience that the depicted persons do not have any human subjectivity or none that should be attributed any positive moral value are dehumanizing. In most cases, the answer to the question whether depictions and treatments involve dehumanization thus depends on the attitudes, beliefs, and viewpoints of the perpetrators. Although this renders it difficult to determine when dehumanization takes place, it reflects the reality that dehumanization not only concerns the ways in which people are treated or portrayed, but also, and importantly, how they are perceived.

Dehumanizing migrants

The perspective of dehumanization presented in this chapter helps elucidate when the moral exclusion of refugees, asylum seekers, and unwanted migrants involves dehumanization. Since dehumanization, on my view, consists in blindness for the moral relevance of the human subjectivity of the victim(s), establishing whether dehumanization takes place generally requires insight into the attitudes, beliefs, and viewpoints held by the perpetrators. In some cases, it is evident that the suffering of victims counts for nothing, as with the infliction of gratuitous violence. Dehumanization can therefore be recognized most easily in situations characterized by wanton abuse or other forms of mistreatment that signal that the human subjectivity of the victims is not morally valued. In other cases, perpetrators express their views in what they say about their victims, how they represent them, or the ways in which they treat them.

Definite dehumanization

Chapter 2 introduced the idea that some practices may be universally dehumanizing because they rule out recognition of the moral status that victims hold as human beings. Now that we have delineated what the distinctive denial of moral standing that characterizes dehumanization consists in, we can establish whether treatments exist that always are dehumanizing. In the discussion above we concluded that the infliction of gratuitous violence and wanton suffering are definitely dehumanizing because these acts entail that the human subjectivity of victims is attributed not even minimal moral relevance.

The challenge here lies in establishing when violence is wanton. In testimonies from refugees, asylum seekers, and other (forced) migrants, people often describe forms of abuse that seem uncalled for and without sense. Yet, it is important to recognize that every move across international borders takes place within a political context that establishes rights and obligations. Much is therefore at stake for all parties involved. The fact that victims did not do anything to provoke violence therefore does not entail that abuses are without (political) reason. The frequent references to violent or humiliating treatment involved in policies of border control may be read within this light.

We may recall here the testimony of the young Moroccan man, discussed in Chapter 2, who told about the violence he endured during his attempt to cross the Serbian-Croatian border: 'The policeman threw me to the floor and just started kicking and kicking. I don't understand. We have the papers from Greece, Macedonia and Serbia but they didn't let us pass and sent us back, like animals'.[27] The man explicitly indicates he did not understand why police officials hurt him as there was no immediate motive that could justify the violence. Yet, the use of violence in this case may be seen as a technique of social control, conveying to refugees, asylum seekers, and other migrants the message to stay away from the border. Violence may be used as an instrument of communication, which is partially directed at the immediate victim(s), but also seeks to appeal to a wider audience, particularly of people in similar circumstances who might be dissuaded from coming to the same place through stories of the fate that awaits them.

The politicized nature of the accommodation of refugees, asylum seekers, and other (unwanted) migrants thus renders it more difficult to assess when violence is truly wanton as the interest in dissuasion makes the use of seemingly incomprehensible forms of mistreatment politically expedient. That is to say, if people who travel to countries that are reluctant to take them in experience suffering through forms of mistreatment that appear aimless and uncalled for, their stories contribute to creating a general image of an unwelcoming space, which offers no safe haven for people in need. This image, in turn, may dissuade others from venturing there, thereby contributing to the political goal of lowering the number of (forced) migrants arriving in these

144 Dehumanization in the Global Migration Crisis

countries. This should put us on our guard not too quickly to characterize mistreatment as wanton within a political climate that securitizes and criminalizes particular forms of migration, as the appearance of gratuitous abuse may serve underlying purposes to keep people out.

In Chapter 2 and Chapter 3, we considered enslavement and torture as potential practices that should be considered de facto dehumanizing, since both include ways of treating people that conflict with core beliefs about what minimal recognition of the moral status of human beings requires. This is the case for enslavement because it effectively takes away people's ownership of their own lives, bodies, and actions. If basic recognition of moral human status entails at least a minimal respect for people's autonomy, engaging in this type of action would not be conceivable while recognizing victims as minimally human in a moral sense.

Stories of enslavement are recounted by refugees, asylum seekers, and other migrants from sub-Saharan Africa. In Chapter 3, the experiences of Amadou were discussed who was held captive in camps in Libya where he was tortured and extorted for money: 'There are many prisons. They are all the same thing. They mistreat people for money'. In an interview with the journalist Ruth Sherlock, Boubaker Nassou, an African man who managed to escape to Tunisia from a similar situation of incarceration in Libya, talks about how he was captured and sold as a slave. One of the prisons in which he was held was used as a slave market: 'This man would come and say, I need one person. They said this one is for $400–400 dinar. This one is for 500. This one is for 300, and this one is for 200. They sell like that'.[28] Boubaker also recounts that people were sometimes bought to be sold again at a higher price: 'You buy me for 200, you sell me for 1,000 or 500 so that you can make some profit out of it'.[29] Many people died from beatings and other forms of mistreatment in the prisons.

The shocking stories recounted by Amadou, Boubaker, and others like them illustrate that enslavement is not a practice from a faraway past but something that continues in our current day and age. Treating people like mere resources to be bought and sold or mistreated for money speaks to a fundamental failure to acknowledge the moral status that the victims hold as human beings. If we consider enslavement through the lens of disregard for the moral relevance of people's human subjectivity, a similar image arises. The definition of slavery that I draw on here is the one proposed by the philosopher Joshua Cohen, who argues that history displays a tension between the way enslaved people were commonly portrayed in legal, moral, and religious sources and the roles they performed in society. Cohen thus argues that

one of the great challenges in understanding slavery and its evolution is to appreciate the ways in which slaves exercised their will and contributed as agents to their
own history under highly constrained circumstances, where one of the many con-
straints upon them was precisely the denial in the public culture of their capacity
for deliberate action.[30]

Cohen notes that some people who were legally classified as enslaved should
not be considered de facto so because of their ability to pursue their own will.
Following the same logic, persons who would not legally classify as enslaved
should be considered de facto enslaved because of their inability to follow
their own will—an idea that is particularly relevant in the current world order
where slavery is officially prohibited yet continues to exist in practice. Cohen
thus proposes to characterize the enslaved as follows:

A slave is, in the first instance, someone largely lacking the power to dispose of his
or her physical and mental powers, including the capacity to produce and control
the body more generally (extending to sexuality and reproduction); the power to
dispose of the means of production; the power to select a place of residence; the
power to associate with others and establish stable bonds; the power to decide on
the manner in which one's children will be raised; and the (political) power to fix
the rules governing the affairs of the state in which one resides.[31]

The denial of the power to dispose of one's own physical and mental powers
is a denial that strikes at the heart of respect for people's human subjectivity.
Enslaved persons, in the true sense of the word, are in a position of suffering treatment from others—as well as having to perform any act that they are
ordered to—without having the power to object. In some cases of enslavement, the human subjectivity of victims is denied. These include cases in
which the enslaved are regarded as cattle, or their subjectivity is denied, as
they are viewed, portrayed, and treated as brute labour force. In other cases,
the human subjectivity of the enslaved is acknowledged but not considered a
reason that counts decisively against their enslavement. In all cases, the moral
relevance of people's human subjectivity is denied. To attribute even minimal
moral relevance to people's human subjectivity entails that we acknowledge
they have a right to direct their own life. The position of the enslaved is therefore per definition dehumanizing, I argue, because persons who are enslaved
cannot be recognized as having a right to direct their own life, given that
this right cannot be acknowledged without them losing their de facto status as enslaved. Approaching another person as a slave therefore rules out
acknowledgement of their human subjectivity in a moral sense.

146 Dehumanization in the Global Migration Crisis

Torture, at least in some of its guises, similarly transgresses fundamental moral limits in interpersonal relations because it involves using people's bodies and minds against them to break their will. Torture expresses contempt for the moral status of human beings, which expresses itself in disregard for the significance of the human subjectivity of victims as a moral factor that should be taken into consideration in how to treat them. In torture, the suffering of victims counts as a reason in favour of mistreating them, rather than against it. In fact, torture requires the infliction of suffering on the victim. The logic of torture dictates that the suffering of victims is used against them as a means of coercion. The suffering of the victim is therefore something to be inflicted, rather than avoided. Imagine a scenario where a victim of torture would ask the torturer to inflict more pain out of sadomasochistic desire. The act of inflicting pain would cease to be torture because the request of the victim would fundamentally change the dynamics of the situation. Torture, furthermore, constitutes an affront to human subjectivity in a further sense. Torture is a form of breaking people. Minimal respect for people's human subjectivity rules out attempts to fundamentally violate and undermine this subjectivity.

The infliction of gratuitous violence, torture, and enslavement thus constitute practices that are de facto dehumanizing because they cannot take place without perpetrators failing to recognize the moral relevance of the human subjectivity of their victims. This sheds light on the situations of Musa and Amadou in Libya, as described in Chapter 3. The testimony of Musa about the ordeals he endured while he was staying in Sabratha and leaving by boat for Europe speaks of the inhumane and brutal treatment of refugees and migrants. Recalling the distressing situation on the boat, Musa observed that

> it was very crazy. All the way to reach here it was. There was a group firing at us while there was a group trying to help us off the boat. They don't care about you. They try to get things from you. If they can't get anything, they just leave you.

Musa describes how the gang used the people on the boat to obtain money and valuables without concern for their interests, as shown by the fact that they were shooting at them to compel them to hand over their belongings. Still, keeping Garrard's distinction between wrong- and evil-doing in mind, we cannot tell whether the group firing at the passengers did so because their suffering counted for nothing or because the advantages of engaging in the armed robbery, in the eyes of the perpetrators, outweighed the importance of their suffering.

The situation in the torture camps in Libya, as described by Amadou, is different. Recounting the abuse and torture he endured in prison camps in

Sabha and Tripoli where human traffickers sought to extort money from prisoners and their relatives, Amadou narrates how people who were unable to raise the requested amount were killed or left to die. The kind of mistreatment that occurred in these camps falls under that exceptional category of acts that are always dehumanizing. This is the case because it is not possible to torture a person to death to extort money without failing to recognize the moral relevance of their human subjectivity. This treatment combines elements of torture and enslavement. The deprivation of freedom as a means of extortion is dehumanizing to people who are unable to pay the ransom as they are forced in a position of slavery. Basic recognition of the moral relevance of human subjectivity entails at least minimal respect for their autonomy, which does not permit this kind of treatment. The elements of torture also entail that minimal respect for the moral relevance of people's human subjectivity was lacking. Even minimal respect for subjectivity rules out torture because the suffering of victims becomes a factor that counts in favour of their mistreatment rather than against it.

Brutalization, as a practice through which perpetrators seek to turn their victims into something less than human, is related to human subjectivity in a complex manner. Like torture, brutalization can be understood as a practice that aims to harm the victim's human subjectivity. The stories by refugees, asylum seekers, and migrants who experienced brutalizing treatments and recount feeling like zombies, ghosts, or dead inside, as discussed in Chapter 4, testify of the detrimental impact that brutalization has had on their subjectivity. The intent to undermine human subjectivity entails a failure to positively value this subjectivity. When perpetrators purposefully seek to brutalize their victims this is therefore dehumanizing, not because it necessarily impedes victims from recognizing their own sense of humanity—which it allegedly usually does not succeed at—but because acts that seek to negate human subjectivity cannot coincide with minimal regard for the moral value of that subjectivity.

Recognizing dehumanization

In cases where torture, enslavement, wanton violence, or intentional brutalization are absent, we may consider the ways in which victims are portrayed and treated, in order to consider whether perpetrators demonstrate disregard for the moral significance of the human subjectivity of victims and therefore engage in dehumanization. There are three steps that can help us in this process. First, it is important to consider whether the human subjectivity of victims is recognized. If this subjectivity is not recognized, it follows that it cannot be attributed any minimal moral value either. Second, we should assess whether the human subjectivity of victims is attributed any moral relevance. If there is factual acknowledgement of the fact that the victims are human beings with subjectivity but the moral relevance of this subjectivity is denied, people are dehumanized. This happens when victims are considered people who can make choices, pursue goals in their lives, and have experiences typical of human beings, yet perpetrators are indifferent to these facts in the sense that these do not affect their decisions on how to treat them. Third, we should take note if the moral value ascribed to the human subjectivity of victims is positive rather than negative. Dehumanization also occurs if the human subjectivity of victims counts as a reason against, rather than in favour of their mistreatment, as their human subjectivity is not valued in this case.

Let us consider first cases of dehumanization that involve a failure to recognize the human subjectivity of victims. This category is made up of treatments, representations, and perceptions that quite literally cast people as animals or mere objects, lacking an inner life of thoughts, feelings, and experiences typical of human beings. It seems that such occurrences are rare, since people tend to recognize the humanity of their victims. The moral relevance of this subjectivity is what is usually at stake in cases of dehumanization. Consider, for example, the situation at the slave market, described above by Boubaker. He recounts how people are bought and sold like merchandise. While this treatment signals contempt for the moral human status of the victims, it is hard to tell whether their human subjectivity is not recognized at all. This may be the case for slavers who only look at people as goods to be traded, and thereby forget about the thoughts, feelings, and experiences that mark the lives of the persons they subjugate. Yet other traders may recognize the fact that their victims have uniquely human traits and mental states and for this reason consider them more valuable merchandise than, for example, cows or sheep. What is evident is that the human subjectivity of victims is not attributed any moral relevance in any case, be it because it is not recognized in the first place or because it is not properly valued.

It seems to be difficult to uphold the denial of victims' human subjectivity while engaging in close interpersonal interactions. Particularly when communication occurs, minimal recognition of a shared human subjectivity seems to mark the situation. After all, communication requires acknowledgement of certain uniquely human capacities. Failures to recognize the human subjectivity of victims, in my view, are therefore more likely to occur at a distance, following Bauman's description of the ways in which 'human waste' is taken 'care' of in the modern world by being made 'invisible by not looking and unthinkable by not thinking'.[32]

In light of these reflections, Barry Malone's appeal that the term 'migrant' should no longer be used, as discussed in Chapter 1, gains new meaning. Malone claims that the word 'dehumanizes and distances' and contributes to a loss of compassion:

> It is not hundreds of people who drown when a boat goes down in the Mediter-ranean, not even hundreds of refugees. It is hundreds of migrants. It is not a person—like you, filled with thoughts and history and hopes—who is on the tracks delaying a train. It is a migrant. A nuisance.[33]

While the morally reductive framing of this term may contribute to making the suffering of migrants 'invisible' and 'unthinkable', I still maintain it would be better, rather than avoiding the term, to infuse it with its original meaning, complemented with a view of the rich life worlds of the persons who are concealed behind it. Babak, who comes from Iran and used to live in the Calais camp, emphasizes this aspect when he highlights: 'A migrant is not only a word, not only news, not only a problem for society: a human is living behind this word. He has feelings, hope for future, and there are some people waiting for him to come back, and a family waiting for good news'.[34]

The more central question to assess whether a particular case involves dehumanization, on my understanding, then is not whether the human subjectivity of victims is recognized, but whether the human subjectivity of victims is attributed any moral relevance, and if so, whether the value ascribed to it is positive. Perpetrators may fail to attribute moral relevance to their victims' human subjectivity in various ways. An evident example is found in Katie Hopkins's column for *The Sun*, discussed in Chapter 2, in which she likens migrants arriving by boat in Europe to cockroaches.[35] The view that gunships should be used to make boats return shows disregard for the moral relevance of the human subjectivity of the persons involved as it displays disdain for the fact that migrants are human beings whose subjective experiences, particularly in terms of suffering, should be a matter of at least minimal concern. Hopkins even explicitly attests not to care about 'pictures of coffins' or 'bodies floating in water'.[36] These words mark the fact that even the deaths of migrants count for nothing in her eyes. Recognizing contempt for the moral status of human beings, as expressed in disregard for the moral significance of their human subjectivity, thus does not always prove difficult.

150 Dehumanization in the Global Migration Crisis

Let us consider some more complex cases. How about depictions that liken migrants to waste or pliable material, as discussed in Chapter 3? Likening people to garbage is dehumanizing because their designation as waste highlights their complete lack of worth in the eyes of the people who liken them to refuse. Like garbage, these people can be discarded without concern. By portraying people as waste, the moral relevance of their human subjectivity is denied as their experiences, mental states, and views are not seen to matter. The depiction as pliable material, which may be used for the economy, is more neutral in terms of ascribing specific characteristics to migrants, yet this neutrality derives precisely from the fact that, following this representation, they have no defining features. On my understanding, this does not amount to dehumanization, since the reason why migrants can be used in this way is precisely because of their uniquely human attributes. It is the human flexibility to adapt and meet existing needs that accounts for their potential to contribute. The human subjectivity of migrants is thereby minimally morally valued in this representation.

What about cases where the human subjectivity of victims is attributed moral relevance, but in a negative sense? The example of the detainee of the processing centre, located in a former zoo, in Tripoli, Libya, who recounted how he and the other inmates were treated and depicted as animals by the guards seems a case in point wherein human subjectivity is considered a reason in favour of mistreatment. The detainee spoke about the different ways in which the staff of the centre sought to humiliate the inmates: 'They don't even enter our room because they say that we smell and have illnesses. They constantly insult us, and call us "You donkey, you dog". When we are moving in their way, they look disgusted and slap us'.[37]

The combination of likening the detainees to donkeys and dogs, expressions of disgust, and abuse signals that the guards attribute the inmates a status below that of human beings, more similar to that of a donkey or a dog, which meant that they could be beaten without concern. Recognition of humanity plays an ambivalent role here. To recognize can mean 'to acknowledge formally', 'to acknowledge or take notice in some definite way', or 'to perceive to be something or someone previously known'.[38] These different meanings suggest that recognition contains a cognitive and a behavioural dimension. While the guards recognized the human subjectivity of the inmates in a cognitive sense, they fail to recognize it in a behavioural sense. By treating the prisoners in the described way, the guards dehumanize the detainees by treating them in a way that suggests that their normative standing is more similar to that of animals, rather than that of fellow human beings. In order to signal this message, the guards

Dehumanization **151**

need to recognize the human subjectivity of their victims. While people can look disgusted at animals and slap them, they would not tell animals they smell or have diseases, insult them, or call them a different kind of animal to humiliate them. The recognized human subjectivity of the victims thus appears to function as a reason that counts in favour of their mistreatment, rather than against it, resulting in forms of abuse and insults, which express utter contempt for the moral value of the human subjectivity of the victims.

Conclusion

This chapter developed an original account of dehumanization as a particular form of moral exclusion that is characterized by neglect of or contempt for the moral status of human beings, which expresses itself in blindness for the significance of the human subjectivity of victims as a moral factor that should be taken into consideration in decisions regarding how to treat them. When persons are dehumanized, so I argued, their experiences, particularly in terms of suffering, no longer matter in the eyes of the dehumanizer(s), or at least not as a moral reason that counts against their mistreatment. Those who are dehumanized are thereby not simply attributed a lower moral standing than persons whom we include in our inner moral circle(s), but excluded from the moral category of humanity altogether. Dehumanization therefore constitutes a uniquely radical form of exclusion.

This perspective has a number of strengths. First, it offers a view of dehumanization that draws a sharp distinction with infra-humanization by focusing on what it entails for people's moral human standing to be fully denied, rather than undermined in a more limited sense. Second, the focus on the denial of the moral significance of human subjectivity helps make sense of different forms of dehumanization that involve various emotions ranging from indifference to hate. Third, this view can account for the fact that perpetrators who allegedly engage in dehumanization frequently interact with victims in ways that seemingly acknowledge their uniquely human traits and mental states. By including two sides to dehumanization, consisting in the denial of human subjectivity itself and the denial of the moral relevance of this subjectivity, the perspective presented here is able to make sense of forms of dehumanization that consist in blindness to the human subjectivity of victims, involve a failure to ascribe moral value to the subjective experiences of victims, or regard the human subjectivity of the victims as a factor in favour of their mistreatment.

152 Dehumanization in the Global Migration Crisis

The attitudes, beliefs, and viewpoints held by the perpetrator(s) are important to determine when dehumanization occurs on my account. Given that perpetrators, at least in certain cases, do not openly share their views of the victims, it can prove difficult to assess when dehumanization occurs. Dehumanization can be recognized most easily in situations characterized by torture, slavery, and wanton abuse, or other forms of treatment that signal that the human subjectivity of the victims is not morally valued. In other situations, perpetrators express their views in their speech and actions. By paying close attention to the way in which perpetrators speak, portray, and act towards victims, we can distil whether dehumanization happens. Now that we know how to recognize dehumanization, let us turn to the final chapter to consider what we can do counteract it.

Notes

1. Charles Taylor, 'Self-Interpreting Animals', in *Human Agency and Language: Philosophical Papers Volume 1* (Cambridge: Cambridge University Press, 1985), pp. 45–76.
2. Edouard Machery, 'Dehumanization and the Loss of Moral Standing', in *The Routledge Handbook of Dehumanization*, edited by Maria Kronfelder (London and New York: Routledge, 2021), p. 146.
3. Idem, 147.
4. Eve Garrard, 'The Nature of Evil', *Philosophical Explorations* 1 (1998): 53, https://doi.org/10.1080/10001998018538689.
5. Ibid.
6. For my earlier work on this account, see: de Ruiter, 'Failing to See' and de Ruiter, 'To Be or Not to Be Human'.
7. Haslam, 'What Is dehumanization?'.
8. I draw, for example, from the work of the social psychologist Susan Opotow, who argues that dehumanization consists in a form of moral exclusion that places people 'outside the boundary in which moral values, rules, and considerations of fairness apply' (p. 1). On her account, dehumanization constitutes an extreme form of moral exclusion, casting victims as 'nonentities, expendable, or underserving' (p. 1). As people are placed outside the circle of persons who are seen to matter, it follows that they can be harmed and exploited without concern. My view seeks to specify what this form of radical exclusion involves and how it differs from other ways in which people may be excluded from moral consideration and regard. See: Susan Opotow, 'Moral Exclusion and Injustice: An Introduction', *Journal of Social Issues* 46 (1990): 1–20, https://doi.org/10.1111/j.1540-4560.1990.tb00268.x.
9. I first learned about dehumanization through Kelman's work. His insights on dehumanization in state-sanctioned atrocities left a deep mark on my thinking and inspired my curiosity on the subject.
10. Kelman, 'Violence Without Moral Restraint', 48–9.
11. Idem, 48.

12. Idem, 49.
13. Ibid.
14. Honneth, *Reification*.
15. Idem, 57–8.
16. Judith Butler, 'Taking Another's View: Ambivalent Implications', in Axel Honneth, *Reification: A New Look at an Old Idea* (Berkeley Tanner Lectures) (Oxford: Oxford University Press, 2012), pp. 97–119 and Raymond Geuss, 'Philosophical Anthropology and Social Criticism', in Axel Honneth, *Reification: A New Look at an Old Idea* (Berkeley Tanner Lectures) (Oxford: Oxford University Press, 2012), pp. 120–30.
17. Lang, 'Questioning Dehumanization', Lang, 'The Limited Importance of Dehumanization', Manne, *Down Girl*, Over, 'Seven Challenges', and Rai, 'Dehumanization Increases Instrumental Violence'.
18. Manne, *Down Girl*, 135.
19. Lang, 'Questioning Dehumanization', 226.
20. Over, 'Seven Challenges', 21.
21. Harmfulness appears as an important factor that impacts on the moral status that is ascribed. A study by the psychologists Jared Piazza, Justin Landy, and Geoffrey Goodwin about the moral standing attributed to animals found that ascribed moral status was negatively impacted by how harmful animals were perceived to be. Similarly, marketing scholar Mansur Khamitov, political scientist Jeremy Rotman, and Piazza found that perceived harmfulness leads to the attribution of lower moral standing to human beings. When people regard others as mean, aggressive, and hostile, they tend to think it is less morally wrong to harm them and that it would be less important to protect them or treat them with compassion or fairness. See: Jared Piazza, Justin F. Landy, and Geoffrey P. Goodwin, 'Cruel Nature: Harmfulness as an Important, Overlooked Dimension in Judgments of Moral Standing', *Cognition* 131 (2014): 108–24, https://doi.org/10.1016/j.cognition.2013.12.013 and Mansur Khamitov, Jeff D. Rotman, and Jared Piazza, 'Perceiving the Agency of Harmful Agents: A Test of Dehumanization Versus Moral Typecasting Accounts', *Cognition* 146 (2016): 33–47, https://doi.org/10.1016/j.cognition.2015.09.009.
22. Mikkola, *The Wrong of Injustice*.
23. Idem, 168.
24. Idem, 165 and 170.
25. Anna Galeotti, 'Respect as Recognition: Some Political Implications', in *The Plural States of Recognition*, edited by Michel Seymour (Basingstoke: Palgrave Macmillan, 2010), p. 85.
26. I use the original pronouns from Garrard's text to stay close to the original formulation and favour readability. I do not hereby intend to imply that victims of rape are always women and perpetrators are necessarily men.
27. Médecins Sans Frontières, *Obstacle Course to Europe*, 44.
28. Sherlock and Al-Arian, 'Migrants Captured in Libya'.
29. Ibid.
30. Joshua Cohen, 'The Arc of the Moral Universe', in *The Arc of the Moral Universe and Other Essays* (Cambridge MA: Harvard University Press, 2010), p. 24.
31. Idem, 25.
32. Bauman, *Wasted Lives*, 27.
33. Malone, 'Why Al Jazeera'.

34. *Voices from the 'Jungle'*, 126.
35. Hopkins, 'Rescue Boats?'
36. Ibid.
37. As cited in Vaughan-Williams, '"We Are Not Animals!"', 1.
38. 'Recognize', *Merriam Webster Dictionary*, https://www.merriam-webster.com/dictionary/recognize.

Conclusion

> When someone possesses a bit of humanity you should feel for people
> with these difficult experiences.
>
> **Hanan, refugee from Syria**

Countering dehumanization

Hanan is a young Syrian woman who fled from Aleppo to Germany. When asked what humanity means to her, she explains it involves showing empathy for strangers in need: 'As a human you help one another. When someone does not know me and he helps me, he empathizes with me and helps me, that is for me humanity'. She believes that the treatment of refugees does not always demonstrate this kind of compassionate engagement. Humanity, in her eyes, requires that people feel for others who flee their homes and seek to help them. A double movement is visible in her narrative. Her words reveal hope for humanity demonstrating concern and care for the plea of refugees. At the same time, her claim that people should empathize with persons with difficult experiences if they are to possess even a bit of humanity involves the risk of denying the humanity of those who do not feel for them. Her words reflect the danger of continuing a vicious circle of dehumanization where the denial of care for victims can lead them to doubt the humanity of those who disregard the moral relevance of their suffering.

Hanan's story speaks to the difficulty of putting an end to dehumanization. This final chapter brings the analysis in this book to a close by considering the opportunities and challenges involved in efforts to resist dehumanization. The ultimate aim of this book is to understand dehumanization better in the hopes that it may one day be dispelled altogether. While this prospect may be optimistic, examining ways to mitigate dehumanization can yield insights into how it can be challenged and counteracted, if not avoided completely. This chapter therefore considers what could and should be done to resist dehumanization through attempts to counteract, challenge, and mitigate its exclusionary logic.

Dehumanization in the Global Migration Crisis. Adrienne de Ruiter, Oxford University Press. © Adrienne de Ruiter (2024).
DOI: 10.1093/oso/9780198893400.003.0007

156   Dehumanization in the Global Migration Crisis

The first part identifies three constitutive elements of our response to dehumanization—persuasion, support, and coercion—and sets out why strategies of persuasion should form the basis of our approach. The second part explains how support for the victims of dehumanization is required to rebuild trust in the moral human community and affirm the moral significance of their human subjectivity. Beyond persuasion and support, coercive means may be needed to resist dehumanization in light of its detrimental impact on victims. The third part therefore considers what forms of coercion, aimed at restricting the space for action and expression available to perpetrators, are conceivable and permissible to counteract dehumanization. The final part brings the various lines of the argument together.

Persuasion against dehumanization

The previous chapter developed an account of dehumanization as a particular form of moral exclusion that is characterized by disregard for the moral status of human beings, which expresses itself in blindness for the significance of the human subjectivity of victims as a moral factor that should be taken into consideration in decisions on how to treat them. Since dehumanization springs from the mind of the perpetrator(s), I argue that our attempts to counter it should focus foremost on resisting attitudes, beliefs, and viewpoints that support dehumanization.

The perspective of dehumanization presented in this book highlights that there are two ways in which the moral status of human beings can be denied in a dehumanizing way: by failing to recognize that victims have human subjectivity or by failing to acknowledge the moral relevance of this subjectivity as a factor that counts against their mistreatment. Given these two pathways to dehumanization, there may be two paths out of dehumanization as well. When the human subjectivity of victims is denied, perpetrators should be persuaded that their victims do in fact hold such subjectivity. When the moral relevance of their subjectivity is denied, a different path should be followed.

On my view, people tend to recognize the fact that other human beings experience the world in similar ways as a reason not to callously mistreat them, even if circumstances can lead to other reasons outweighing concerns about harming them. Persuasion against dehumanization therefore does not require convincing perpetrators of views that are wholly alien to them. It is rather about reminding them of beliefs they already hold and bringing about the realization that their attitude towards and treatment of victims is in tension with these core values. The question is how this can be done most effectively.

The philosopher Richard Rorty argues that the tendency to dehumanize is best downplayed by a sentimental education that nurtures people's sympathy for others by extending the boundaries of the community of persons that are seen as 'people like us'. Based on a view of morality inspired by the ideas of the philosopher David Hume, Rorty claims that people are more likely to come to recognize others as fellow human beings through the telling of 'sad and sentimental stories' than through rationalist teachings that uphold the fundamental equality of human beings as moral agents.[1]

On the one hand, I am sympathetic to Rorty's proposition that a Humean 'sentimental education' can be helpful in countering dehumanization. This proposal corresponds to the findings of studies in psychology, which suggest that affective engagement is necessary for the claims of people to be perceived as moral claims.[2] As we have seen in previous chapters, without this type of engagement, people may treat others in ways similar to psychopaths, without concern for their vulnerability to suffering.[3] On the other hand, I am concerned that if we would make people more empathetic by telling them the 'right stories', which make them feel for refugees, asylum seekers, and other migrants, who is to say that when other storytellers come along that tell them less benign tales, they may not just as well be swayed in this other direction.

Endeavours to encourage affective engagement with people may be insufficient to counter dehumanization, furthermore, because these efforts can lead to recognition of similarity in too limited a sense. A similar concern is expressed by the English scholar Lynn Festa, who notes that the focus on pity that characterizes sentimentalism produces a definition of humanity tied to suffering.[4] In my view, pity is an elementary way to come to appreciate the moral value of the subjective experiences of other living beings. Yet, recognizing the moral relevance of people's human subjectivity requires more than just pity for their suffering. It also requires respect for their agency and freedom.

A further limit to Rorty's account, in my view, is that the strategy of countering dehumanization through the recounting of sentimental stories ignores the larger societal, institutional, and political influences that encourage people to hold dehumanized perceptions in the first place. This sentimental education targets the symptoms of dehumanization, but not its root causes. To get to these root causes it is important to appreciate the way in which dehumanization constitutes a social and political phenomenon.

We thus need to consider the conditions under which dehumanization comes about. People usually do not spontaneously engage in dehumanization, I maintain, but are brought to dehumanize others through the

158   Dehumanization in the Global Migration Crisis

manipulation of their perceptions through propaganda and ideology.[5] Dehumanization is induced by social factors. I draw this conclusion from the fact that people generally develop dehumanized perceptions at particular times in history and in particular societies, namely when and where societies are characterized by the dissemination of dehumanizing images and representations, such as, for instance, frequently occurs in times of war. The conclusion that dehumanization should be seen as a political phenomenon is also supported by the observation that dehumanization generally involves the opposition between an 'us' versus a 'them' rather than an 'I' versus a 'you'.

If dehumanization contains an important collective dimension, it follows that efforts to counter dehumanization should also focus on the collective, and not just the individual, level. Efforts to prevent and mitigate dehumanization should therefore aim at countering the dissemination of dehumanizing images and representations in propaganda and hate speech as well as blaming and shaming governments that employ, allow, condone, or permit dehumanization. Countering the dissemination of dehumanizing images and representations often has a double aim, namely to halt the spread of dehumanizing perceptions and to counter and prevent incitement to mass atrocity crimes.[6] As the ideology scholar Jonathan Leader Maynard insightfully points out, efforts to counter ideologies that legitimate the use of excessive violence can take 'persuasive' or 'coercive' forms.[7] Persuasive forms aim at contesting the content of incendiary messages, whereas coercive forms seek to block the transmission of dehumanizing propaganda and hate speech.[8]

Which of these two strategies is the most appropriate is context-dependent. If dehumanizing propaganda and hate speech are produced by a single source, it may be opportune to block their transmission. This can take the form of 'jamming' hate radio and television broadcasts, seizing broadcasting transmitters, or destroying radio and television stations.[9] While coercive means of countering dehumanizing ideology and hate speech may be appropriate when there is a need to rapidly interfere with broadcasts, for example, in a context of increasing antagonism turning violent, such interventions are often risky and costly. For instance, the possibility of coercive intervention was considered in the case of the radio channel Radio-Télévision Libre des Milles Collines in Rwanda, but this idea was rejected because of the high costs involved.[10] Nowadays, with information spreading over the internet, it seems even less feasible to counter dehumanizing propaganda and hate speech through a blockade of the sources of dehumanizing contents.[11] Blocking transmissions can also seemingly provide legitimacy to limiting free press and freedom of speech, which is likely to strengthen the hand of politicians who seek to use media to spread antagonistic and polarizing views.[12]

Conclusion   159

Interfering with broadcasts, furthermore, does not engage with the content of the messages and can therefore not contribute to changing the viewpoints of people.

A more promising way of countering dehumanizing ideology and hate speech seems to lie in challenging its content through persuasive means, such as the dissemination of counter-messages or the diversification of the audience of broadcasts. Journalist and dangerous speech scholar Susan Benesch notes, for example, that the KTN television network in Kenya changed its policies after the widespread political violence of 2007–2008 to broadcast clips of Kenyan politicians with subtitles in Swahili or English in order to discourage the use of inflammatory speech in vernacular languages.[13] A broader campaign was set up in Kenya to prevent new violent outbreaks and to mitigate social polarization before the 2013 elections. This campaign included initiatives by civil society groups to monitor media, the raising of awareness among journalists of their responsibility in informing the public about politics, and the distribution of messages of peace and union in radio and television broadcasts.[14] The case of Kenya suggests that efforts to counter propaganda and hate speech through counter-messages can contribute to dissuading people from engaging in violent acts and promoting more positive views of other groups in society.[15]

Media campaigns to alter public perceptions of refugees, asylum seekers, and migrants hold promise to challenge perspectives on global migration. Considering a campaign organized by the Canadian government in late 2015, the social psychologists Victoria Esses, Stelian Medianu, and Alina Sutter report that changes in discourse that cast the accommodation of refugees in a positive light led to a shift in public opinion.[16] While this effect did not occur among all ranks of society, private sponsorship of refugees by citizens increased, which could in turn contribute towards the further humanization of refugees: 'The personal contact and provision of direct assistance to refugees on a regular basis surely served to individuate them and promote an understanding of their thoughts, feelings, and intentions, with consequent further humanization. This suggests that once rehumanization is initiated, it may have a burgeoning effect'.[17]

The digital economy and culture scholar Yasmin Ibrahim and journalism scholar Anita Howarth highlight the importance of the creation of (media) spaces where migrants can tell their stories in their own words. Against distanced framings frequently used in mainstream media, Ibrahim and Howarth argue that letting migrants speak for themselves can give rise to an image that is more relatable and authentic.[18] In a similar vein, the communication studies scholar Roy Schwartzman calls for the use of first-hand testimonies to

160 Dehumanization in the Global Migration Crisis

counter xenophobic portrayals of migrants in political rhetoric, highlighting how personal narratives can bring in more nuanced individual viewpoints, bring out the similarities and differences between migrant experiences, and shed light on the political and situational contexts within which people's lives unfold.[19] While I am critical of considering de-individualization in media frames a form of dehumanization for reasons set out in Chapter 1, I believe that first-hand stories by refugees, asylum seekers, and other migrants can help humanize these groups as telling one's own story in one's own words is a powerful way of displaying one's human's subjectivity.

Persuasion should be central, then, to our efforts to counter and mitigate dehumanization, since dehumanization springs from the attitudes, beliefs, and perceptions of perpetrators, which are elicited by social and political influencing. Dehumanization comes about in dialogical relations where people come to doubt that others have human subjectivity or that it holds any positive moral weight. Persuasive means are needed to change the viewpoints of the perpetrator(s) by emphasizing the moral relevance of the human subjectivity of the victims through both emotive and rational means. Ideally, refugees, asylum seekers, and migrants themselves take part in this process of countering dehumanizing frames. Telling one's own story is a powerful way of displaying one's human's subjectivity. By raising their voice, people may dispel the denial of their agency. Displaced persons should therefore be included in attempts to counter their dehumanization through persuasive means, whenever possible.

Standing with the victims

Besides efforts to dissuade people from engaging in dehumanization and persuading those who do of the wrongness of their views and actions, it is important to stand with the victims. Support is required to rebuild trust in the moral human community and affirm the moral significance of their human subjectivity. Since dehumanization is a social and political phenomenon, the reality of dehumanization is not determined by the relation between the perpetrator and the victim alone. A social universe surrounds them, which is made up of persons who can strengthen the position of the perpetrator (through action or inaction), aid the victim, standby as witnesses, or look away.

The role of onlookers, in moral terms, is always to stand with the victims. First, supporting the victims is key to expressing that they still belong to the moral community of humanity from which perpetrators seek to expel them.

Second, the moral disregard that characterizes the position that perpetrators take towards their victims entails that the latter are deprived of effective means to object against the treatment they are given. Since no positive moral value is attributed to the human subjectivity of victims, their appeals against the treatment they receive are effectively voided. Victims are silenced, at least in the interactions with perpetrators who dehumanize them, by the fact that the attitude of moral disregard that dehumanizers take towards them makes their appeals inaudible as moral appeals. This lack of means to make a moral appeal adds to the collective moral obligation on the side of bystanders to stand up for victims whose pleas become inaudible for those who mistreat them.

This moral obligation to counter dehumanization derives from the need(s) and value of the victim(s), rather than from liability on the side of bystanders for the wrong done to the victim(s). The argument here is similar to the one that suggests that people who see someone drowning have an obligation to rescue him or her, irrespective of whether they had any role in how the person ended up in the water.[20] Although a person who pushed someone in the water would be under a greater duty to rescue him or her, because of his or her causal responsibility, this fact does not discharge bystanders from their collective obligation to prevent the person from drowning, if capable of doing so. In a similar way, the obligation to prevent and counter dehumanization should be seen as a collective moral obligation because it derives from the need(s) and value of the victim(s), rather than from causal responsibility on the side of identifiable persons (other than the perpetrators) for the wrong done to the victim(s). This moral obligation is shared by all those who witness dehumanization and have adequate capacities to respond to it. These two criteria are crucial because people cannot be held responsible for what they are not aware of or what they are unable to do something about.[21]

On the individual and local level, people can resist dehumanization and stand by victims by raising their voice. Smith notes that there is a duty on people to fight against dehumanization 'in small ways in daily life, calling it out where you see it, objecting when people you speak to or people who represent you employ its dangerous rhetoric, and, crucially opposing it in the voting booth.'[22] Two things are gained by speaking out. Not only are perpetrators confronted with the fact that their views and representations are not deemed acceptable by everyone, potentially placing strain on their views. Victims may also note that people speak up for them, reaffirming their moral standing as fellow human beings.

On the political level, efforts to prevent and mitigate dehumanization can be directed at blaming and shaming governments that employ, allow, permit,

162   Dehumanization in the Global Migration Crisis

or condone dehumanization.[23] It is most effective if these actions are taken by political actors with influence. The point of capacity, mentioned above, is important here because it suggests that states as well as (inter)national institutions and organizations may have a greater responsibility in preventing, countering, and punishing dehumanization than do individuals, given that states, institutions, and organizations generally have a greater capacity to act and intervene than individuals do.[24] This is especially the case when we recall that dehumanization should be seen as a collective phenomenon, which is often induced by social and political factors.

Blaming and shaming are important forms of resisting dehumanization because they respond to the experience of the victims who are unable to effectively call their wrongdoers to account. It can have an important psychological effect on the victims as well in demonstrating that their normatively human status is acknowledged by others. In this way, blaming can be understood as form of protest against the way in which people are treated.[25] Acts of blaming and shaming furthermore signal normative expectations and can contribute to the creation of a normative environment that is less permissive of dehumanization, in general.[26]

Standing with victims may also be the only way of seeking to suture the broken bonds and restore a sense of community and trust in others on the side of victims. Dehumanization may leave deep psychological marks as the chapter on brutalization in particular has shown. It is crucial that witnesses stand against dehumanization to strengthen the resources of victims to consider themselves as persons who stand in supportive relations to others. The philosopher James Sias notes how the recognition of one's moral status by others may be important for one's self-understanding and ability to engage with others partaking in a shared moral community: 'If this is right, then failures of recognition are not just wrongful omissions, but harmful ones as well, and the particular harm involved is a matter of ruining (even if only temporarily) another's conception of himself or herself as fully deserving of others' respect'.[27]

The harmful effects on people's sense of self and relations to others present a forceful claim to prevent dehumanization. If it is proves too late for that, it is important to stand with victims in seeking to put an end to their moral exclusion by perpetrators. After dehumanization ends, attention should be paid to caring for the victims in terms of attending to the wounds that their exclusion from the moral community may have left. Here, standing by victims entails creating space for listening to their stories, using imaginative means to seek to place ourselves in their position, and reaffirming their belonging.[28]

Conclusion   **163**

Vladimir Jović from the Center for Rehabilitation of Torture Victims in Belgrade, Serbia, highlights that counselling should constitute an important element of the process of rehumanization of refugees who experienced torture and other traumatic events.[29] This author indicates that their suffering is caused by interpersonal trauma. Safety, in both a legal and a psychological sense, is therefore required to help in the process of recovery. Standing with victims of dehumanization thus entails providing them with 'psychological space in which a traumatized person can feel safe and start to recover, and give meaning to their experiences, and develop attachments to individuals and objects in a new environment'.[30]

Ending dehumanization through coercive means

Beyond countering dehumanizing messages through persuasion, supporting the victims in reaffirming their belonging to the human community, blaming and shaming governments that employ, enable, condone, or permit dehumanization, coercive means may also be needed to resist dehumanization. Persuasion may take time to achieve results. Standing with victims while allowing their mistreatment to continue may seem like a farce. Blaming and shaming actors may not be enough to bring an end to dehumanization. It is therefore important to consider when coercion may be used to counteract dehumanization.

Coercive means only seem useful as a response to dehumanizing portrayals or treatment. Perception falls outside of the domains that can reasonably be expected to be influenced by coercion, unless we would be willing to use brainwashing techniques. While the mind is better left to persuasion, coercion may be required to resist dehumanizing treatments and depictions in light of their detrimental impact on victims.

In terms of representation, the analysis above considered the use of coercive means to block the transmission of dehumanizing propaganda and hate speech. While this approach may offer the quickest means of mitigating the spread of dehumanizing viewpoints, it comes at a high price. In our current world, where information is quickly shared through diverse information networks, it seems unlikely that transmissions can be successfully blocked through this type of interventions. Blocking does not help change the views of people and offers ammunition for authoritarian rulers to allegedly justify limitations to free press and freedom of speech. Coercion therefore seems less promising in this context than persuasion.

164 Dehumanization in the Global Migration Crisis

Coercive means may be more at their place to respond to dehumanizing forms of treatment. Indeed, the prosecution of perpetrators of crimes in which dehumanization plays a key role, such as torture and enslavement, is crucial. Putting wrongdoers on trial is important for several reasons. The prosecution of slavery and torture (as well as other crimes in which dehumanization often plays a significant role, such as genocide and war crimes) is imperative in the first place because these acts constitute egregious violations of non-derogable human rights. Admittedly, prosecution is not directed against dehumanization but against the callous forms of mistreatment that coincide with dehumanization. It is important to note, however, that these legal actions do communicate a powerful message that contradicts the central belief in dehumanization that victims are excluded from a moral community that sets limits to the ways in which people are to be treated. The fact that victims of these crimes are protected by law, as illustrated by the fact that the violation of their rights results in legal prosecution, demonstrates victims are included in the moral category of humanity and thereby reaffirms their status as persons whose experiences merit moral consideration.

In this sense, the coercive force that underpins prosecution is expressive of the idea of moral inclusion. Prosecution therefore contains elements of persuasion, which may dissuade perpetrators of dehumanization from acting on their belief that victims hold no relevant moral standing, and support for victims, whose moral status is acknowledged through the legal attention for their cause. While these factors are important, coercive means to counter dehumanization are limited by the fact that rights entitle people to particular forms of treatment, but cannot control the ways in which people are perceived.

As noted in the previous chapter, Galeotti offers an insightful discussion of the distinction between respect and rights, which is also relevant to the point I wish to make here. Galeotti notes that to be recognized as a subject of rights is a necessary, but not a sufficient condition for being respected.[31] This is the case because a claim to respect transcends claims for a particular form of treatment, which could be expressed in the terms of specific rights. Galeotti thus notes that a right claim is claim for an 'an acknowledging attitude which escapes definition and precise behaviour'.[32] Since dehumanization involves the denial of a particular form of respect, it follows that coercive means to end rights violations and persecute the perpetrators are unlikely to suffice to end dehumanization.

Within the context of the global migration crisis, coercive means may be used to guarantee more humane conditions for migrants held in detention centres. The Manus facility was closed, for example, as a consequence of legal action taken by the government of Papua New Guinea.[33] In general, however, it seems difficult to effectuate change through legal actions as parties are generally reluctant to go beyond blaming and shaming. This tendency is illustrated, for example, by the International Criminal Court's prosecutor's decision not to take further legal action to investigate contraventions of human rights law in the Australian offshore detention centres in spite of the conclusion that the conditions in facilities amount to 'cruel, inhuman, or degrading treatment'.[34] At the national level, legal scholar Esna Abdulamit proposes contract reforms and stricter oversight to promote the 're-humanization' of the US immigration detention system, presenting another potential path to reconfiguring the conditions under which migrants are detained using legal measures.[35]

Coercive means may delimit the ways in which perpetrators can treat their victims, but the underlying perceptions as the fundamental issue in dehumanization, require other means to be effectively addressed. A combination of persuasion, support for victims, and coercive means to end the most flagrant abuses following from in its wake therefore seems most appropriate to counter dehumanization.

The wrongs that remain

The perspective of dehumanization set forth in this book entails both good and bad news. My good news is that—on my view—dehumanization is less common than is generally assumed. My bad news is that dehumanization is far worse than we tend to think. Through dehumanization, people are not considered as lesser human beings, but no longer regarded as morally human at all. This exclusion from the moral category of humanity entails that the experiences of the dehumanized no longer hold any positive moral weight in the eyes of perpetrators.

Chapter 1 showed that dehumanization is often conflated with related processes in scholarly writing, human rights commentary, and journalistic opinion pieces on the ongoing migration crisis. The imprecise use of the notion is problematic, so I argued, because it may well render claims that refugees, asylum seekers, and unwanted migrants are dehumanized less convincing. There is a risk involved in the manner in which advocates for the rights of displaced persons appeal to the notion of dehumanization in underdetermined, vague, and overly inclusive ways to bring home the point that certain treatments and portrayals of refugees and migrants are inadmissible. In overusing this term, the distinct nature and wrong of dehumanization

166 Dehumanization in the Global Migration Crisis

become more difficult to discern and people may come to feel that advocates for a more humane treatment of refugees, asylum seekers, and other (forced) migrants overstate their case and present the plea of the displaced in more forceful terms than circumstances justify. De-individualization, stigmatization, marginalization, criminalization, and infra-humanization unsettle the social and moral position that refugees, asylum seekers, and migrants hold. Still, these practices only turn into dehumanization when morally degrading portrayals or treatments deny the moral status that victims hold as human beings. Many cases of mistreatment and misrepresentation fall short of this. Dehumanization involves expelling people from the moral category of humanity, rather than assigning them a low or marginal position within this category. If we ignore this distinction, we lose sight of what dehumanization is and why it requires a robust response.

Chapter 2 showed that the moral sense of humanity is central to dehumanization by illustrating how animalization becomes dehumanizing when the distinctively human quality of the feelings, thoughts, and life of the person(s) involved is discredited by attributing to it a lower, animalistic, status. Through dehumanizing forms of animalization, people are usually seen, portrayed, or treated as mere vermin or other lowly animals, who are devoid of a human inner life, or as dangerous predators, whose experiences need not concern us because of their viciousness or depravity.

Chapter 3 illustrated that objectification turns into a form of dehumanization when treating, portraying, or viewing people as objects entails a failure to ascribe them human subjectivity. While in cases of animalization, the distinctively human quality of the feelings, thoughts, and inner life of the person(s) involved is discredited, these feelings, thoughts, and inner life are denied or ignored in cases of objectification. Objectification is therefore foremost marked by an absence. It is characterized by a lack of connection as the subjectivity of the victim(s) does not resonate with the perpetrator(s). In cases of representation, the likening to an object works in a metaphoric sense to signal that the victim holds no inner life, and is more similar to a thing without agency, rather than a living, thinking, and feeling subject. This kind of portrayal justifies indifference to the well-being of the victims as there is nothing 'there' to be concerned about. With treatment, objectification tends towards disregard for the interests, needs, and viewpoints of the persons involved. This is reflected in cases of inhumane treatment where the perpetrators recognize nothing of moral importance in their victims that would count against their abuse. Objectification furthermore characterizes failures to act on behalf of victims when these omissions result from utter indifference to their fate.

Chapter 4 argued that it is uncommon for brutalizing treatment to genuinely alienate people from their own sense of humanity. The human mind often turns out to be resilient and the complete disavowal of one's own sense of humanity seems exceptionally uncommon. We should therefore not too easily buy into the logic of perpetrators who hold that victims can truly be made less than human through brutalizing treatment. Generally, victims are not turned into something less than human but impeded from enjoying or expressing their full range of human qualities. Only when the human spirit is utterly broken is it possible to claim that brutalization dehumanizes people in the sense that they come to fail to recognize their own human subjectivity. What brutalizing treatment does tend to bring about, however, is a weakening of the sense of one's humanity and belonging to the world.

Chapter 5 reconceptualized the notion of moral exclusion that is central to understanding dehumanization. Dehumanization, on this view, consists in a particular form of moral exclusion that is characterized by neglect of or contempt for the moral status of human beings, which expresses itself in blindness to the significance of the human subjectivity of victims as a moral factor that should be taken into consideration in decisions on how to treat them. This means that when persons are dehumanized, their experiences no longer matter in the eyes of the dehumanizer(s), or at least not as moral factors that count against their mistreatment. Those who are dehumanized are thereby not simply attributed a lower moral standing than persons whom we include in our inner moral circle(s), but excluded from the moral category of humanity altogether. Dehumanization, therefore, constitutes a uniquely radical form of exclusion.

An implication of this view of dehumanization is that many wrongs remain even if we would be able to put an end to dehumanizing practices. Banning dehumanization would not entail that people are always guaranteed proper rights and respect. Discrimination, marginalization, stigmatization, infra-humanization, and inhumane treatment would continue to lead to suffering and produce unfair disadvantages in life. Our moral duties therefore do not end with resisting dehumanization.

Although this book has set out that dehumanization occurs less frequently than is commonly assumed, this does not entail that we should be less concerned about it. The reason for this is that dehumanization is an unusual, but exceptionally severe, form of moral exclusion. While we should view dehumanization as an extreme phenomenon that does not occur frequently, it warrants serious attention because the wrong that is done to victims is of a particularly grave kind. Dehumanization, I conclude, constitutes the most

168 Dehumanization in the Global Migration Crisis

acute status wrong that can be inflicted on people because the failure to recognize the minimal moral relevance of people's subjectivity casts them out from the moral category of humanity.

Notes

1. Rorty, 'Human Rights, Rationality, and Sentimentality', 172.
2. Elisa Aaltola, 'Affective Empathy as Core Moral Agency: Psychopathy, Autism and Reason Revisited', *Philosophical Explorations* 17 (2004): 81, https://doi.org/10.1080/13869795. 2013.825004.
3. Ibid. This conclusion also relates to the discussion of Honneth's study of dehumanization as a form of reification in Chapter 3 and Chapter 5.
4. Lynn Festa, 'Humanity without Feathers', *Humanity: An International Journal of Human Rights, Humanitarianism, and Development* 1 (2010): 13, https://doi.org/10.1353/hum. 2010.0007.
5. Similar points are brought up by Honneth and Smith. David Livingstone Smith notes, for example: 'Thinking of others as less than human isn't something that arises spontaneously from within as a response to "difference."' See: Smith, *On Inhumanity*, 7.
6. The idea that countering dehumanizing propaganda and hate speech can aid the prevention and mitigation of mass atrocity crimes is presented, for example, in Jamie Metzl, 'Information Intervention: When Switching Channels Isn't Enough', *Foreign Affairs* 76 (1997): 15–20, https://doi.org/10.2307/20048273, Alexander Dale, 'Countering Hate Messages that Lead to Violence: The United Nations' Chapter VII Authority to Use Radio Jamming to Halt Incendiary Broadcasts', *Duke Journal of Comparative & International Law* 11 (2001): 109–32, https://scholarship.law.duke.edu/djcil/vol11/iss1/6, Monroe E. Price and Mark Thomson (eds.), *Forging Peace: Intervention, Human Rights and the Management of Media Space* (Edinburgh: Edinburgh University Press, 2002), and Susan Benesch, 'Words as Weapons', *World Policy Journal* 29 (2012): 7–12, https://doi.org/10. 1177/0740277512443794. See also Scott Straus, 'What is the Relationship between Hate Radio and Violence? Rethinking Rwanda's "Radio Machete"', *Politics & Society* 35 (2007): 609–37, https://doi.org/10.1177/0032329207308181 for a critical analysis of the impact of propaganda broadcasts during the Rwandan genocide.
7. Jonathan Leader Maynard, 'Combating Atrocity-Justifying Ideologies', in *The Responsibility to Prevent: Overcoming the Challenges to Atrocity Prevention*, edited by Serena K. Sharma and Jennifer M. Welsh (Oxford: Oxford University Press, 2015), p. 219.
8. Ibid.
9. See: Metzl, 'Information Intervention', 18, Dale, 'Countering Hate Messages', Monroe E. Price, 'Information Intervention: Bosnia, the Dayton Accords, and the Seizure of Broadcasting Transmitters', *Cornell International Law Journal* 33 (2000): 67–112, http:// scholarship.law.cornell.edu/cilj/vol33/iss1/2, Leader Maynard, 'Combating Atrocity-Justifying Ideologies', 219, and Larry May, *Genocide: A Normative Account* (Cambridge and New York: Cambridge University Press, 2010), p. 232.
10. May notes regarding the case of the RTML that '[t]he radio station's tower could have been destroyed, the broadcasts could have been jammed, or there could have been

"counter-broadcasts" transmitted through the auspices of foreign States. Here, according to Samantha Power, the United States was best placed to act. A Pentagon analysis concluded that the jamming would be too difficult and costly' (p. 232).

11. For a discussion of the legal aspects involved, see: Janice Yu, 'Regulation of Social Media Platforms to Curb ISIS Incitement and Recruitment: The Need for an International Framework and Its Free Speech Implications', *Journal of Global Justice and Public Policy* 4 (2018): 1–29. See also: Monroe E. Price, 'Orbiting Hate? Satellite Transponders and Free Expression', in *The Content and Context of Hate Speech: Rethinking Regulation and Responses*, edited by Michael Herz (Cambridge and New York: Cambridge University Press, 2012), pp. 514–38.

12. Smith, *On Inhumanity*, 187.

13. Benesch, 'Words as Weapons', 10.

14. See: Serena K. Sharma, 'The 2007–8 Post-Election Crisis in Kenya', in *The Responsibility to Prevent: Overcoming the Challenges to Atrocity Prevention*, edited by Serena K. Sharma and Jennifer M. Welsh (Oxford: Oxford University Press, 2015), p. 300 and Jessica Gustafsson, 'Media and the 2013 Kenyan Election: From Hate Speech to Peace Preaching', *Conflict & Communication* 15 (2016): 1–13.

15. It is important to note, however, that initiatives to counter impunity accompanied these communication campaigns. The obtained results may therefore not be attributed solely to the effects of the media reforms. See: Sharma, 'The 2007–8 Post-Election Crisis in Kenya'.

16. Esses, Medianu, and Sutter, 'The Dehumanization and Rehumanization of Refugees', 285.

17. Idem, 286.

18. Yasmin Ibrahim and Anita Howarth, 'Sounds of the Jungle: Rehumanizing the Migrant', *JOMEC Journal Journalism Media and Cultural Studies* 7 (2015): 1–18.

19. Roy Schwartzman, 'Rehumanizing the Alien "Invaders": How Testimony Can Counteract Xenophobia', *International Journal of Communication and Media Studies* 10 (2020): 5–12.

20. An important difference between these cases lies in the fact that a person who is left to drown will die, whereas a person who is dehumanized often may not. The harms that are involved in these situations are thus not the same and the obligations on the side of third parties to intervene are therefore not the same either.

21. Regarding the second point, the philosopher Onora O'Neill notes that 'both institutions and individuals can have obligations *if, but only if*, they have adequate capabilities to fulfil or discharge those obligations'. See: Onora O'Neill, *Justice Across Boundaries: Whose Obligations?* (Cambridge: Cambridge University Press, 2016), p. 169.

22. Smith, *On Inhumanity*, 185.

23. An exception should be made for governments that are unable, rather than unwilling, to act against dehumanization employed by other actors in society. In this case, a more appropriate response would be to provide assistance to help strengthen the government's capacities for governance.

24. This argument corresponds to the one made by James Pattison for effectiveness as one of the main criteria for determining the legitimacy of humanitarian intervention. See: James Pattison, 'Effectiveness and the Moderate Instrumentalist Approach', in *Humanitarian Intervention & The Responsibility to Protect: Who Should Intervene?* (Oxford: Oxford University Press, 2010), pp. 69–97. Another factor that can play a role in the attribution of collective responsibility is whether special ties exists between victims and bystanders,

170 Dehumanization in the Global Migration Crisis

as is suggested by David Miller. See: David Miller, 'Distributing Responsibilities', *Journal of Political Philosophy* 9 (2001): 453–71, https://doi.org/10.1111/1467-9760.00136.

25. The philosopher Angela Smith notes, for example, that blaming has two functions: 'first, to *register* the fact that the person wronged did not deserve such treatment by *challenging* the moral claim implicit in the wrongdoer's action; second, to prompt moral recognition and acknowledgment of this fact on the part of the wrongdoer and/or others in the moral community' (p. 43). See: Angela M. Smith, 'Moral Blame and Moral Protest', in *Blame: Its Nature and Norms*, edited by D. Justin Coates and Neal A. Tognazzini (Oxford and New York: Oxford University Press, 2013), pp. 27–48. Similar accounts of the function of blaming are provided by Pamela Hieronymi in 'Articulating An Uncompromising Forgiveness', *Philosophy and Phenomenological Research* 62 (2001): 529–55, https://doi.org/10.2307/2653535, and Christopher Evan Franklin, 'Valuing Blame', in *Blame: Its Nature and Norms*, edited by D. Justin Coates and Neal A. Tognazzini (Oxford and New York: Oxford University Press, 2013), pp. 207–23.

26. The notion of a normative environment of permissiveness is presented by Jennifer M. Welsh and Serena K. Sharma in 'Operationalizing the Responsibility to Prevent' (Oxford Institute for Ethics, Law, and Armed Conflict), April 2012, https://www.oxfordmartin.ox.ac.uk/downloads/briefings/201204ELACResponsibility-to-Prevent.pdf, p. 7.

27. James Sias, *The Meaning of Evil* (London: Palgrave Macmillan, 2016), p. 195.

28. Rehumanization is often analysed within the context of the aftermath of atrocities. See, for example: Luigi Corrias, 'Crimes against Humanity, Humanity, Dehumanization and Rehumanization: Reading the Case of Duch with Hannah Arendt', *The Canadian Journal of Law and Jurisprudence* 29 (2016): 351–70, https://doi.org/10.1017/cjlj.2016.15, Pumla Gobodo-Madikizela, 'Remorse, Forgiveness, and Rehumanization: Stories from South Africa', *Journal of Humanistic Psychology* 42 (2002): 7–32, https://doi.org/10.1177/0022167802421002, Jodi Halpern and Harvey M. Weinstein, 'Rehumanizing the Other: Empathy and Reconciliation', *Human Rights Quarterly* 26 (2004): 561–83, and Rianna Oelofsen, 'Re- and Dehumanization in the Wake of Atrocities', *South African Journal of Philosophy* 28 (2009): 178–88, https://doi.org/10.4314/sajpem.v28i2.46677. The focus in this literature lies on how to resuture bonds between former enemies. My arguments here concentrate on the needs of victims of dehumanization in terms of what they need to recover and find a place in the moral community shared by fellow human beings.

29. Vladimir Jović, 'Refugees, Torture, and Dehumanization', in *Oxford Textbook of Migrant Psychiatry*, edited by Dimesh Bhugra (Oxford: Oxford University Press, 2021), pp. 351–8.

30. Idem, 356.

31. Galeotti, 'Respect as Recognition', 79.

32. Idem, 85.

33. Giannacopoulos and Loughnan, '"Closure" at Manus Island'.

34. Doherty, 'Australia's Offshore Detention'.

35. Esna Abdulamit, 'Nothing Human Is Alien: The Re-humanization of The US Immigration Detention System through Contract Reform', *Public Contract Law Journal* 46 (2016): 117–34.

References

Aaltola, Elisa. 'Affective Empathy as Core Moral Agency: Psychopathy, Autism and Reason Revisited'. *Philosophical Explorations* 17 (2004): 76–92, https://doi.org/10.1080/13869795.2013.825004.

Abdulamit, Esna. 'Nothing Human Is Alien: The Re-humanization of The US Immigration Detention System Through Contract Reform'. *Public Contract Law Journal* 46 (2016): 117–34.

Abid Raith Zeher, Shakila Abdul Manan, and Zuhair Abdul Amir Abdul Rahman. '"A Flood of Syrians Has Slowed to a Trickle": The Use of Metaphors in the Representation of Syrian Refugees in the Online Media News Reports of Host and Non-Host Countries'. *Discourse & Communication* 11 (2017): 121–40, https://doi.org/10.1177/1750481317691857.

Agamben, Giorgio. *Homo Sacer: Sovereign Power and Bare Life*, translated by Daniel Heller-Roazen (Stanford: Stanford University Press, 1998).

Agier, Michel. *On the Margins of the World: The Refugee Experience Today*, translated by David Fernbach (Cambridge: Polity, 2008).

Agier, Michel. *Managing the Undesirables: Refugee Camps and Humanitarian Government*, translated by David Fernbach (Cambridge: Polity, 2010).

Améry, Jean. *At the Mind's Limits: Contemplations by a Survivor on Auschwitz and Its Realities*, translated by Sidney Rosenfeld and Stella Rosenfeld (Bloomington: Indiana University Press, 1980 [1966]).

Amnesty International. '"Island of Despair": Australia's "Processing" of Refugees on Nauru'. 17 October 2016, https://www.amnesty.org.au/island-of-despair-nauru-refugee-report-2016/.

Amnesty International. *Libya's Dark Web of Collusion: Abuses Against Europe-Bound Refugees and Migrants*. 11 December 2017, https://www.amnesty.org/en/documents/mde19/7561/2017/en/.

Amnesty International. 'Turkey/EU: Refugees Must Not Pay the Price in Political Game'. 28 February 2020, https://www.amnesty.org/en/latest/news/2020/02/turkeyeu-refugees-must-not-pay-the-price-in-political-game/.

Anderson, Bridget. 'The Politics of Pests: Immigration and the Invasive Other'. *Social Research: An International Quarterly* 84 (2017): 7–28, doi:10.1353/sor.2017.0003.

Andersson, Ruben. 'Hunter and Prey: Patrolling Clandestine Migration in the Euro-African Borderlands'. *Anthropological Quarterly* 87 (2014): 119–49, https://www.jstor.org/stable/43652723.

Andrighetto, Luca, Cristina Baldissarri, Sara Lattanzio, Steve Loughnan, and Chiara Volpato. 'Human-itarian Aid? Two Forms of Dehumanization and Willingness to Help after Natural Disasters'. *British Journal of Social Psychology* 53 (2014): 573–84, https://doi.org/10.1111/bjso.12066.

Appiah, Kwame Anthony. *Experiments in Ethics* (Cambridge, Massachusetts: Harvard University Press, 2008).

Arcimaviciene, Liudmila and Sercan Hamza Baglama. 'Migration, Metaphor and Myth in Media Representations: The Ideological Dichotomy of "Them" and "Us"'. *SAGE Open* 8 (2018), https://doi.org/10.1177/2158244018768657.

Arendt, Hannah. *The Origins of Totalitarianism* (New York: Harvest, 1973 [1951]).

172 References

Arendt, Hannah. 'We Refugees'. In *Altogether Elsewhere: Writers on Exile*, edited by Marc Robinson (London: Faber & Faber, 1994), pp. 110–19.

Arendt, Hannah. *The Human Condition. Second edition* (Chicago: Chicago University Press, 1999 [1958]).

Atran, Scott. *Talking to the Enemy: Violent Extremism, Sacred Values, and What It Means to Be Human* (London: Penguin, 2011).

Azevedo, Ruben T., Sophie De Beukelaer, Isla L. Jones, Lou Safra, and Manos Tsakiris. 'When the Lens Is Too Wide: The Political Consequences of the Visual Dehumanization of Refugees'. *Humanities and Social Sciences Communications* 8 (2021): 1–16, https://doi.org/10.1057/s41599-021-00786-x.

Bain, Paul, Jeroen Vaes, and Jacques-Philippe Leyens (eds.). *Humanness and Dehumanization* (New York and London: Routledge, 2014).

Bandura, Albert, Bill Underwood, and Michael Fromson. 'Disinhibition of Aggression through Diffusion of Responsibility and Dehumanization of Victims'. *Journal of Research in Personality* 9 (1975): 253–69, https://doi.org/10.1016/0092-6566(75)90001-X.

Basaran, Tugba. 'The Saved and the Drowned: Governing Indifference in the Name of Security'. *Security Dialogue* 46 (2015): 205–20, https://doi.org/10.1177/09670106145575.

Batziou, Athanasia. 'Framing "Otherness" in Press Photographs: The Case of Immigrants in Greece and Spain'. *Journal of Media Practice* 12 (2011): 41–60, https://doi.org/10.1386/jmpr.12.1.41_1.

Bauman, Zygmunt. *Wasted Lives: Modernity and Its Outcasts* (New Jersey: Wiley, 2003).

Bauman, Zygmunt. *Strangers at Our Door* (Cambridge: Polity Press, 2016).

BBC. 'Migrant Crisis: EU's Juncker Announces Refugee Quota Plan'. 9 September 2015, http://www.bbc.com/news/world-europe-34193568.

BBC. 'Food Wristbands Scrapped for Cardiff Asylum Seekers'. 25 January 2016, http://www.bbc.com/news/uk-wales-35397109.

Bender, Felix. 'Why the EU Condones Human Rights Violations of Refugees in Hungary'. *Open Democracy*, 15 April 2018, https://www.opendemocracy.net/en/can-europe-make-it/why-eu-condones-human-rights-violations-of-refugees-in-hungary/.

Benesch, Susan. 'Words as Weapons'. *World Policy Journal* 29 (2012): 7–12, https://doi.org/10.1177/0740277512443794.

Benjamin, an asylum seeker. 'Detained on Nauru: "This Is the Most Painful Part of My Story—When You Realise No One Cares"'. *The Guardian*, 24 March 2017, https://www.theguardian.com/world/australia-books-blog/2017/mar/24/detained-on-nauru-this-is-the-most-painful-part-of-my-story-when-you-realise-no-one-cares.

Berry, Mike, Inaki Garcia-Blanco, and Kerry Moore. Press Coverage of the Refugee and Migrant Crisis in the EU: A Content Analysis of Five European Countries. Report Prepared for the United Nations High Commission for Refugees. 2015. https://www.unhcr.org/protection/operations/56bb369c9/press-coverage-refugee-migrant-crisis-eu-content-analysis-five-european.html.

Betts, Alexander and Paul Collier. *Refuge: Transforming a Broken Refugee System* (London: Allen Lane, 2017).

Betts, Alexander and Gil Loescher. *Refugees in International Relations* (Oxford: Oxford University Press, 2010).

Bishop, Mac William. 'Bulgarian Vigilantes Patrol Turkey Border to Keep Migrants Out'. *NBC News*, 10 March 2017, https://www.nbcnews.com/storyline/europes-border-crisis/bulgarian-vigilantes-patrol-turkey-border-keep-migrants-out-n723481.

Bleiker, Roland, David Campbell, Emma Hutchison, and Xzarina Nicholson. 'The Visual Dehumanisation of Refugees'. *Australian Journal of Political Science* 48 (2013): 398–416, https://doi.org/10.1080/10361146.2013.840769.

References   173

Bloom, Paul. *Just Babies: The Origins of Good and Evil* (New York: Broadway Books, 2013).

Boochani, Behrouz. *A Letter from Manus Island* (Adamstown, County Wexford, Ireland: Borderstream Books, 2018).

Borderline-Europe. 'At the Limen: The Implementation of the Return Directive in Italy, Cyprus, and Spain'. 2013, https://www.borderline-europe.de/sites/default/files/readingtips/at%20the%20limen_12_2013.pdf.

Borderline-Europe. '"That Is the Worst: The Political Normality to Lock People Up" Interview with Borderline-Lesvos'. 2020, https://www.borderline-europe.de/sites/default/files/readingtips/Interview%20borderline%20lesvos.pdf.

'Brutal'. *Online Etymology Dictionary*, https://www.etymonline.com/search?q=brutal.

'Brutalize'. *Merriam-Webster Online*, https://www.merriam-webster.com/dictionary/brutalize.

Brunwasser, Matthew. 'Bulgaria's Vigilante Migrant "Hunter"'. *BBC News*, 30 March 2016, https://www.bbc.co.uk/news/magazine-35919068.

Buber, Martin. *Hasidism and Modern Man* (New York: Horizon Press, 1958).

Buber, Martin. 'From *I and Thou* (1923)'. In *The Martin Buber Reader: Essential Writings*, edited by Asher D. Biemann (New York: Palgrave MacMillan, 2002), pp. 181–8.

Buber, Martin. 'Distance and Relation (1950)'. In *The Martin Buber Reader: Essential Writings*, edited by Asher D. Biemann (New York: Palgrave MacMillan, 2002), pp. 206–13.

Buckels, Erin E. and Paul D. Trapnell. 'Disgust Facilitates Outgroup Dehumanization'. *Group Processes & Intergroup Relations* 16 (2013): 771–80, https://doi.org/10.1177/1368430212471738.

Butler, Judith. *Frames of War: When Is Life Grievable?* (London and New York: Verso, 2010).

Butler, Judith. 'Taking Another's View: Ambivalent Implications'. In Axel Honneth, *Reification: A New Look at an Old Idea* (Berkeley Tanner Lectures) (Oxford: Oxford University Press, 2012), pp. 97–119.

Cabot, Heath. '"Refugee Voices": Tragedy, Ghosts and the Anthropology of Not Knowing'. *Journal of Contemporary Ethnography* 45 (2016): 645–72, https://doi.org/10.1177/0891241615625567.

Calais Writers. *Voices from the 'Jungle': Stories from the Calais Refugee Camp* (London: Pluto Press, 2017).

Čehajić, Sabina, Rupert Brown, and Roberto Gonzalez. 'What Do I Care? Perceived Ingroup Responsibility and Dehumanization as Predictors of Empathy Felt for the Victim Group'. *Group Processes & Intergroup Relations* 12 (2009): 715–29, https://doi.org/10.1177/1368430209347727.

Ćerimović, Emina. 'Asylum Seekers' Hell in a Greek "Hotspot"'. *Human Rights Watch*, 30 November 2017, https://www.hrw.org/news/2017/11/30/asylum-seekers-hell-greek-hotspot.

Chlopak, Erin. 'Dealing with the Detainees at Guantanamo Bay: Humanitarian and Human Rights Obligations under the Geneva Conventions'. *Human Rights Brief* 9 (2002): 6–9, 13, https://digitalcommons.wcl.american.edu/hrbrief/vol9/iss3/2/.

Chouliaraki, Lilie and Rafal Zaborowski. 'Voice and Community in the 2015 Refugee Crisis: A Content Analysis of News Coverage in Eight European Countries'. *The International Communication Gazette* 79 (2017): 613–35. https://doi.org/10.1177/1748048517727173.

Cisneros, David. 'Contaminated Communities: The Metaphor of "Immigrant as Pollutant" in Media Representations of Immigration'. *Rhetoric & Public Affairs* 11 (2008): 569–601, doi:10.1353/rap.0.0068.

Cohen, Joshua. 'The Arc of the Moral Universe'. In *The Arc of the Moral Universe and Other Essays* (Cambridge, Massachusetts: Harvard University Press, 2010), pp. 15–74.

174 References

Corrias, Luigi. 'Crimes Against Humanity, Dehumanization and Rehumanization: Reading the Case of Duch with Hannah Arendt'. *The Canadian Journal of Law and Jurisprudence* 29 (2016): 351–70, https://doi.org/10.1017/cjlj.2016.15.

Crary, Alice. 'Dehumanization and the Question of Animals'. In *The Routledge Handbook of Dehumanization*, edited by Maria Kronfelder (New York: Routledge, 2021), pp. 159–72.

'Crisis'. *Online Etymology Dictionary*, https://www.etymonline.com/word/crisis.

Crofts, Penny and Anthea Vogl. 'Dehumanized and Demonized Refugees, Zombies and World War Z'. *Law and Humanities* 13 (2019): 29–51, https://doi.org/10.1080/17521483.2019.1572290.

Dale, Alexander. 'Countering Hate Messages That Lead to Violence: The United Nations' Chapter VII Authority to Use Radio Jamming to Halt Incendiary Broadcasts'. *Duke Journal of Comparative & International Law* 11 (2001): 109–32, https://scholarship.law.duke.edu/djcil/vol11/iss1/6.

DeBono, Daniela. '"Less than Human": The Detention of Irregular Migrants in Malta'. *Race & Class* 55 (2013): 60–81, https://doi.org/10.1177/0306396813497880.

De Genova, Nicholas. 'Bare Life, Labor-Power, Mobility, and Global Space: Toward a Marxian Anthropology?' *The New Centennial Review* 12 (2012): 129–52, https://doi.org/10.2307/41949805.

de Ruiter, Adrienne. 'Failing to See What Matters Most: Towards a Better Understanding of Dehumanisation', *Contemporary Political Theory* (2022) https://doi.org/10.1057/s41296-022-00569-2.

de Ruiter, Adrienne. 'To Be or Not To Be Human: Resolving the Paradox of Dehumanisation', *European Journal of Political Theory* 22 (2023): 73–95, https://doi.org/10.1177/1474885120984605.

de Waal, Frans. *The Age of Empathy: Nature's Lessons for a Kinder Society* (New York: Three Rivers Press, 2009).

Dickerson, Caitlin. '"There Is a Stench": Soiled Clothes and No Baths for Migrant Children at a Texas Center'. *New York Times*, 21 June 2019, https://www.nytimes./2019/06/21/us/migrant-children-border-soap.html?module=inline.

Dines, Nick, Nicola Montagna, and Vincenzo Ruggiero. 'Thinking Lampedusa: Border Construction, the Spectacle of Bare Life and the Productivity of Migrants'. *Ethnic and Racial Studies* 38 (2015): 430–45, https://doi.org/10.1080/01419870.2014.936892.

Doherty, Ben. 'UN Countries Line Up to Criticise Australia's Human Rights Record'. *The Guardian*, 9 November 2015, https://www.theguardian.com/law/2015/nov/10/un-countries-line-up-to-criticise-australias-human-rights-record.

Doherty, Ben. 'International Criminal Court Told Australia's Detention Regime Could Be a Crime against Humanity'. *The Guardian*, 13 February 2017, https://www.theguardian.com/australia-news/2017/feb/13/international-criminal-court-told-australias-detention-regime-could-be-a-against-humanity.

Doherty, Ben. 'Australia's Offshore Detention Is Unlawful, Says International Criminal Court Prosecutor'. *The Guardian*, 15 February 2020, https://www.theguardian.com/australia-news/2020/feb/15/australias-offshore-detention-is-unlawful-says-international-criminal-court-prosecutor.

Doty, Roxanne. 'Bare Life: Border-Crossing Deaths and Spaces of Moral Alibi'. *Environment and Planning D: Society and Space* 29 (2011): 599–612, https://doi.org/10.1068/d3110.

Douglas, Mary. *Purity and Danger: An Analysis of Concepts of Pollution and Taboo* (New York: Routledge, 1966).

Downey, Anthony. 'Zones of Indistinction: Giorgio Agamben's Bare Life and the Politics of Aesthetics'. *Third Text* 223 (2009): 109–25, https://doi.org/10.1080/09528820902840581.

References 175

Doherty, Ben and Daniel Hurst. 'UN Accuses Australia of Systematically Violating Torture Convention'. *The Guardian*, 10 March 2015, https://www.theguardian.com/australia-news/2015/mar/09/un-reports-australias-immigration-detention-breaches-torture-convention.

The Economist. 'Bulgaria Tries to Restrain Its Vigilante "Migrant Hunters"'. 19 April 2016, https://www.economist.com/europe/2016/04/19/bulgaria-tries-to-restrain-its-vigilante-migrant-hunters.

el Daoi, Racha. 'Syrian Refugees Deprived of Basic Human Rights'. *Norwegian Refugee Council*, 10 December 2017, https://www.nrc.no/syrian-refugees-deprived-of-basic-human-rights.

El-Enany, Nadine. 'Aylan Kurdi: The Human Refugee'. *Law Critique* 27 (2016): 13, https://doi.org/10.1007/s10978-015-9175-7.

Elgot, Jessica and Matthew Taylor. 'Calais Crisis: Cameron Condemned for "Dehumanising" Description of Migrants'. *The Guardian*, 30 July 2015, https://www.theguardian.com/uk-news/2015/jul/30/david-cameron-migrant-swarm-language-condemned.

El Refaie, Elisabeth. 'Metaphors We Discriminate By: Naturalized Themes in Austrian Newspaper Articles about Asylum Seekers'. *Journal of Sociolinguistics* 5 (2001): 352–71, https://doi.org/10.1111/1467-9481.00154.

Epley, Nicholas. *Mindwise: Why We Misunderstand What Others Think, Believe, Feel, and Want* (New York: Vintage Books, 2015).

Esses, Victoria, Stelian Medianu, and Andrea Lawson. 'Uncertainty, Threat, and the Role of Media in Promoting the Dehumanization of Immigrants and Refugees'. *Journal of Social Issues* 69 (2013): 518–36, https://doi.org/10.1111/josi.12027.

Esses, Victoria, Stelian Medianu, and Alina Sutter. 'The Dehumanization and Rehumanization of Refugees'. In *The Routledge Handbook of Dehumanization*, edited by Maria Kronfelder (London and New York: Routledge, 2021) pp. 275–91.

Esses, Victoria, Scott Veenvliet, Gordon Hodson, and Ljiljana Mihic. 'Justice, Morality, and the Dehumanization of Refugees'. *Social Justice Research* 21 (2008): 4–25, https://doi.org/10.1007/s11211-007-0058-4.

Euromed Rights. 'Refugees Must Not Be Used as Bargaining Chips!' 3 March 2020, https://euromedrights.org/publication/refugees-must-not-be-used-as-bargaining-chips/.

European Parliament. *Resolution of 14 April 2016 on the 2015 Report on Turkey*, 2015/2898(RSP) (2016), https://www.europarl.europa.eu/doceo/document/TA-8-2016-0133_EN.html?redirect.

Festa, Lynn. 'Humanity without Feathers'. *Humanity: An International Journal of Human Rights, Humanitarianism, and Development* 1 (2010): 3–27, https://doi.org/10.1353/hum.2010.0007.

Fiske, Lucy. 'Human Rights and Refugee Protest against Immigration Detention: Refugees' Struggles for Recognition as Human'. *Refuge* 32 (2016): 22, https://doi.org/10.25071/1920-7336.40380.

Franklin, Christopher Evan. 'Valuing Blame'. In *Blame: Its Nature and Norms*, edited by D. Justin Coates and Neal A. Tognazzini (Oxford and New York: Oxford University Press, 2013), pp. 207–23.

Frelick, Bill. 'Dispatches: Why We Should Outlaw "Illegal"'. *Human Rights Watch*, 24 June 2014, https://www.hrw.org/news/2014/06/24/dispatches-why-we-should-outlaw-illegal.

Galeotti, Anna. 'Respect as Recognition: Some political implications'. In *The Plural States of Recognition*, edited by Michel Seymour (Basingstoke: Palgrave Macmillan, 2010), pp. 79–97.

Garrard, Eve. 'The Nature of Evil', *Philosophical Explorations* 1 (1998): 43–60, https://doi.org/10.1080/10001998018538689.

176 References

Geertz, Clifford. 'Thick Description: Toward an Interpretive Theory of Culture'. In *The Interpretation of Cultures: Selected Essays* (New York: Basic Books, 1973), pp. 310–23.

Geras, Norman. *Solidarity in the Conversation of Humankind: The Ungroundable Liberalism of Richard Rorty* (London: Verso, 1995).

Geuss, Raymond. 'Philosophical Anthropology and Social Criticism'. In *Reification: A New Look at an Old Idea*, edited by Axel Honneth (Berkeley Tanner Lectures) (Oxford: Oxford University Press, 2012), pp. 120–30.

Giannacopoulos, Maria and Claire Loughnan. '"Closure" at Manus Island and Carceral Expansion in the Open Air Prison'. *Globalizations* 17 (2020): 1118–35, https://doi.org/10.1080/14747731.2019.1679549.

Gibson, Janice T. and Mika Haritos-Fatouras. 'The Education of a Torturer', *Psychology Today* 20 (1986): 50–8.

Glick, Megan. *Infrahumanisms: Science, Culture, and the Making of Modern Non/personhood* (Durham and London: Duke University Press, 2018).

Gobodo-Madikizela, Pumla. 'Remorse, Forgiveness, and Rehumanization: Stories from South-Africa'. *Journal of Humanistic Psychology* 42 (2002): 7–32, https://doi.org/10.1177/0022167802421002.

Goffman, Erving. *Stigma: Notes on the Management of Spoiled Identity* (London: Penguin, 1963).

Goodman, Simon, Ala Sirriyeh, and Simon McMahon. 'The Evolving (Re)Categorisations of Refugees throughout the "Refugee/Migrant Crisis"'. *Journal of Community and Applied Social Psychology* 27 (2017): 105–14, https://doi.org/10.1002/casp.2302.

Graham, David A. 'Trump Says Democrats Want Immigrants to "Infest" the U.S.'. *The Atlantic*, 19 June 2018, https://www.theatlantic.com/politics/archive/2018/06/trump-immigrants-infest/563159/.

Gray, Harriet and Anja K. Franck. 'Refugees as/at Risk: The Gendered and Racialized Underpinnings of Securitization in British Media Narratives'. *Security Dialogue* 50 (2019): 275–91, https://doi.org/10.1177/0967010619830590.

Greenhill, Kelly M. *Weapons of Mass Migration: Forced Displacement, Coercion, and Foreign Policy* (Ithaca, New York: Cornell University Press, 2016).

Gumbel, Andrew. '"They Were Laughing At Us": Immigrants Tell of Cruelty, Illness, and Filth in US Detention'. *The Guardian*, 12 September 2018, https://www.theguardian.com/us-news/2018/sep/12/us-immigration-detention-facilities.

Gündüz, Orhun. '"Burden on our Shoulders" Rhetoric: Objectification of Syrian Refugees in Turkey through Political and Economic Discourse'. *Refugee Review* 3 (2017): 34–45.

Gustafsson, Jessica. 'Media and the 2013 Kenyan Election: From Hate Speech to Peace Preaching'. *Conflict & Communication* 15 (2016): 1–13.

Haidt, Jonathan. *The Righteous Mind: Why Good People Are Divided by Politics and Religion* (London: Penguin, 2013).

Halpern, Jodi and Harvey M. Weinstein. 'Rehumanizing the Other: Empathy and Reconciliation'. *Human Rights Quarterly* 26 (2004): 561–83.

Hartley, Lisa and Caroline Fleay. '"We Are like Animals": Negotiating Dehumanising Experiences of Asylum-Seeker Policies in the Australian Community'. *Refugee Survey Quarterly* 36 (2017): 45–63, https://doi.org/10.1093/rsq/hdx010.

Haslam, Nick. 'Dehumanization: An Integrative Approach'. *Personality and Social Psychology Review* 10 (2006): 252–64, https://doi.org/10.1207/s15327957pspr1003_4.

Haslam, Nick. 'What Is Dehumanization?' In *Humanness and Dehumanization*, edited by Paul Bain, Jeroen Vaes, and Jacques-Philippe Leyens (New York and London: Routledge, 2014), pp. 34–48.

References   177

Hegel, Georg Wilhelm Friedrich. 'Lordship and Bondage'. In *The Phenomenology of Spirit*, translated by Arnold Miller (Oxford: Oxford University Press, 1977 [1807]), pp. 110–19.

Hieronymi, Pamela. 'Articulating An Uncompromising Forgiveness'. *Philosophy and Phenomenological Research* 62 (2001): 529–55, https://doi.org/10.2307/2653535.

Hintjens, Helen. 'Failed Securitisation Moves During the 2015 "Migration Crisis"'. *International Migration* 57 (2019): 181–96, https://doi.org/10.1111/imig.12588.

Holmes, Seth M. and Heide Casteñada. 'Representing the "European Refugee Crisis" in Germany and Beyond: Deservingness and Difference, Life and Death'. *American Ethnologist* 43 (2016): 12–24, https://doi.org/10.1111/amet.12259.

Holzberg, Billy, Kristina Kolbe, and Rafal Zaborowski. 'Figures of Crisis: The Delineation of (Un)Deserving Refugees in the German Media'. *Sociology* 53 (2018): 534–50, https://doi.org/10.1177/0038038518759460.

Honneth, Axel. *Reification: A New Look at an Old Idea* (Berkeley Tanner Lectures) (Oxford: Oxford University Press, 2012).

Hopkins, Katie. 'Rescue Boats? I'd Use Gunships to Stop Migrants'. *The Sun*, 17 April 2015, http://www.gc.soton.ac.uk/files/2015/01/hopkins-17april-2015.pdf.

'Humanity'. *Merriam-Webster Online*, https://www.merriam-webster.com/dictionary/humanity.

Human Rights Watch. '"I Wanted to Lie Down and Die": Trafficking and Torture of Eritreans in Sudan and Egypt'. 11 February 2014, https://www.hrw.org/report/2014/02/11/i-wanted-lie-down-and-die/trafficking-and-torture-eritreans-sudan-and-egypt.

Ibrahim, Yasmin and Anita Howarth. 'Sounds of the Jungle: Rehumanizing the Migrant'. *JOMEC Journal Journalism Media and Cultural Studies* 7 (2015): 1–18.

Innes, Alexandria J. 'When the Threatened Become the Threat: The Construction of Asylum Seekers in British Media Narratives'. *International Relations* 24 (2010): 456–77, https://doi.org/10.1177/0047117810385882.

Jahoda, Gustav. *Images of Savages: Ancient Roots of Modern Prejudice in Western Culture* (New York: Routledge, 1999).

Janmyr, Maja. 'Precarity in Exile: The Legal Status of Syrian refugees in Lebanon'. *Refugee Survey Quarterly* 35 (2016): 58–78, https://doi.org/10.1093/rsq/hdw016.

Janmyr, Maja. 'UNHCR and the Syrian Refugee Response: Negotiating Status and Registration in Lebanon'. *International Journal of Human Rights* 22 (2018): 393–419, https://doi.org/10.1080/13642987.2017.1371140.

Janmyr, Maja and Lama Mourad. 'Modes of Ordering: Labelling, Classification and Categorization in Lebanon's Refugee Response'. *Journal of Refugee Studies* 31 (2018): 544–65, https://doi.org/10.1093/jrs/fex042.

Jones, Reece. *Violent Borders: Refugees and the Right to Move* (London and New York: Verso, 2016).

Jović, Vladimir. 'Refugees, Torture, and Dehumanization'. In *Oxford Textbook of Migrant Psychiatry*, edited by Dimesh Bhugra (Oxford: Oxford University Press, 2021), pp. 351–8.

Kathrani, Paresh. 'Object or Subject? The Ongoing "Objectification" of Asylum Seekers', *International Comparative Jurisprudence* 3 (2017): 1–7, https://doi.org/10.13165/j.icj.2017.03.001.

Keen, Sam. *Faces of the Enemy: Reflections of the Hostile Imagination* (New York: HarperCollins Publishers, 1991).

Kelman, Herbert. 'Violence without Moral Restraint: Reflections on the Dehumanization of Victims and Victimizers'. *Journal of Social Issues* 29 (1973): 25–61, https://doi.org/10.1111/j.1540-4560.1973.tb00102.x.

178 References

Khamitov, Mansur, Jeff D. Rotman, and Jared Piazza. 'Perceiving the Agency of Harmful Agents: A Test of Dehumanization Versus Moral Typecasting Accounts'. *Cognition* 146 (2016): 33–47, https://doi.org/10.1016/j.cognition.2015.09.009.

Kil, Sang H. and Cecilia Menjívar. 'The War on the Border: Criminalizing Immigrants and Militarizing the US-Mexico Border'. In *Immigration and Crime: Race, Ethnicity, and Violence*, edited by Ramiro Martinez Jr. and Abel Valenzuela Jr. (New York: New York University Press, 2006), pp. 164–88.

Kil, Sang H., Cecilia Menjívar, and Roxanne Doty. 'Securing Borders: Patriotism, Vigilantism and the Brutalization of the US American Public'. In *Immigration, Crime and Justice (Sociology of Crime, Law and Deviance, Vol. 13)*, edited by William F. McDonald (Bingley: Emerald Group Publishing Limited, 2009), pp. 297–312.

Kingsley, Patrick. 'The Death of Alan Kurdi: One Year On, Compassion Towards Refugees Fades'. *The Guardian*, 2 September 2016, https://www.theguardian.com/world/2016/sep/01/alan-kurdi-death-one-year-on-compassion-towards-refugees-fades.

Kingsley, Patrick. *The New Odyssey: The Story of Europe's Refugee Crisis* (London: Guardian Faber Publishing, 2016).

Kristeva, Julia. *Powers of Horror: An Essay on Abjection* (New York: Columbia University Press, 1984).

Kronfelder, Maria (ed.). *The Routledge Handbook of Dehumanization* (London and New York: Routledge, 2021).

Kteily, Nour, Emile Bruneau, Adam Waytz, and Sarah Cotterill. 'The Ascent of Man: Theoretical and Empirical Evidence for Blatant Dehumanization'. *Journal of Personality and Social Psychology* 109 (2015): 901–31, https://doi.org/10.1037/pspp0000048.

Kukathas, Chandran. 'Are Refugees Special?' In *Migration in Political Theory: The Ethics of Movement and Membership*, edited by Sarah Fine and Lea Ypi (Oxford: Oxford University Press, 2016, pp. 249–68).

Kymlicka, Will. 'Human Rights without Human Supremacism'. *Canadian Journal of Philosophy* 48 (2018): 763–92, https://doi.org/10.1080/00455091.2017.1386481.

Lakoff, George and Mark Johnson, *Metaphors We Live By* (Chicago: University of Chicago Press, 1980).

Lang, Johannes. 'Questioning Dehumanization: Intersubjective Dimensions of Violence in the Nazi Concentration and Death Camps'. *Holocaust and Genocide Studies* 24 (2010): 225–46, https://doi.org/10.1093/hgs/dcq026.

Lang, Johannes. 'The Limited Importance of Dehumanization in Collective Violence'. *Current Opinion in Psychology* 35 (2020): 17–20, https://doi.org/10.1016/j.copsyc.2020.02.002.

Leader Maynard, Jonathan. 'Combating Atrocity-Justifying Ideologies'. In *The Responsibility to Prevent: Overcoming the Challenges to Atrocity Prevention*, edited by Serena K. Sharma and Jennifer M. Welsh (Oxford: Oxford University Press, 2015), pp. 189–225.

Levi, Primo. *The Drowned and the Saved*, translated by Raymond Rosenthal (London: Abacus, 1989).

Leyens, Jacques-Philippe, Stéphanie Demoulin, Jeroes Vaes, Ruth Gaunt, and Maria Paola Paladino. 'Infra-humanization: The Wall of Group Differences'. *Social Issues and Policy Review* 1 (2007): 139–72, https://doi.org/10.1111/j.1751-2409.2007.00006.x.

Lifton, Robert. The Nazi Doctors: Medical Killing and the Psychology of Genocide (London: Basic Books, 1988).

Lynn, Nick and Susan Lea. 'A Phantom Menace and the New Apartheid: The Social Construction of Asylum-Seekers in the United Kingdom'. *Discourse and Society* 14 (2003): 425–52, https://doi.org/10.1177/0957926503014004002.

References 179

Machery, Edouard. 'Dehumanization and the Loss of Moral Standing'. In *The Routledge Handbook of Dehumanization*, edited by Maria Kronfelder (London and New York: Routledge, 2021), pp. 145–58.

Mahendran, Kesi, Nicola Magnusson, Caroline Howarth, and Sarah Scuzzarello. 'Reification and the Refugee: Using a Counterposing Dialogical Analysis to Unlock a Frozen Category'. *Journal of Social and Political Psychology* 7 (2019): 577–97, https://doi.org/10.5964/jspp.v7i1.656.

Malkki, Liisa. 'National Geographic: The Rooting of Peoples and the Territorialization of National Identity among Scholars and Refugees'. Cultural Anthropology (1992): 24–44, https://doi.org/10.1525/can.1992.7.1.02a00030.

Malkki, Liisa. 'Speechless Emissaries: Refugees, Humanitarianism, and Dehistoricization'. *Cultural Anthropology* 11 (1996): 377–404, https://doi.org/10.1525/can.1996.11.3.02a00050.

Malone, Barry. 'Why Al Jazeera Will Not Say Mediterranean "Migrants"'. *Al Jazeera English*, 20 August 2015, http://www.aljazeera.com/blogs/editors-blog/2015/08/al-jazeera-mediterranean-migrants-150820082226309.html.

Manne, Kate. *Down Girl: The Logic of Misogyny* (Oxford: Oxford University Press, 2019).

Mannik, Lynda. 'Public and Private Photographs of Refugees: The Problem of Representation'. *Visual Studies* 27 (2012): 262–76, https://doi.org/10.1080/1472586X.2012.717747.

Marder, Lev. 'Refugees Are Not Weapons: The "Weapons of Mass Migration" Metaphor and Its Implications'. *International Studies Review* 20 (2018): 576–88, https://doi.org/10.1093/isr/vix055.

Margalit, Avishai. *The Decent Society*, translated by Naomi Goldblum (Cambridge, Massachusetts and London: Harvard University Press, 1996).

Marr, David and Oliver Laughland. 'Australia's Detention Regime Sets Out to Make Asylum Seekers Suffer, Says Chief Immigration Psychiatrist'. *The Guardian*, 4 August 2014, https://www.theguardian.com/world/2014/aug/05/-sp-australias-detention-regime-sets-out-to-make-asylum-seekers-suffer-says-chief-immigration-psychiatrist.

Marshall, Shantal and Jessica Shapiro. 'When "Scurry" vs "Hurry" Makes the Difference: Vermin Metaphors, Disgust, and Anti-Immigrant Attitudes'. *Journal of Social Issues* 74 (2018): 774–89, https://doi.org/10.1111/josi.12298.

May, Larry. *Genocide: A Normative Account* (Cambridge and New York: Cambridge University Press, 2010).

Médecins Sans Frontières. *Obstacle Course to Europe: A Policy-Made Humanitarian Crisis at EU Borders*. January 2016, https://www.doctorswithoutborders.org/sites/usa/files/2016_01_msf_obstacle_course_to_europe_-_final_-_low_res.pdf.

Mehdi. 'I Am Leaving Australia's Torture Chambers after Nine Years—But What I Have Is the Worst Kind of Freedom'. *The Guardian*, 4 March 2022, https://www.theguardian.com/commentisfree/2022/mar/04/i-am-leaving-australias-torture-chambers-after-nine-years-but-what-i-have-is-the-worst-kind-of-freedom.

Mendoza, Martha and Garance Burke. 'US Gov't Moves Children after AP Exposes Bad Treatment'. Associated Press, 25 June 2019, https://apnews.com/article/border-patrols-az-state-wire-tx-state-wire-michael-pence-caribbean-a7a9acc4c6a546829a258e008d10d705.

Metzl, Jamie. 'Information Intervention: When Switching Channels Isn't Enough'. *Foreign Affairs* 76 (1997): 15–20, https://doi.org/10.2307/20048273.

Mikkola, Mari. *The Wrong of Injustice: Dehumanization and Its Role in Feminist Philosophy* (Oxford: Oxford University Press, 2016).

Miller, David. 'Distributing Responsibilities'. *Journal of Political Philosophy* 9 (2001): 453–71, https://doi.org/10.1111/1467-9760.00136.

180 References

Ministry of Foreign Affairs of the Italian Republic. *Memorandum d'Intesa Sulla Cooperazione nel Campo dello Sviluppo, del Contrasto all'Immigrazione Illegale, al Traffico di Esseri Umani, al Contrabbando e sul Rafforzamento della Sicurezza delle Frontiere tra lo Stato della Libia e la Repubblica Italiana*. 2 February 2017, itra.esteri.it/vwPdf/wfrmRenderPdf.aspx?ID=50975.

Mittelstaedt, Juliana von and Maximilian Popp. 'One Year after the Lampedusa Tragedy' (translated by Christopher Sultan). *Spiegel Online*, 9 October 2014, http://www.spiegel.de/international/europe/lampedusa-survivors-one-year-after-the-refugee-tragedy-a-994887.html.

Muir, Hugh. 'Indefinite Detention Is Dehumanizing For Refugees: This Practice Must End'. *The Guardian*, 19 July 2017, https://www.theguardian.com/commentisfree/2017/jul/19/indefinite-detention-refugees-journeys-refugee-tales.

Nussbaum, Martha C. 'Objectification', *Philosophy & Public Affairs*, 24 (1995): 249–91, https://doi.org/10.1111/j.1088-4963.1995.tb00032.x.

O'Brien, Gerald V. 'Indigestible Foods, Conquering Hordes, and Waste Materials: Metaphors of Immigrants and the Early Immigration Restriction Debate in the United States'. *Metaphor and Symbol* 18 (2003): 33–47, https://doi.org/10.1207/s15327868ms1801_3.

O'Neill, Onora. *Justice across Boundaries: Whose Obligations?* (Cambridge: Cambridge University Press, 2016).

Oelofsen, Rianna. 'Re- and Dehumanization in the Wake of Atrocities'. *South African Journal of Philosophy* 28 (2009): 178–88, https://doi.org/10.4314/sajpem.v28i2.46677.

Office of the United Nations High Commissioner for Human Rights. *Detained and Dehumanised: Report on Human Rights Abuses Against Migrants in Libya*, 13 December 2016, http://www.ohchr.org/Documents/Countries/LY/DetainedAndDehumanised_en.pdf.

Opotow, Susan. 'Moral Exclusion and Injustice: An Introduction'. *Journal of Social Issues* 46 (1990): 1–20, https://doi.org/10.1111/j.1540-4560.1990.tb00268.x.

Over, Harriet. 'Seven Challenges for the Dehumanization Hypothesis'. *Perspectives on Psychological Science* 16 (2021): 3–13.

Owens, Patricia. '"Reclaiming "Bare Life"? Against Agamben on Refugees'. *International Relations* 23 (2009): 567–82, https://doi.org/10.1177/0047117809350545.

Parekh, Serena. *Refugees and the Ethics of Forced Displacement* (Milton Park, Oxfordshire: Taylor & Francis, 2016).

Parekh, Serena. *No Refuge: Ethics and the Global Refugee Crisis* (Oxford: Oxford University Press: 2020).

Parfit, Derek. 'As a Means and Merely as a Means'. In *On What Matters: Volume One* (Oxford: Oxford University Press, 2011), pp. 221–28.

Parker, Ashley, Nick Miroff, Sean Sullivan, and Tyler Pager. '"No End in Sight": Inside the Biden's Administration's Failure to Contain the Border Surge'. *Washington Post*, 22 March 2021, www.washingtonpost.com%2fpolitics%2fbiden-border-surge%2f2021%2f03%2f20%2f21824e94-8818-11eb-8a8b-5cf82c3dffe4_story.html.

Pattison, James. 'Effectiveness and the Moderate Instrumentalist Approach'. In *Humanitarian Intervention & The Responsibility to Protect: Who Should Intervene?* (Oxford: Oxford University Press, 2010), pp. 69–97.

Phillips, Anne. *The Politics of the Human* (Cambridge: Cambridge University Press, 2015).

Philo, Greg, Emma Briant, and Pauline Donald. *Bad News for Refugees* (London: Pluto Press, 2013).

Piazza, Jared, Justin F. Landy, and Geoffrey P. Goodwin. 'Cruel Nature: Harmfulness as an Important, Overlooked Dimension in Judgments of Moral Standing'. *Cognition* 131 (2014): 108–24, https://doi.org/10.1016/j.cognition.2013.12.013.

References 181

Price, Monroe E. 'Information Intervention: Bosnia, the Dayton Accords, and the Seizure of Broadcasting Transmitters'. *Cornell International Law Journal* 33 (2000): 67–112, http://scholarship.law.cornell.edu/cilj/vol33/iss1/2.

Price, Monroe E. 'Orbiting Hate? Satellite Transponders and Free Expression'. In *The Content and Context of Hate Speech: Rethinking Regulation and Responses*, edited by Michael Herz (Cambridge and New York: Cambridge University Press, 2012), pp. 514–38.

Price, Monroe E. and Mark Thomson (eds.). *Forging Peace: Intervention, Human Rights and the Management of Media Space* (Edinburgh: Edinburgh University Press, 2002).

Pro Asyl. *Walls of Shame: Accounts from the Inside: The Detention Centers of Evros.* 2012, https://www.proasyl.de/en/material/walls-of-shame-accounts-from-the-inside-the-detention-centres-of-evros/.

Rai, Tage, Piercarlo Valdesolo, and Jesse Graham. 'Dehumanization Increases Instrumental Violence, But Not Moral Violence'. *Proceedings of the National Academy of Sciences* 114 (2017): 8511–16, https://doi.org/10.1073/pnas.1705238114.

Rawlence, Ben. 'Refugees Shouldn't Be Bargaining Chips'. *New York Times*, 17 May 2016, https://www.nytimes.com/2016/05/17/opinion/refugees-shouldnt-be-bargaining-chips.html.

'Recognize'. *Merriam-Webster Dictionary*, https://www.merriam-webster.com/dictionary/recognize.

Rector, John. *The Objectification Spectrum: Understanding and Transcending Our Diminishment and Dehumanization of Others* (Oxford: Oxford University Press, 2014).

Riva, Paolo and Luca Andrighetto. '"Everybody Feels a Broken Bone, But Only We Can Feel a Broken Heart": Group Membership Influences the Perception of Targets' Suffering'. *European Journal of Social Psychology* 42 (2012): 801–06, https://doi.org/10.1002/ejsp.1918.

Rorty, Richard. 'Human Rights, Rationality, and Sentimentality'. In *Truth and Progress: Philosophical Papers. Volume 3* (Cambridge: Cambridge University Press, 1998), pp. 167–85.

Rothwell, James. 'Afghan Migrant "Shot Dead by Hunting Party" in Serbian Woods'. *The Telegraph*, 24 August 2016, https://www.telegraph.co.uk/news/2016/08/24/afghan-migrant-shot-dead-by-hunting-party-in-serbian-woods/.

Sabo, Samantha, Susan Shaw, Maia Ingram, Nicolette Teufel-Shone, et al. 'Everyday Violence, Structural Racism and Mistreatment at the EU-Mexico Border'. *Social Science & Medicine* 109 (2014): 66–74, https://doi.org/10.1016/j.socscimed.2014.02.005.

Sacks, Oliver. *The Man Who Mistook His Wife For a Hat, and Other Clinical Tales* (New York: Touchstone, 1998 [1985]).

Sajir, Zakaria and Miriyam Aouragh. 'Solidarity, Social Media, and the "Refugee Crisis": Engagement Beyond Affect'. *International Journal of Communication* 13 (2019): 550–77, https://ijoc.org/index.php/ijoc/article/view/9999.

Schininá, Guiglielmo. 'Objectification and Abjectification of Migrants: Reflections to Help Guide Psychosocial Workers'. *Intervention* 15 (2017): 100–5, http://doi.org/10.1097/WTF.0000000000000146.

Schinkel, Willem. '"Illegal Aliens" and the State, or: Bare Bodies vs. the Zombie'. *International Sociology* 24 (2009): 779–806, https://doi.org/10.1177/0268580909343494.

Schwartzman, Roy. 'Rehumanizing the Alien "Invaders": How Testimony Can Counteract Xenophobia', *International Journal of Communication and Media Studies* 10 (2020): 5–12.

Scottish Refugee Policy Forum. 'A Fairer Scotland for Asylum Seekers and Refugees in Times of Austerity?' February 2012, https://scottishrefugeecouncil.org.uk/wp-content/uploads/2019/10/A-fairer-Scotland-for-asylum-seekers-and-refugees-in-a-time-of-austerity-Scottish-Refugee-Policy-Forum-report-PDF.pdf.

182 References

Serena K. Sharma, 'The 2007–8 Post-Election Crisis in Kenya'. In *The Responsibility to Prevent: Overcoming the Challenges to Atrocity Prevention*, edited by Serena K. Sharma and Jennifer M. Welsh (Oxford: Oxford University Press, 2015), pp. 280–303.

Sherlock, Ruth and Lama Al-Arian. 'Migrants Captured in Libya Say They End Up Sold as Slaves'. *NPR*, 21 March 2018, https://www.npr.org/sections/parallels/2018/03/21/595497429/migrants-passing-through-libya-could-end-up-being-sold-as-slaves.

Shetty, Salil. 'Tackling the Global Refugee Crisis: Sharing, Not Shirking Responsibility'. *Amnesty International*, 4 October 2016, https://www.amnesty.org/en/latest/campaigns/2016/10/tackling-the-global-refugee-crisis-sharing-responsibility/.

Sias, James. *The Meaning of Evil* (London: Palgrave Macmillan, 2016).

Slovic, Paul, Daniel Västfjäll, Arvid Erlandsson, and Robin Gregory. 'Iconic Photographs and the Ebb and Flow of Empathic Response to Humanitarian Disasters'. *Proceedings of the National Academy of Sciences of the United States of America* 114 (2017): 640–44, https://doi.org/10.1073/pnas.1613977114.

'Sly Fox, Fat Cat: Animals Names for People: Anthropomorphic names for the human animal'. *Merriam-Webster*, https://www.merriam-webster.com/words-at-play/anthropomorphic-animal-names-for-humans/duck.

Smeulers, Alette and Fred Grünfeld. 'Training and Education of Perpetrators'. In *International Crimes and Other Gross Human Rights Violations* (Leiden: Martinus Nijhoff Publishers, 2011), pp. 267–94.

Smith, Angela M. 'Moral Blame and Moral Protest'. In *Blame: Its Nature and Norms*, edited by D. Justin Coates and Neal A. Tognazzini (Oxford and New York: Oxford University Press, 2013), pp. 27–48.

Smith, David Livingstone. *Less than Human: Why we Demean, Enslave and Exterminate Others* (New York: St. Martin's, 2012).

Smith, David Livingstone. *On Inhumanity: Dehumanization and How to Resist It* (Oxford: Oxford University Press, 2020).

Smith, David Livingstone. *Making Monsters: The Uncanny Power of Dehumanization*, (Cambridge, Massachusetts: Harvard University Press, 2021).

Smith, Jonathan, Paul Flowers, and Michael Larkin. *Interpretative Phenomenological Analysis: Theory, Method and Research* (London: Sage, 2009).

Smith, Merril (ed.). 'Warehousing Refugees: A Denial of Rights, a Waste of Humanity'. *World Refugee Survey* 38 (2004): 38–56, https://www.refugees.org/wp-content/uploads/2021/06/Warehousing_Refugees_A_Denial_of_Rights-English.pdf.

Spindler, William. '2015: The Year of Europe's Refugee Crisis'. *UNHCR*, 8 December 2015, https://www.unhcr.org/news/stories/2015/12/56ec1ebde/2015-year-europes-refugee-crisis.html.

Steizinger, Johannes. 'The Significance of Dehumanization: Nazi Ideology and Its Psychological Consequences'. *Politics, Religion & Ideology* 19 (2018): 139–57, https://doi.org/10.1080/21567689.2018.1425144.

Stollznow, Karen. 'Dehumanization in Language and Thought'. *Journal of Language and Politics* 7 (2008): 177–200, https://doi.org/10.1075/jlp.7.2.01sto.

Stratton, Jon. 'Zombie Trouble: Zombie Texts, Bare Life and Displaced People'. *European Journal of Cultural Studies* 14 (2011): 265–81, https://doi.org/10.1177/1367549411400103.

Straus, Scott. 'What Is the Relationship between Hate Radio and Violence? Rethinking Rwanda's "Radio Machete"'. *Politics & Society* 35 (2007): 609–37, https://doi.org/10.1177/0032329207308181.

Sydney Morning Herald. 'Think Australia's Treatment of Refugees and Asylum Seekers Is OK? Read This. An Open Letter From a Refugee on Nauru to the Leaders of the UN's Summit for Refugees and Migrants'. 19 September 2016, http://www.smh.com.au/comment/think-australias-treatment-of-refugees-and-asylum-seekers-is-ok-read-this-20160919-grjjz2.html.

Tatter, Grace and Meghna Chakrabarti. '"Torture Facilities": Eyewitnesses Describe Poor Conditions At Texas Detention Centers For Migrant Children'. WBUR, 25 June 2019, https://www.wbur.org/onpoint/2019/06/25/texas-border-control-facilities-migrant-children.

Taylor, Charles. 'Self-Interpreting Animals'. In *Human Agency and Language: Philosophical Papers Volume 1* (Cambridge: Cambridge University Press, 1985), pp. 45–76.

Tileagă, Cristian. 'Ideologies of Moral Exclusion: A Critical Discursive Reframing of Depersonalization, Delegitimization and Dehumanization'. *British Psychological Society* 46 (2007): 717–37, https://doi.org/10.1348/014466607X186894.

Tirrell, Lynne. 'Genocidal Language Games'. In *Speech and Harm: Controversies over Free Speech*, edited by Ishani Maitra and Mary Kate McGowan (Oxford: Oxford University Press, 2002), pp. 174–221.

Todorov, Tzvetan. *Facing the Extreme: Moral Life in the Concentration Camps*, translated by Arthur Denner and Abigail Pollak (New York: Henry Holt and Company, 1996).

Tomico Ellis, Izzy. 'Don't Call It the "Refugee Crisis", It's a Humanitarian Issue—Failing to Recognise That Creates Even More Suffering'. Independent, 13 November 2019, https://www.independent.co.uk/voices/refugee-migrant-crisis-humanitarian-greece-syria-turkey-eu-a9201006.html.

Tuğal, Cihan. 'Syrian Refugees in Turkey Are Pawns in a Geopolitical Game'. *The Guardian*, 15 February 2016, https://www.theguardian.com/commentisfree/2016/feb/15/refugees-turkey-government-eu-crisis-europe.

Turner, Victor. *The Forest of Symbols: Aspects of Ndembu Ritual* (New York.: Cornell University Press, 1967).

United Nations. Report of the Special Rapporteur on Torture and Other Cruel, Inhuman or Degrading Treatment or Punishment, Juan E. Méndez: Addendum. 5 March 2015, https://digitallibrary.un.org/record/793910.

United Nations. 'Refugees, Migrants Branded "Threats", Dehumanized in Campaigns Seeking Political Gain, High Commissioner Tells Third Committee, Appealing for Return to Dignity'. General Assembly Third Committee, Seventy-third Session, 41st Meeting, 31 October 2018, https://www.un.org/press/en/2017/gashc4247.doc.htm.

UNHCR. 'Mouhamad's Journey, Greece', Refugee Stories, 2014, http://stories.unhcr.org/mouhamads-story-greece-p60137.html.

U.S. Committee for Refugees and Immigrants. 'Lives in Storage: Refugee Warehousing and the Overlooked Humanitarian Crisis'. December 2019, https://reliefweb.int/sites/reliefweb.int/files/resources/USCRI-Warehousing-Dec2019-v4.pdf.

Varvin, Sverre. 'Our Relations to Refugees: Between Compassion and Dehumanization'. *Academic Journal of Psychoanalysis* 77 (2017): 359–77, https://doi.org/10.1057/s11231-017-9119-0.

Vaughan-Williams, Nick. '"We Are Not Animals!" Humanitarian Border Security and Zoopolitical Spaces in EUrope'. *Political Geography* 45 (2015): 1–10, https://doi.org/10.1016/j.polgeo.2014.09.009.

Vaughan-Williams, Nick. *Europe's Border Crisis: Biopolitical Security and Beyond* (Oxford: Oxford University Press, 2015).

'Vermin'. *Online Etymology Dictionary*, https://www.etymonline.com/word/vermin.

Walzer, Michael. *Just and Unjust Wars: A Moral Argument with Historical Illustrations* (New York: Basic Books, 2006).

Welsh, Jennifer. *The Return of History: Conflict, Migration, and Geopolitics in the Twenty-First Century* (Toronto: House of Anansi Press, 2016).

184   References

Welsh, Jennifer M. and Serena K. Sharma. 'Operationalizing the Responsibility to Prevent' (Oxford Institute for Ethics, Law, and Armed Conflict), April 2012, http://www.elac.ox.ac.uk/downloads/elac%20operationalising%20the%20responsibility%20to%20prevent.pdf.

Wiesel, Elie. *Night*, translated by Marion Wiesel (London: Penguin, 2008).

Wilmott, Annabelle C. 'The Politics of Photography: Visual Depictions of Syrian Refugees in U.K. Online Media'. *Visual Communication Quarterly* 24 (2017): 67–82, https://doi.org/10.1080/15551393.2017.1307113.

Wroe, Lauren. 'Social Workers Have a Duty to Speak Up about the Humanitarian Crisis in Calais'. *The Guardian*, 4 August 2015, https://www.theguardian.com/social-care-network/2015/aug/04/social-workers-humanitarian-crisis-calais.

Wroe, Lauren E. '"It Really Is about Telling People Who Asylum Seekers Are, Because We Are Human like Anybody Else": Negotiating Victimhood in Refugee Advocacy Work'. *Discourse & Society* 29 (2018): 324–43.

Yinanç, Barçın. 'Treating Migrants like Natural Disasters "Dehumanizing"'. *Hürriyet*, 7 September 2015, http://www.hurriyetdailynews.com/treating-migrants-like-natural-disasters-dehumanizing.aspx?PageID=238&NID=88054&NewsCatID=359.

Yu, Janice. 'Regulation of Social Media Platforms to Curb ISIS Incitement and Recruitment: The Need for an International Framework and Its Free Speech Implications'. *Journal of Global Justice and Public Policy* 4 (2018): 1–29.

Zhang, Xu and Lea Hellmueller. 'Visual Framing of the European Refugee Crisis in Der Spiegel and CNN International: Global Journalism in News Photographs'. *International Communication Gazette* 79 (2017): 483–510, https://doi.org/10.1177/1748048516688134.

Zimbardo, Philip. *The Lucifer Effect: How Good People Turn Evil* (London: Rider, 2008).

Index

For the benefit of digital users, indexed terms that span two pages (e.g., 52–53) may, on occasion, appear on only one of those pages.

Abid, Manan, and Rahman, 78, 82–84
abjectification, 84–85
abuse and severe mistreatment, 98, 140, 165
  animals, of, 48, 57
  concentration and extermination camps, in Nazi, 56, 110, 112–113
  dehumanization, as linked to, 137–138, 142, 152
  factor in brutalization, as a, 99, 110, 113, 121–124, 130
  immigration detention centres, in, 14–15, 47, 69, 117–120, 150–151
  refugees and migrants travelling, of, 45, 54–56, 68–69, 86–87, 90–93, 102 n.41, 144, 146–147
  related to moral disengagement, as, 53, 98–99, 108–109, 166
  wanton violence, as, 142–144
affective engagement, 25, 40 n.9, 135–137, 157
Agamben, Giorgio, 32, 64, 84, 114
agency,
  denial of, 77–78, 85–89, 98, 130, 166
  enslaved persons, of, 144–145
  expressions of, 65, 86, 160
  limitations to, 88–89, 97, 99, 101 n.30
  moral standing, as criterion for attributing, 131
  moral valuing of, 147–148, 157
alienation,
  between people, 2, 16 n.6
  from one's own humanity, 14–15, 47–48, 99, 105–113, 119, 121, 123–124, 167. *See also* ambivalence towards one's own humanity and humanity, denial of: one's own
ambivalence towards one's own humanity, 48, 108, 111, 113, 115, 121–122. *See also* alienation: from one's own humanity and humanity, denial of: one's own
Améry, Jean, 110–111, 113
Anderson, Bridget, 38, 50–51
Andersson, Ruben, 38
Andrighetto, Baldissarri, Lattanzio, Loughnan, and Volpato, 53–54
animalization, 45–71, 120–121
  brutalization, as linked to, 107–108, 111, 113, 121–123

dehumanization, as a form of, 9–10, 14, 70–71, 130, 148, 150, 166
  lens to study dehumanization, as a, 13–14, 38
  loss of dignity, as a, 35
  making people resemble animals, as, 47, 61–62, 111
  objectification, as compared to, 71, 82–83, 96
  refugees and migrants, of, 4, 14, 23, 38, 46–48, 54–55, 57, 66–70, 113, 121–122
animal-human distinction, 45–46, 48, 54, 57, 62–63, 106
animals
  apes, 52, 63. *See also* animals: chimpanzees
  bats, 63
  cattle, 145. *See also* animals: cows
  chickens, 51–52
  chimpanzees, 57
  cockroaches, 10, 38, 46–47, 49, 51–52, 56, 63, 66–68, 149
  cows, 148
  dogs, 4, 18 n.15, 29, 47, 57, 69, 150–151
  donkeys, 47, 69, 150–151
  ducks, 51
  insects, 46, 49, 50–52, 67–68, 113
  lovebirds, 51
  monkeys, 52, 74 n.60
  rats, 38, 49, 67–68
  rodents, 49–52
  sheep, 55–56, 148
  turtle doves, 51
  vermin, 14, 18 n.15, 29, 49–53, 56, 67–68, 166
  worms, 50–51, 119, 121–122
animals, moral status of, *see* status, moral: hierarchy of
Appiah, Kwame Anthony, 56
Arendt, Hannah, 64–66, 84, 101 n.29
as if, treatment, 56–58, 61, 94
atrocities and mass violence, 53, 133, 134–135, 137–138, 158. *See also* genocide
Auschwitz, 27, 74 n.51, 106, 110–113, 123–124, 125 n.15. *See also* concentration and extermination camps
Australia, media representations of refugees and migrants in, 31–32

186 Index

Australia, off-shore detention, 4, 47, 65, 107–108, 115–119, 121–123, 164–165
autonomy, 58, 87, 92, 144, 146–147
Azevedo, De Beukelaer, Jones, Safra, and Tsakiris, 33–34

barbarism, 26
bare life, 32, 43 n.37, 114–115. *See also*: representation of refugees and migrants: as bare or raw humanity
Bauman, Zygmunt, 1–2, 42 n.27, 100 n.15, 148–149
Benesch, Susan, 159
blaming and shaming governments, 158, 161–165, 170 n.25
Bleiker, Campbell, Hutchison, and Nicholson, 31–32
Bloom, Paul, 51–52, 62
Boochani, Behrouz, 118–119, 121, 122
border control, 3, 10, 12, 31–32, 38, 46–47, 54–55, 108–109, 114, 143
border crisis, 12. *See also* migration crisis
brutalization, 105–124
  animalization, as linked to, 69–70, 107–108, 111, 113, 121–122
  definition of, 106
  dehumanization, as a form of, 14–15, 123–124, 130, 138, 140, 147, 162, 167
  inhumane treatment, as related to, 106–107
  lens to study dehumanization, as a, 13–14, 38, 99
  objectification, as linked to, 99, 123
  refugees and migrants, of, 14–15, 38, 107–109, 113, 115–123
Buber, Martin, 94–95, 120
Bulgaria, (experiences of) refugees and migrants in, 26, 54, 55
bystanders, 59, 62, 70, 123, 160–162

Cabot, Heath, 116
cages, 47, 54, 57, 68–69
Calais camp, 46, 126 n.37, 149
Cameron, David, 46, 67, 82–83
Canada, accommodation of refugees in, 2, 159
civility, denial of, 26–27, 61–62, 71 n.1, 74 n.51. *See also* hygiene, denial of
coercive action against dehumanization, 15–16, 156, 163–165
Cohen, Joshua, 144–145
compassion, 1–2, 31–32, 42 n.27, 53–54, 57, 91–92, 103 n.59, 107–109, 120–121, 124 n.1, 149, 153 n.21, 155. *See also* empathy
concentration and extermination camps, 56, 110–113, 125 n.15, 137. *See also* Auschwitz

contempt, 53–54, 68–69, 71, 96, 107, 129, 136–137
  for moral human status, 15, 129, 132, 139, 146, 148, 149–151, 167
counteracting dehumanization, 4–5, 15–16, 29, 134, 155–168
  as a collective obligation, 161
Crary, Alice, 48
criminalization, 13–14, 23–26, 34, 35–37, 39, 60, 68, 108–109, 120–121, 143–144, 165–166
crisis of humanity, 2, 35
Croatia, experiences of refugees and migrants at the border with, 55–56, 143
Crofts and Vogl, 114
cruel, inhuman or degrading treatment, *see* inhumane treatment
cruelty, 51–52, 56, 106, 137–138

death, 108, 110–111, 114, 115–116, 118, 121, 135–136, 147
DeBono, Daniela, 47
decent living conditions, minimally, (absence of), immigration detention centres, in, 47–48, 89–90, 117–118, 164–165
  refugee camps, in, 34–35, 37
degradation, *see* humiliation
dehumanization as a denial of human status, 4–5, 27, 32, 45–46, 78
dehumanization as a denial of human moral status, 9–10, 30, 34, 37, 39, 58–59, 90, 97–98, 129, 130, 165–166
  animalization, in, 9–10, 54, 56, 62–63, 66, 70, 130
  brutalization, in, 106–107, 123, 130. *See also* dehumanization as a denial of one's own humanity
  enslavement and torture, in, 58, 91, 92, 98, 144
  infra-humanization, in contrast to, 28–29, 65–66, 134
  objectification, in, 10, 83, 85–86, 88, 91–92, 96–98, 130
dehumanization as a denial of one's own humanity, 14–15, 47–48, 69–70, 105–106, 109–110, 113, 122–124, 130, 147, 167
dehumanization as a denial of the moral significance of human subjectivity, 8–9, 15, 129, 131–133, 135, 136–138, 142, 144–151, 156, 165, 167
dehumanization as a form of moral exclusion, 4–5, 8–9, 15, 26–30, 33, 36–37, 39, 46–47, 85, 95, 99, 129, 134, 136–137, 139, 142, 151, 152 n.8, 165, 167
dehumanization as a social and political phenomenon, 4–5, 157–158, 161–162
dehumanization as a spectrum concept, 133–134

dehumanization as an umbrella term, 5, 37–39, 165–166
dehumanization as turning people into something less than human, 14–15, 106–107, 110, 113, 123, 124, 147, 167
dehumanization, de facto, 58–59, 69, 92, 98, 142–147
dehumanization, preliminary definition of, 8–10
dehumanization, three forms of, 9–10
    perception, as, *see* perception, dehumanization as
    representation, as, *see* representation, dehumanization as
    treatment, as, *see* treatment, dehumanization as
de-individualization, 13–14, 23, 24–25, 31–34, 37, 39, 53, 78–79, 83, 134–135, 159–160, 165–166
demonization, 29, 101 n.25
denial of humanity, *see* humanity, denial of
denial of one's own humanity, *see* humanity, denial of: one's own
depiction of refugees and migrants, *see* representation of refugees and migrants
depravity, 14, 138, 166
deprivation, 14–15, 25, 34–35, 37, 45, 47, 99, 105, 108, 110, 113, 119, 121–124
desensitization, 48, 106–109, 111, 112, 118, 120–122
destitution, *see* deprivation
detention, 4, 26, 35, 45, 47–48, 54, 57, 65, 69–70, 86–87, 91, 92, 98, 107–108, 117–118, 119, (of children), 121, 123, 144, 150, 164–165. *See also* immigration detention centres
deviance, 13–14, 24–26
dignity, 2, 4
    denial of, 13–14, 24–25, 34–37
    regaining, 118–119, 122
    violation of, 69
discrimination, 3, 63–68, 91–92, 138–139, 141, 167. *See also* racism
disengagement, moral, 3, 8, 13–14, 24–25, 31–34, 36–37, 51–54, 62, 63, 66–67, 70, 82–83, 134, 135–137, 149
disease, 27–28, 34–35, 37, 49, 56, 61–62, 89–90, 97–98, 135–136, 150–151. *See also* representation of refugees and migrants: as (carriers of) disease
disgust, 27–28, 47, 51–53, 61–62, 66–67, 69, 71, 74 n.51, 83–84, 96, 103 n.60, 150–151
disregard, moral, 8–9, 25, 83–84, 86–87, 89–92, 95–99, 118, 119–120, 129, 130–133, 138, 139–142, 144, 146, 149, 155, 160–161, 166. *See also* indifference
Douglas, Mary, 72 n.23

empathy, 1–2, 53–54, 71 n.1, 107–109, 120–121, 155. *See also* compassion
enemies, *see* hostility
enslavement, 58, 91, 92, 98, 144–148, 152, 164
Epley, Nicholas, 8
Esses, Medianu, and Lawson, 26–30
Esses, Medianu, and Sutter, 159
EU-Turkey deal, 11
evil, 131–132
exclusion, moral, *see* moral exclusion
extermination, 50–51, 56, 67–68, 125 n.4

fear, 26, 103 n.60, 105, 109, 110–111, 114–116,
Festa, Lynn, 157
Fiske, Lucy, 65–66
freedom, 26, 35, 88–89, 92, 97, 99, 113, 122–123, 138–139, 146–147, 157. *See also* autonomy
freedom of speech, 158–159, 163
Frelick, Bill, 34–36
fully human, *see* human, fully

Galeotti, Anna, 139–140, 164
garbage, *see* waste
Garrard, Eve, 131–132, 140, 146
Geertz, Clifford, 59–60
gender-based violence, 55, 137. *See also* sexual violence and rape
genocide, 9, 56, 134–138, 164. *See also* atrocities and mass violence and Rwandan genocide
Geras, Norman, 18 n.15, 29
Germany, experiences of refugees and migrants in, 4, 26, 85, 105, 155
ghosts, 48, 107–108, 115–117, 121, 123–124, 147
Goffman, Erving, 27–28
Grandi, Filippo, 35, 37
Greece, experiences of refugees and migrants in, 47, 61–62, 113, 116
Guantanamo Bay, 30

Haslam, Nick, 28–29, 71 n.1, 100 n.3
hate, 71, 96, 107, 133, 136–137, 151
hate speech, 158–159, 163
Hintjens, Helen, 120
historical representations of refugees and migrants, 50, 80–81
Honneth, Axel, 8, 95–96, 136–137
Hopkins, Katie, 46–47, 63, 66–67, 149
hostility, 3–4, 16 n.6, 25, 53, 91–92, 108–109, 120, 153 n.21, 170 n.28
human, fully, 24, 26–28, 34, 35, 99, 106–107, 121–122, 134, 135–136, 140–141
    in contrast to minimally human, 135
human, minimally, 32–33, 58, 144
    in contrast to fully human, 135–136

188 Index

humanitarian crisis, 12
humanitarianism, 11–12, 31–32, 40 n.9, 53–54, 65, 66–67, 85, 89, 120, 169 n.24
humanity as a moral category, 4, 72 n.23, 84
  exclusion from, 5–6, 15, 28–29, 36–37, 39, 86, 95, 97, 99, 129, 134, 139, 151, 165–168
  inclusion in, 27–30, 97, 164
humanity as a moral status, 9. *See also* humanity, denial of: as a moral status and humanity, recognition of: as a moral status
humanity as a polysemous concept, 9, 21 n.30, 34, 124 n.1. *See also* humanity, three senses of
humanity as a scalar notion, 63–64
humanity, denial of, 3–5, 8, 9, 14–15, 27, 28–29
humanity, denial of, as a moral status,
  animalization, in, 9, 14, 54, 62, 63, 67–69, 130, 150–151
  brutalization, in, 106–107, 121–122, 130
  disregard, expressed as, 8–9, 15, 155. *See also* contempt: for moral human status
  disengagement, as a factor in moral, 53
  dehumanization, as a form of, *see* dehumanization as a denial of human moral status
  denial of dignity, as a, 25, 34, 35–36
  objectification, in, 77, 79, 82–83, 85, 98, 130
  supra-humanization, in, 21 n.31
  one's own, 108, 118. *See also* alienation: from one's own humanity, ambivalence towards one's own humanity, and dehumanization as a denial of one's own humanity
humanity, recognition of, 8, 25, 34, 56, 57–58, 60, 62–63, 65–66, 89, 91–92, 94, 95–96, 131, 136–138, 148, 150–151, 157
  as a moral status, 5, 20 n.29, 53, 58, 85, 88, 92, 95, 98, 135, 138–140, 144, 157, 162
  one's own, 14–15, 48, 99, 106, 108, 110, 111–113, 118–119, 121–122, 124, 147, 167. *See also*: ambivalence towards one's own humanity
humanity, three senses of, 9, 21 n.30
  biological, 9, 32–34, 64–66, 114, 130
  traits-based, 9, 38, 71 n.1, 83, 133, 137–138, 148, 151. *See also* qualities, (uniquely) human
  moral, 9, 14, 33–34, 54, 61, 66, 70–71, 86, 92, 106–107, 130, 138, 150–151, 165–166
humanity, views of, 5–6, 19 n.21, 155
humanization, 31–32, 65, 159–160, 163, 170 n.28
human rights, 1–3, 13, 29–30, 34–35. *See also* rights, (fundamental)
human rights advocacy, 7, 34–35, 37, 39, 61–62, 65, 82, 89–90, 97–98, 102 n.41, 109, 117–118, 165–166

human rights violations, 1, 10–12, 17 n.14, 24, 90–93, 108–110, 117–118, 164–165
humane conditions, *see* decent living conditions, minimally, (absence of),
humiliation, 5, 55–58, 62–63, 77, 85, 122, 129, 140, 150–151
Huxley, Aldous, 52–53
hygiene, denial of, 47, 61–62, 69, 74 n.51, 89–90, 150. *See also* civility, denial of

Ibrahim and Howarth, 159–160
identification, moral, 1–3, 31, 118–119, 122
identity, 51–52, 65, 69, 79, 84–85, 93, 94–95, 101 n.29, 106, 108, 118–119, 121–122, 134–135, 162
ideology, 15–16, 65, 95–96, 109, 136, 157–159. *See also* propaganda
immigration detention centres, 4, 14–15, 26, 38, 47, 57, 61–62, 69, 91, 106, 107–108, 117, 119, 164–165. *See also* Australia, off-shore detention
inclusion, moral, *see* moral inclusion
indifference, 2, 51–52, 71, 93–96, 98–99, 123–124, 129, 130–131, 133, 136–137, 147–148, 151, 166. *See also* disregard, moral
infestation, 49–52, 67–68
infra-humanization, 9, 23–24, 28–30, 37, 39, 50, 61, 63–69, 85, 86, 96, 97, 99, 109, 120–121, 123, 133–136, 139, 141, 151, 165–167
inhumane conditions, *see* inhumane treatment and decent living conditions, minimally, (absence of)
inhumane treatment, 5, 7, 19 n.21, 23, 38, 57, 91–92, 98–99, 106, 107, 116–120, 146, 164–167
inhumanity, 19 n.21, 106–107, 137
instrumentalization, 38, 79, 81–82, 86–88, 91, 97, 129, 130, 144, 148
insults, 47, 51–52, 69, 150–151
interviews, 7–8, 19 n.20, n.21. *See also* refugee and migrant testimonies
Italy-Libya Memorandum of Understanding, 11
Italy, experiences of refugees and migrants in, 4, 26, 47, 69, 108

Jović, Vladimir, 163

Kafka, Franz, 113
Kelman, Herbert, 134–136, 152 n.9
Kil and Menjívar, 108–109, 120
Kil, Menjívar, and Doty, 108–109, 120
killing, 26, 52, 53, 91, 92, 114, 131–132, 134–135, 140, 144, 146–147
Klein, Fritz, 27
Kteily, Nour, 63–64

Kristeva, Julia, 84–85
Kurdi, Alan, 1–3
Kymlicka, Will, 48

Lang, Johannes, 137
Leader Maynard, Jonathan, 158
Lebanon, experiences of refugees and migrants in, 31, 77, 99 n.1, 100 n.2, 129
Levi, Primo, 74 n.51, 110–113
Leyens, Demoulin, Vaes, Gaunt, and Paladino, 28
Libya, experiences of refugees and migrants in, 45, 47, 55, 61–62, 69, 86–87, 90–92, 98, 117, 144, 146–147, 150
liminality, 84–85, 114–117

Machery, Edouard, 131
Mahendran, Magnusson, Howarth, and Scuzzarello, 84
Malkki, Liisa, 32–34, 64, 84, 116
Malone, Barry, 36–37, 149
Malta, experiences of refugees and migrants in, 47, 69–70, 107–108
Manne, Kate, 91, 137–138
Margalit, Avishai, 21 n.31, 56, 94
marginalization, 3, 5, 7, 13–14, 23–24, 27, 35, 37, 39, 65–68, 97, 114–115, 120–121, 165–167
media campaigns against polarisation and dehumanization, 159–160
media depictions of refugees and migrants, 1–4, 24, 25–27, 31–34, 36, 77–78, 82, 108–109, 114, 120, 159–160
metaphor, 49–51, 70, 80, 98, 115
   animal, 49, 52, 63. See also representation of refugees and migrants
   object-related, 78–86. See also representation of refugees and migrants
   water-related, 78–79, 82–84, 96–97. See also representation of refugees and migrants: as natural disasters
   war, 50, 52–54
metaphor, use of,
   derogatory, 51–52, 81
   positive, 51, 81–82
migrant deaths, 1–3, 16 n.7, 36, 66–67, 91, 92, 144, 146–147, 149
migrant label, 36–37, 149
migration crisis, 2, 10–13
Mikkola, Mari, 8, 138–141
minimally human, see human, minimally
mistreatment, (severe), see abuse
monsters, 114. See also ghosts and zombies
moral inclusion, 5, 18 n.15, 29, 65, 97, 135, 160–161, 164
moral exclusion, 3, 7–8, 13–14, 19 n.21, 21 n.31, 23–24, 27–28, 30, 38–39, 43 n.37, 130,

134–135, 162, 164. See also dehumanization as a form of moral exclusion
moral sensibilities, 26, 56, 57 (in animals), 62–63, 131
moral status,
   hierarchy of, 9, 21 n.31, 48, 50–51, 69, 83
   human, see humanity as a moral status

Nauru, see Australia, off-shore detention
needs, basic, 25, 32, 34–35, 77–80, 87–90, 97, 98–99, 117–119, 138–139, 166
Nussbaum, Martha, 87–88

objectification, 77–99
   animalization, as compared to, 71, 81–83, 96
   brutalization, as linked to, 99, 123
   dehumanization, as a form of, 10, 14, 96–99, 130, 136–137, 148, 166
   lens to study dehumanization, as a, 13–14, 38
   refugees and migrants, of, 14, 38, 78–81, 86–87, 90–93
   typology of, 55–87
O'Brien, Gerald, 50, 80–81
Opotow, Susan, 152 n.8
Over, Harriet, 137–138

paradox of dehumanization, 20 n.29, 56–58, 133, 137–138
parasites, 29, 32. See also representations of refugees and migrants: parasites
Parfit, Derek, 86–87, 89, 97–98
perception, dehumanization as, 5–6, 9–10, 59, 60–66, 70, 80, 91–96, 98, 138–140, 152, 163, 165
persecution, 1, 17 n.14, 23–24, 35, 40 n.9, 101 n.29
personhood, 35–36, 93–94, 105, 118–119, 149
persuasive action against dehumanization, 15–16, 156–160, 163, 164–165
pestilence, see representation of refugees and migrants: as pestilence or vermin
poison, 29, 81, 83. See also representation of refugees and migrants: as poison
pollution, 50–52, 80–84, 114
portrayal, dehumanization as, see representation, dehumanization as
predators, 14, 166
propaganda, 8, 15–16, 136, 157–158. See also ideology
   countering, 158–159, 163, 168 n.6
   Nazi, 27, 49
   Stalinist, 49
   war, 52–54, 157–158

190 Index

psychopaths, 95–96, 103 n.59, 136, 157
public health, concern for, 25–26, 49, 81, 83

qualities, (uniquely) human, 14–15, 38, 61–62,
    89, 106, 111–113, 115, 124, 133, 137–138,
    148–151, 167

racism, 26, 63, 91–92, 114, 115. *See also*
    discrimination
rape, 55–56, 92, 109, 120, 137–141. *See also*
    gender-based violence and sexual violence
recognition, moral, 4–6, 20 n.29, 25, 53, 65–66,
    95, 140, 157, 162. *See also* humanity,
    recognition of: as a moral status
recognition of human status, *see* humanity,
    recognition of
reification, 95–96, 136–137
refugee camps, 3–4, 11, 88–90, 97, 99, 101 n.30.
    See also Calais camp
refugee crisis, 2, 10–12, 31, 33–34, 50–51. *See also*
    migration crisis
refugee hunting, *see* vigilante border control
refugees
    category, as a, 79, 84–86, 97
    definition, 12, 17 n.14
    distinction from migrants, 12
    historical change in meaning, 101 n.29
    moral counterparts, as, 2–3
    victims, as, 2–3, 77–79, 84, 85–86, 97, 101 n.25
refugee and migrant testimonies, 7–8, 159–160
    from author's interviews
      Abdul, 31, 57
      Amadou, 91–92, 144, 146–147
      Amira, 26
      Ammar, 105
      Hanan, 85, 155
      Hassan, 77, 129
      Joseph, 35
      Musa, 45, 90–92, 146
      Salim, 26, 31, 38, 108, 114–115
      Suha, 85
      Tariq, 23, 26, 54–55, 58
    from other sources
      Ali, 126 n.37
      Babak, 149
      Benjamin, 108, 118, 121
      Boubaker Nassou, 144, 148
      Hadish, 4
      Ibrahim, 4, 35, 38
      Mehdi, 108, 118, 119, 121–122
      Milkesa, 102 n.41
      Mouhamad, 113
rehumanization, *see* humanization
relative and absolute denials of humanity, 28–29,
    133–134

representation, dehumanization as, 5–6, 9–10,
    14–15, 60, 61–62, 70, 80, 98, 106, 122–124,
    138, 141–142, 152, 163
representation of refugees and migrants,
    as bare or raw humanity, 32–34, 79, 84, 116
    as bargaining chips or pawns, 77–78. *See also*
      treatment of refugees and migrants: as
      bargaining chips or pawns
    as cockroaches, 46–47, 51–52, 63, 66–67, 149
    as criminals, 3–4, 24–26, 108–109, 120. *See*
      also criminalization
    as (carriers of) diseases, 14, 23, 24–30, 32, 47,
      50, 61–62, 69, 78, 86, 150
    as dogs, 47, 69, 150–151
    as donkeys, 47, 69, 150–151
    as frauds, 3–4, 29–30
    as ghosts, 48, 107–108, 116–117
    as human animals, 64–66
    as indigestible foods, 77–78, 80, 96–97
    as insects, 46, 49, 50–52, 113
    as illegal, 34–36, 65
    as intruders, 23, 25, 53
    as natural disasters, 14, 25, 38, 50, 78–84,
      96–97
    as parasites, 50–52
    as pestilence or vermin, 29–30, 38, 49–53,
      67–68
    as (potential) terrorists, 23, 25–27, 30, 42 n.27,
      114
    as poison, 77–78, 80–83, 96–97
    as polluting factors, 80–83
    as queue-jumpers, 3–4, 23, 27–30
    as raw material, 81–82, 150
    as savage beasts, 47, 69
    as swarms, 46, 49, 50, 67, 82–83
    as (helpless) victims, 2–3, 77–78, 84, 85–86, 97,
      101 n.25
    as waste, 14, 38, 77–78, 80, 81–83, 86, 96–97,
      100 n.15 ('wasted humans'), 148–149
      ('human waste'), 150
representation, politics of, 49–51
resilience, 14–15, 113, 118–119, 123–124, 167
respect, 4, 25, 34–35, 58, 92, 105, 139–140, 144,
    145–147, 157, 162, 164, 167
rhetoric, dehumanizing, 3–4, 9, 38, 46–47, 49,
    66–68, 120
    countering, 16 n.6, 159–161
rights, (fundamental), 37–38, 65, 77–80, 87–89,
    91, 97–99, 118–119, 122, 138–140, 143,
    164, 167. *See also* human rights
Rohingya crisis, 11–12
Rorty, Richard, 8, 157
Rwandan genocide, 49, 158–159
Ryle, Gilbert, 59–60

Sacks, Oliver, 93–94
Schininá, Guglielmo, 84–85
Schwartzman, Roy, 159–160
search and rescue missions, 16 n.7, 46–47, 66–67, 120
secondary emotions, denial of, 26–27
securitization, 25–26, 31–32, 40 n.10, 48, 108–109, 120–121, 143–144
semiotic sensibilities, 56–57, 62–63, 131
sense of self, *see* identity
sentience, 50–51, 54, 57, 131
sentimental education, 157
sexual violence, 55–56, 68–69, 117–118. *See also* gender-based violence and rape
shame, 27–28, 85, 103 n.59, 111–112
Shetty, Shalil, 34–35, 37, 82, 89–90, 97–98
Sias, James, 162
silencing, 32, 52, 160–161
Smith, David Livingstone, 8, 52, 72 n.23, 101 n.25, 161
slavery, *see* enslavement
social values, higher order, 26–28
solidarity, 1–3, 65
stigmatization, 3, 5, 7, 13–14, 23–24, 27–30, 35–37, 39, 56, 67–68, 120–121, 165–167
Stollznow, Karen, 8, 124 n.1
Stratton, Jon, 114–115
sub-humanization, 8, 21 n.31, 28, 46–47, 71, 72 n.23, 99, 105, 121. *See also* infra-humanization
subjectivity, human,
    affirming, 15–16, 119, 157, 159–160
    animalization, as denied by, 14, 130, 166
    brutalization, as affected by, 14–15, 122, 130, 147, 167
    definition of, 131
    denial of moral relevance of, as defining Dehumanization, 8–9, 15, 129, 156, 160–161, 167–168
    objectification, as denied by, 14, 85, 87–89, 96, 98, 130, 166
suffering, 135, 167
    disregard for, as signal of dehumanization, 8–9, 129, 130–132, 140, 141–142, 149, 151, 155, 157
    human, 54, 111, 131, 157
    insensitivity to, 38, 51–52, 66–67, 89, 98–99, 157
    morally relevant, as, 6–7, 131
    refugees and migrants, of, 1–2, 10–12, 31, 143–144, 146–147, 149, 163
    torture, and, 130, 146–147
support for victims of dehumanization, 15–16, 156, 160–165
supra-humanization, 21 n.31

Taylor, Charles, 131
terrorism, 23, 25–27, 30, 33, 42 n.27, 114
threat, 13–14, 24–26, 31–32, 35, 53, 78–79, 81, 83, 114, 115–116, 131–132, 138
Todorov, Tzvetan, 125 n.4
torture, 42 n.25, 52, 56, 58, 91, 92, 98, 102 n.41, 107, 114–115, 117–118, 120, 137–138, 144, 146–147, 152, 163–164
trafficking, human, 45, 55, 90–91, 102 n.41, 120, 144, 146–147
treatment, dehumanization as, 5–6, 9–10, 54–62, 70, 86–93, 98–99, 123, 124, 138–139, 141–142, 150–152, 163
treatment of refugees and migrants
    animals, like, 47, 54–62, 70, 143
    bargaining chips or pawns, as, 38, 79–80, 86–88, 97
    helpless victims, as, 77–78
    inhumane, 19 n.21, 23, 38, 57, 91–92, 116–120, 146
    mere things, as, 14, 86–87, 90
    warehousing, 86–89, 97
    weapons, as, 86–87
Trump, Donald, 11–12, 49, 67–68, 119
trust (loss of), 2, 15–16, 109, 116–117, 123–124, 156, 160, 162
Turkey, refugees and migrants in, 1–2, 11
Turner, Victor, 84

United Kingdom, treatment of refugees and migrants in,
    accommodation policies, 3–4, 23
    brutalizing or dehumanizing perceptions and representations, 46–47, 63, 66–67, 109, 149
    political rhetoric, 46, 67, 82–83
United Nations High Commissioner for Refugees, 35
United States, treatment of refugees and migrants in,
    experiences of refugees and migrants, 57
    historical representations, 50, 80–81
    immigration policies, 11–12, 119
    political rhetoric, 49, 67–68
'unlawful combatants', 30
US-Mexico border, 11–12, 68, 108–109, 119, 120

value, 77, 79, 81–85, 88, 129, 138–140, 152 n.8, 156, 161
Vaughan-Williams, Nick, 16 n.7, 47
vermin, *see* animals: vermin
viciousness, 14, 166
vigilante border patrol, 38, 54, 55, 58–61, 108–109

192 Index

violence, 10–11, 52–54, 70, 90–92, 108–109, 119, 120, 137, 138. *See also* abuse and severe mistreatment, atrocities and mass violence, and gender-based violence
  border control, and, 3, 12, 54–56, 58–61, 68–69, 143
  detention centres, in immigration, 47, 69, 117–118, 150
  gratuitous, 141–144, 146, 152
  Nazi concentration and extermination camps, in, 112–113, 137
vulnerability, human, 54, 56, 131, 157

war, 12, 19 n.19, 24, 26, 34–35, 40 n.8, 45, 84–85, 89–90, 99, 116, 134–136, 157–158
  First World War, 101 n.29
  Second World War, 52, 112

Syria, in, 1, 10–11, 105
Ukraine, in, 11–12
war crimes, 164
war propaganda, *see* propaganda: war
waste, 50–51, 83–84, 103 n.60, 150. *See also* representation of refugees and migrants: as waste
Wiesel, Elie, 112–113
Wilmott, Annabelle, 31
witnesses, *see* bystanders
Wroe, Lauren, 109
wrong, moral, of dehumanization, 6, 23–24, 38, 134, 165–168

xenophobia, 31, 35, 159–160

Zhang and Hellmueller, 31
zombies, 10, 38, 108, 114–116, 123–124, 147